New Perspectives on

Microsoft® Office Excel 2003

Brief

June Jamrich Parsons

Dan Oja

Patrick Carey

Roy Ageloff
University of Rhode Island

THOMSON
★
COURSE TECHNOLOGY

Australia • Canada • Mexico • Singapore • Spain • United Kingdom • United States

THOMSON

COURSE TECHNOLOGY

New Perspectives on Microsoft® Office Excel 2003—Brief

is published by Course Technology.

Managing Editor:
Rachel Goldberg

Senior Product Manager:
Kathy Finnegan

Senior Technology Product Manager:
Amanda Young Shelton

Product Manager:
Karen Stevens

Product Manager:
Brianna Germain

Editorial Assistant:
Abigail Z. Reider

Senior Marketing Manager:
Rachel Stephens

Associate Marketing Manager:
Caitlin Wight

Developmental Editor:
Jane Pedicini

Production Editor:
Philippa Lehar

Composition:
GEX Publishing Services

Text Designer:
Steve Deschene

Cover Designer:
Nancy Goulet

Preface

Real, Thought-Provoking, Engaging, Dynamic, Interactive—these are just a few of the words that are used to describe the New Perspectives Series' approach to learning and building computer skills.

Without our critical-thinking and problem-solving methodology, computer skills could be learned but not retained. By teaching with a case-based approach, the New Perspectives Series challenges students to apply what they've learned to real-life situations.

Our ever-growing community of users understands why they're learning what they're learning. Now you can too!

See what instructors and students are saying about the best-selling New Perspectives Series:

> "The New Perspectives format is a pleasure to use. The Quick Checks and the tutorial Review Assignments help students view topics from a real world perspective."
> — Craig Shaw, Central Community College – Hastings

...and about New Perspectives on Microsoft Office Excel 2003:

> "The layout in this textbook is thoughtfully designed and organized. It is very easy to locate concepts and step-by-step instructions. The Case Problems provide different scenarios that cover material in the tutorial with plenty of exercises."
> — Shui-lien Huang, Mt. San Antonio College

> "I have used the New Perspectives Excel textbooks for several years since they are the best on the market. The New Perspectives Excel 2003 textbook—which can best be described as clear, concise, practical, and interesting—puts the competitors even further behind."
> — Joe Pidutti, Durham College

www.course.com/NewPerspectives

Why *New Perspectives* will work for you

Context

Each tutorial begins with a problem presented in a "real-world" case that is meaningful to students. The case sets the scene to help students understand what they will do in the tutorial.

Hands-on Approach

Each tutorial is divided into manageable sessions that combine reading and hands-on, step-by-step work. Screenshots—now 20% larger for enhanced readability—help guide students through the steps. **Trouble?** tips anticipate common mistakes or problems to help students stay on track and continue with the tutorial.

Review

In New Perspectives, retention is a key component to learning. At the end of each session, a series of Quick Check questions helps students test their understanding of the concepts before moving on. And now each tutorial contains an end-of-tutorial summary and a list of key terms for further reinforcement.

Assessment

Engaging and challenging Review Assignments and Case Problems have always been a hallmark feature of the New Perspectives Series. Now we've added new features to make them more accessible! Colorful icons and brief descriptions accompany the exercises, making it easy to understand, at a glance, both the goal and level of challenge a particular exercise holds.

Reference

While contextual learning is excellent for retention, there are times when students will want a high-level understanding of how to accomplish a task. Within each tutorial, Reference Windows appear before a set of steps to provide a succinct summary and preview of how to perform a task. In addition, a complete Task Reference at the back of the book provides quick access to information on how to carry out common tasks. Finally, each book includes a combination Glossary/Index to promote easy reference of material.

Lab Assignments

Certain tutorials in this book contain Lab Assignments, which provide additional reinforcement of important skills in a simulated environment. These labs have been hailed by students and teachers alike for years as the most comprehensive and accurate on the market. Great for pre-work or remediation, the labs help students learn concepts and skills in a structured environment.

Student Online Companion

This book has an accompanying online companion Web site designed to enhance learning. This Web site includes:
- Internet Assignments and Lab Assignments for selected tutorials
- Student Data Files and PowerPoint presentations
- Microsoft Office Specialist Certification Grids

Review

Apply

Reference Window

Task Reference

Reinforce

www.course.com/NewPerspectives

New Perspectives offers an entire system of instruction

The New Perspectives Series is more than just a handful of books. It's a complete system of offerings:

New Perspectives catalog
Our online catalog is never out of date! Go to the catalog link on our Web site to check out our available titles, request a desk copy, download a book preview, or locate online files.

Coverage to meet your needs!
Whether you're looking for just a small amount of coverage or enough to fill a semester-long class, we can provide you with a textbook that meets your needs.

- Brief books typically cover the essential skills in just 2 to 4 tutorials.
- Introductory books build and expand on those skills and contain an average of 5 to 8 tutorials.
- Comprehensive books are great for a full-semester class, and contain 9 to 12+ tutorials.
- Power Users or Advanced books are perfect for a highly accelerated introductory class or a second course in a given topic.

So if the book you're holding does not provide the right amount of coverage for you, there's probably another offering available. Go to our Web site or contact your Course Technology sales representative to find out what else we offer.

Instructor Resources

We offer more than just a book. We have all the tools you need to enhance your lectures, check students' work, and generate exams in a new, easier-to-use and completely revised package. This book's Instuctor's Manual, ExamView testbank, PowerPoint presentations, data files, solution files, figure files, and sample syllabus are all available on a single CD-ROM or for downloading at www.course.com.

How will your students master Microsoft Office?

SAM (Skills Assessment Manager) 2003 helps you energize your class exams and training assignments by allowing students to learn and test important computer skills in an active, hands-on environment. With SAM 2003, you create powerful interactive exams on critical Microsoft Office 2003 applications, including Word, Excel, Access, and PowerPoint. The exams simulate the application environment, allowing your students to demonstrate their knowledge and to think through the skills by performing real-world tasks. Designed to be used with the New Perspectives Series, SAM 2003 includes built-in page references so students can create study guides that match the New Perspectives textbooks you use in class. Powerful administrative options allow you to schedule exams and assignments, secure your tests, and run reports with almost limitless flexibility. Find out more about SAM 2003 by going to www.course.com or speaking with your Course Technology sales representative.

Distance Learning

Enhance your course with any of our online learning platforms. Go to www.course.com or speak with your Course Technology sales representative to find the platform or the content that's right for you.

www.course.com/NewPerspectives

About This Book

This book provides a short, hands-on introduction to creating spreadsheets for both business and personal use with the latest version of Microsoft Excel.

- Updated for the new software! This book provides coverage of new Excel 2003 features, including the new Research task pane.
- Tutorial 1 gives students the fundamental skills they need to complete basic Excel tasks. In this edition, the tutorial case scenario has been revised and simplified, and the tutorial has been restructured to include topics such as: calculating a total with AutoSum, checking the spelling in a workbook, and displaying formulas in a worksheet.
- For this edition, Tutorial 2 has been restructured and simplified, with a new tutorial case scenario that presents topics related to formulas and functions in a more basic way. The first session includes increased coverage of the more fundamental functions, such as SUM, AVERAGE, and MAX. The *optional* second session presents streamlined coverage of Financial and Logical functions; this session may be skipped without loss of continuity of the instruction.
- Tutorial 3 teaches students how to format a worksheet, including the data in cells, the cells themselves, and the entire worksheet. Students also learn how to format printed worksheets and to include headers and footers.
- Tutorial 4 presents comprehensive coverage of creating and modifying different types of Excel charts. Students also learn how to add and modify drawing objects.

New to this edition!

- Screenshots are now 20% larger for improved readability.
- Sequential page numbering makes it easier to refer to specific pages in the book.
- The new Tutorial Summary and Key Terms sections at the end of each tutorial provide additional conceptual review for students.
- New labels and descriptions for the end-of-tutorial exercises make it easy for you to select the right exercises for your students.

Acknowledgments

We would like to thank the many people whose invaluable contributions made this book possible. First, thanks go to our reviewers: Rory De Simone, University of Florida; Shui-lien Huang, Mt. San Antonio College; Glen Johansson, Spokane Community College; Karleen Nordquist, College of St. Benedict & St. John's University; Joe Pidutti, Durham College; Kate Pulling, Community College of Southern Nevada; Donna Ulmer, St. Louis Community College at Meramec; and Kathy Winters, The University of Tennessee at Chattanooga. At Course Technology we would like to thank Rachel Goldberg, Managing Editor; Kathy Finnegan, Senior Product Manager; Brianna Germain, Product Manager; Abbey Reider, Editorial Assistant; Philippa Lehar, Production Editor; John Bosco and John Freitas, Quality Assurance Managers; Shawn Day, Sean Franey, Marc Sporto, and Ashlee Welz, Quality Assurance Testers; and Steven Freund, Dave Nuscher and Rebekah Tidwell for their work on the Instructor Resources. A special thanks to Jane Pedicini, Developmental Editor, for another great effort, keeping us focused and level-headed as we worked to complete this text.

June Jamrich Parsons
Dan Oja
Patrick Carey
Roy Ageloff

Table of Contents

New Perspectives on

Using Common Features of Microsoft® Office 2003

Preparing Promotional Materials   OFF 3

Read This Before You Begin

To the Student

Data Files

To complete the Using Common Features of Microsoft Office 2003 tutorial, you need the starting student Data Files. Your instructor will either provide you with these Data Files or ask you to obtain them yourself.

The Using Common Features of Microsoft Office 2003 tutorial requires the folder named "OFF" to complete the Tutorial, Review Assignments, and Case Problems. You will need to copy this folder from a file server, a stand-alone computer, or the Web to the drive and folder where you will be storing your Data Files. Your instructor will tell you which computer, drive letter, and folder(s) contain the files you need. You can also download the files by going to www.course.com; see the inside back or front cover for

more information on downloading the files, or ask your instructor or technical support person for assistance.

If you are storing your Data Files on floppy disks, you will need one blank, formatted, high-density disk for this tutorial. Label your disk as shown, and place on it the folder indicated.

▼ Common Features of Office: Data Disk
   OFF folder

When you begin this tutorial, refer to the Student Data Files section at the bottom of the tutorial opener page, which indicates which folders and files you need for the tutorial. Each end-of-tutorial exercise also indicates the files you need to complete that exercise.

To the Instructor

The Data Files are available on the Instructor Resources CD for this title. Follow the instructions in the Help file on the CD to install the programs to your network or standalone computer. See the "To the Student" section above for information on how to set up the Data Files that accompany this text.

You are granted a license to copy the Data Files to any computer or computer network used by students who have purchased this book.

System Requirements

If you are going to work through this book using your own computer, you need:

• **Computer System** Microsoft Windows 2000 or Windows XP Professional or higher must be installed on your computer. This tutorial assumes a typical installation of Microsoft Office 2003. Additionally, to

complete the steps for accessing Microsoft's Online Help for Office, an Internet connection and a Web browser are required.

• **Data Files** You will not be able to complete the tutorals or exercises in this book using your own computer until you have the necessary starting Data Files.

www.course.com/NewPerspectives

Objectives

- Explore the programs that comprise Microsoft Office
- Start programs and switch between them
- Explore common window elements
- Minimize, maximize, and restore windows
- Use personalized menus and toolbars
- Work with task panes
- Create, save, close, and open a file
- Use the Help system
- Print a file
- Exit programs

Using Common Features of Microsoft Office 2003

Preparing Promotional Materials

Case

Delmar Office Supplies

Delmar Office Supplies, a company in Wisconsin founded by Jake Alexander in 1996, sells recycled office supplies to businesses and home-based offices around the world. The demand for quality recycled papers, reconditioned toner cartridges, and renovated office furniture has been growing each year. Jake and all his employees use Microsoft Office 2003, which provides everyone in the company the power and flexibility to store a variety of information, create consistent files, and share data. In this tutorial, you'll review how the company's employees use Microsoft Office 2003.

Student Data Files

▼ OFF folder

  ▽ **Tutorial folder**   ▽ **Review folder**

     (no starting Data Files)   Finances.xls

                              Letter.doc

Exploring Microsoft Office 2003

Microsoft Office 2003, or simply **Office**, is a collection of the most popular Microsoft programs: Word, Excel, PowerPoint, Access, and Outlook. Each Office program contains valuable tools to help you accomplish many tasks, such as composing reports, analyzing data, preparing presentations, compiling information, sending e-mail, and planning schedules.

Microsoft Word 2003, or simply **Word**, is a word-processing program you use to create text documents. The files you create in Word are called **documents**. Word offers many special features that help you compose and update all types of documents, ranging from letters and newsletters to reports, brochures, faxes, and even books—all in attractive and readable formats. You can also use Word to create, insert, and position figures, tables, and other graphics to enhance the look of your documents. The Delmar Office Supplies sales representatives create their business letters using Word.

Microsoft Excel 2003, or simply **Excel**, is a spreadsheet program you use to display, organize, and analyze numerical data. You can do some of this in Word with tables, but Excel provides many more tools for recording and formatting numbers as well as performing calculations. The graphics capabilities in Excel also enable you to display data visually. You might, for example, generate a pie chart or a bar chart to help readers quickly see the significance of and the connections between information. The files you create in Excel are called **workbooks**. The Delmar Office Supplies operations department uses a line chart in an Excel workbook to visually track the company's financial performance.

Microsoft Access 2003, or simply **Access**, is a database program you use to enter, organize, display, and retrieve related information. The files you create in Access are called **databases**. With Access you can create data entry forms to make data entry easier, and you can create professional reports to improve the readability of your data. The Delmar Office Supplies operations department tracks the company's inventory in a table in an Access database.

Microsoft PowerPoint 2003, or simply **PowerPoint**, is a presentation graphics program you use to create a collection of slides that can contain text, charts, pictures, and so on. The files you create in PowerPoint are called **presentations**. You can show these presentations on your computer monitor, project them onto a screen as a slide show, print them, share them over the Internet, or display them on the World Wide Web. You can also use PowerPoint to generate presentation-related documents such as audience handouts, outlines, and speakers' notes. The Delmar Office Supplies sales department has created an effective slide presentation with PowerPoint to promote the company's latest product line.

Microsoft Outlook 2003, or simply **Outlook**, is an information management program you use to send, receive, and organize e-mail; plan your schedule; arrange meetings; organize contacts; create a to-do list; and jot down notes. You can also use Outlook to print schedules, task lists, phone directories, and other documents. Jake Alexander uses Outlook to send and receive e-mail, plan his schedule, and create a to-do list.

Although each Office program individually is a strong tool, their potential is even greater when used together.

Integrating Office Programs

One of the main advantages of Office is **integration**, the ability to share information between programs. Integration ensures consistency and accuracy, and it saves time because you don't have to re-enter the same information in several Office programs. The staff at Delmar Office Supplies uses the integration features of Office daily, including the following examples:

- The accounting department created an Excel bar chart on the previous two years' fourth-quarter results, which they inserted into the quarterly financial report created in Word. They included a hyperlink in the Word report that employees can click to open the Excel workbook and view the original data.
- The operations department included an Excel pie chart of sales percentages by divisions of Delmar Office Supplies on a PowerPoint slide, which is part of a presentation to stockholders.
- The marketing department produced a mailing to promote the company's newest products by combining a form letter created in Word with an Access database that stores the names and addresses of customers.
- A sales representative wrote a letter in Word about a sales incentive program and merged the letter with an Outlook contact list containing the names and addresses of his customers.

These are just a few examples of how you can take information from one Office program and integrate it into another.

Starting Office Programs

You can start any Office program by clicking the Start button on the Windows taskbar, and then selecting the program you want from the All Programs menu. Once the program starts, you can immediately begin to create new files or work with existing ones. If you or another user has recently used one of the Office programs, then that program might appear on the most frequently used programs list on the left side of the Start menu. You can click the program name to start the program.

Starting Office Programs	Reference Window

- Click the Start button on the taskbar.
- Point to All Programs.
- Point to Microsoft Office.
- Click the name of the program you want to start.

or
- Click the name of the program you want to start on the most frequently used programs list on the left side of the Start menu.

You'll start Excel using the Start button.

To start Excel and open a new, blank workbook:

1. Make sure your computer is on and the Windows desktop appears on your screen.

Trouble? If your screen varies slightly from those shown in the figures, then your computer might be set up differently. The figures in this book were created while running Windows XP in its default settings, but how your screen looks depends on a variety of things, including the version of Windows, background settings, and so forth.

2. Click the **Start** button on the taskbar, and then point to **All Programs** to display the All Programs menu.

3. Point to **Microsoft Office** on the All Programs menu, and then point to **Microsoft Office Excel 2003**. See Figure 1. Depending on how your computer is set up, your desktop and menu might contain different icons and commands.

Figure 1	Start menu with All Programs submenu displayed

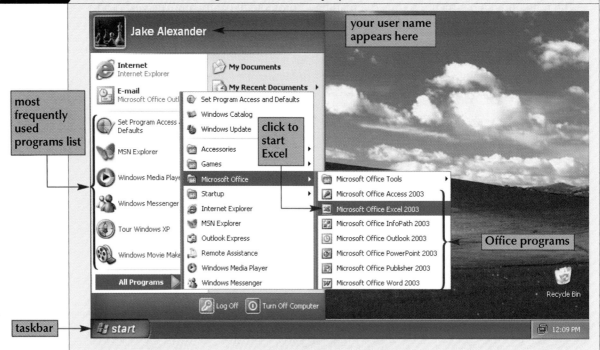

Trouble? If you don't see Microsoft Office on the All Programs menu, point to Microsoft Office Excel 2003. If you still don't see Microsoft Office Excel 2003, ask your instructor or technical support person for help.

4. Click **Microsoft Office Excel 2003** to start Excel and open a new, blank workbook. See Figure 2.

New, blank Excel workbook | **Figure 2**

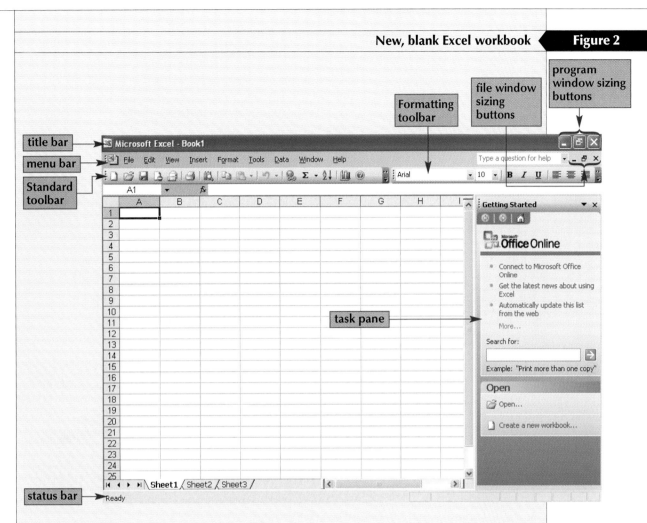

Trouble? If the Excel window doesn't fill your entire screen, the window is not maximized, or expanded to its full size. You'll maximize the window shortly.

You can have more than one Office program open at once. You'll use this same method to start Word and open a new, blank document.

To start Word and open a new, blank document:

1. Click the **Start** button on the taskbar.

2. Point to **All Programs** to display the All Programs menu.

3. Point to **Microsoft Office** on the All Programs menu.

   Trouble? If you don't see Microsoft Office on the All Programs menu, point to Microsoft Office Word 2003. If you still don't see Microsoft Office Word 2003, ask your instructor or technical support person for help.

4. Click **Microsoft Office Word 2003**. Word opens with a new, blank document. See Figure 3.

Figure 3 | New, blank document in Word

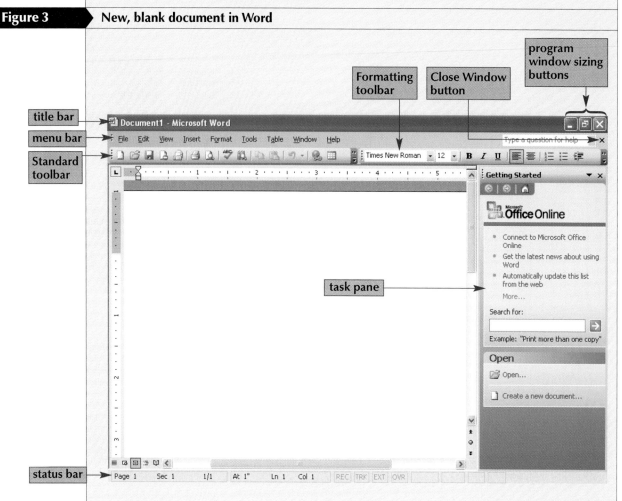

Trouble? If the Word window doesn't fill your entire screen, the window is not maximized. You'll maximize the window shortly.

When you have more than one program or file open at a time, you can switch between them.

Switching Between Open Programs and Files

Two programs are running at the same time—Excel and Word. The taskbar contains buttons for both programs. When you have two or more programs running, or two files within the same program open, you can use the taskbar buttons to switch from one program or file to another. The employees at Delmar Office Supplies often work in several programs at once.

To switch between Word and Excel:

▶ **1.** Click the **Microsoft Excel – Book1** button on the taskbar to switch from Word to Excel. See Figure 4.

Excel and Word programs opened simultaneously ◀ **Figure 4**

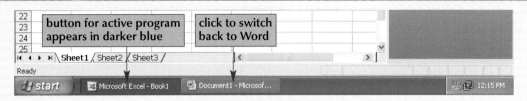

▶ **2.** Click the **Document1 – Microsoft Word** button on the taskbar to return to Word.

As you can see, you can start multiple programs and switch between them in seconds.

Exploring Common Window Elements

The Office programs consist of windows that have many similar features. As you can see in Figures 2 and 3, many of the elements you see in both the Excel program window and the Word program window are the same. In fact, all the Office programs have these same elements. Figure 5 describes some of the most common window elements.

Common window elements ◀ **Figure 5**

Element	Description
Title bar	A bar at the top of the window that contains the filename of the open file, the program name, and the program window sizing buttons
Menu bar	A collection of menus for commonly used commands
Toolbars	Collections of buttons that are shortcuts to commonly used menu commands
Sizing buttons	Buttons that resize and close the program window or the file window
Task pane	A window that provides access to commands for common tasks you'll perform in Office programs
Status bar	An area at the bottom of the program window that contains information about the open file or the current task on which you are working

Because these elements are the same in each program, once you've learned one program, it's easy to learn the others. The next sections explore the primary common features—the window sizing buttons, the menus and toolbars, and the task panes.

Using the Window Sizing Buttons

There are two sets of sizing buttons. The top set controls the program window and the bottom set controls the file window. There are three different sizing buttons. The Minimize button 🗕, which is the left button, hides a window so that only its program button is visible on the taskbar. The middle button changes name and function depending on the status of the window—the Maximize button 🗖 expands the window to the full screen size or to the program window size, and the Restore button 🗗 returns the window to a predefined size. The right button, the Close button 🗙, exits the program or closes the file.

Most often you'll want to maximize the program and file windows as you work to take advantage of the full screen size you have available. If you have several files open, you might want to restore the files so that you can see more than one window at a time or you might want to minimize the programs with which you are not working at the moment. You'll try minimizing, maximizing, and restoring windows now.

To resize windows:

1. Click the **Minimize** button ▬ on the Word title bar to reduce the Word program window to a taskbar button. The Excel window is visible again.

2. If necessary, click the **Maximize** button ▢ on the Excel title bar. The Excel program window expands to fill the screen.

3. Click the **Restore Window** button ⧉ on the Excel menu bar. The file window, referred to as the workbook window in Excel, resizes smaller than the full program window. See Figure 6.

| Figure 6 | Resized Excel windows |

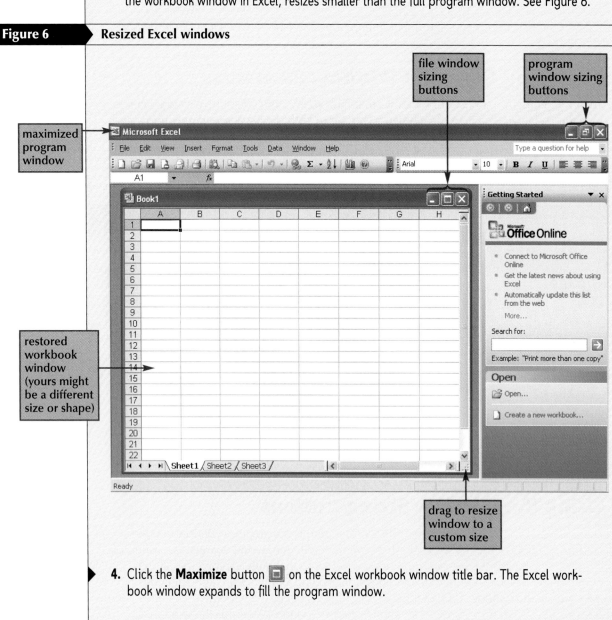

4. Click the **Maximize** button ▢ on the Excel workbook window title bar. The Excel workbook window expands to fill the program window.

▶ **5.** Click the **Document1 - Microsoft Word** button on the taskbar. The Word program window returns to its previous size.

▶ **6.** If necessary, click the **Maximize** button ▣ on the Word title bar. The Word program window expands to fill the screen.

The sizing buttons give you the flexibility to arrange the program and file windows on your screen to best fit your needs.

Using Menus and Toolbars

In each Office program, you can perform tasks using a menu command, a toolbar button, or a keyboard shortcut. A **menu command** is a word on a menu that you click to execute a task; a **menu** is a group of related commands. For example, the File menu contains commands for managing files, such as the Open command and the Save command. The File, Edit, View, Insert, Format, Tools, Window, and Help menus appear on the menu bar in all the Office programs, although some of the commands they include differ from program to program. Other menus are program specific, such as the Table menu in Word and the Data menu in Excel.

A **toolbar** is a collection of buttons that correspond to commonly used menu commands. For example, the Standard toolbar contains an Open button and a Save button. The Standard and Formatting toolbars (as well as other toolbars) appear in all the Office programs, although some of the buttons they include differ from program to program. The Standard toolbar has buttons related to working with files. The Formatting toolbar has buttons related to changing the appearance of content. Each program also has program-specific toolbars, such as the Tables and Borders toolbar in Word for working with tables and the Chart toolbar in Excel for working with graphs and charts.

A **keyboard shortcut** is a combination of keys you press to perform a command. For example, Ctrl+S is the keyboard shortcut for the Save command (you hold down the Ctrl key while you press the S key). Keyboard shortcuts appear to the right of many menu commands.

Viewing Personalized Menus and Toolbars

When you first use a newly installed Office program, the menus and toolbars display only the basic and most commonly used commands and buttons, streamlining the program window. The other commands and buttons are available, but you have to click an extra button to see them (the Expand button on a menu and the Toolbar Options button on a toolbar). As you select commands and click buttons, the ones you use often are put on the short, personalized menu and on the visible part of the toolbars. The ones you don't use remain available on the full menus and toolbars. This means that the Office menus and toolbars might display different commands and buttons on each person's computer.

To view a personalized and full menu:

▶ **1.** Click **Insert** on the Word menu bar to display the short, personalized menu. See Figure 7. The Bookmark command, for example, does not appear on the short menu.

Figure 7 ▶ **Short, personalized menu**

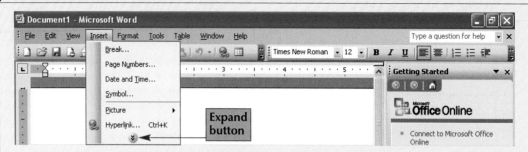

Trouble? If the Insert menu displays different commands than those shown in Figure 7, you need to reset the menus. Click Tools on the menu bar, click Customize (you might need to pause until the full menu appears to see the command), and then click the Options tab in the Customize dialog box. Click the Always show full menus check box to remove the check mark, if necessary, and then click the Show full menus after a short delay check box to insert a check mark, if necessary. Click the Reset menu and toolbar usage data button, and then click the Yes button to confirm that you want to reset the commands. Click the Close button. Repeat Step 1.

You can display the full menu in one of three ways: (1) pause until the full menu appears, which might happen as you read this; (2) click the Expand button at the bottom of the menu; or (3) double-click the menu name on the menu bar.

▶ **2.** Pause until the full Insert menu appears, as shown in Figure 8. The Bookmark command and other commands are now visible.

Figure 8 ▶ **Full, expanded menu**

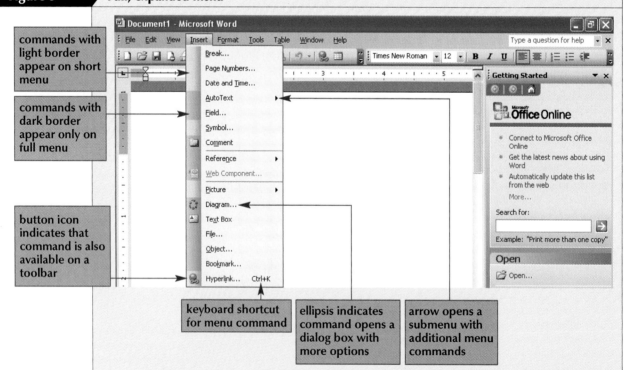

▶ **3.** Click the **Bookmark** command. A dialog box opens when you click a command whose name is followed by an ellipsis (...). In this case, the Bookmark dialog box opens.

▶ **4.** Click the **Cancel** button to close the Bookmark dialog box.

▶ **5.** Click **Insert** on the menu bar again to display the short, personalized menu. The Bookmark command appears on the short, personalized menu because you have recently used it.

▶ **6.** Press the **Esc** key on the keyboard twice to close the menu.

As you can see, the menu changed based on your actions. Over time, only the commands you use frequently will appear on the personalized menu. The toolbars work similarly.

To use the personalized toolbars:

▶ **1.** Observe that the Standard and Formatting toolbars appear side by side below the menu bar.

Trouble? If the toolbars appear on two rows, you need to reset them to their default state. Click Tools on the menu bar, click Customize, and then click the Options tab in the Customize dialog box. Click the Show Standard and Formatting toolbars on two rows check box to remove the check mark. Click the Reset menu and toolbar usage data button, and then click the Yes button to confirm you want to reset the commands. Click the Close button. Repeat Step 1.

▶ **2.** Click the **Toolbar Options** button ⚎ on the Standard toolbar. See Figure 9.

Toolbar Options palette ◀ **Figure 9**

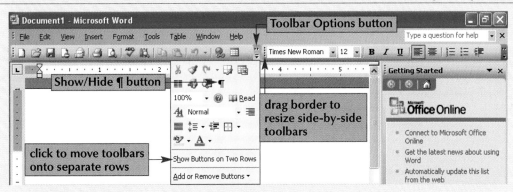

Trouble? If you see different buttons on the Toolbar Options palette, your side-by-side toolbars might be sized differently than the ones shown in Figure 9. Continue with Step 3.

▶ **3.** Click the **Show/Hide ¶** button ¶ on the Toolbar Options palette to display the nonprinting screen characters. The Show/Hide ¶ button moves to the visible part of the Standard toolbar, and another button may be moved onto the Toolbar Options palette to make room for the new button.

Trouble? If the Show/Hide ¶ button already appears on the Standard toolbar, click another button on the Toolbar Options palette. Then click that same button again in Step 4 to turn off that formatting, if necessary.

Some buttons, like the Show/Hide ¶ button, act as a toggle switch—one click turns on the feature and a second click turns it off.

▶ **4.** Click the **Show/Hide ¶** button ¶ on the Standard toolbar again to hide the nonprinting screen characters.

Some people like that the menus and toolbars change to meet their work habits. Others prefer to see all the menu commands or to display the default toolbars on two rows so that all the buttons are always visible. You'll change the toolbar setting now.

To turn off the personalized toolbars:

▶ 1. Click the **Toolbar Options** button ⬚ on the right side of the Standard toolbar.

▶ 2. Click the **Show Buttons on Two Rows** command. The toolbars move to separate rows (the Standard toolbar on top) and you can see all the buttons on each toolbar.

You can easily access any button on the Standard and Formatting toolbars with one mouse click. The drawback is that when the toolbars are displayed on two rows, they take up more space in the program window, limiting the space you have to work.

Using Task Panes

A **task pane** is a window that provides access to commands for common tasks you'll perform in Office programs. For example, the Getting Started task pane, which opens when you first start any Office program, enables you to create new files and open existing ones. Task panes also help you navigate through more complex, multi-step procedures. All the Office programs include the task panes described in Figure 10. The other available task panes vary by program.

Figure 10 ▶ **Common task panes**

Task pane	Description
Getting Started	The home task pane; allows you to create new files, open existing files, search the online and offline Help system by keyword, and access Office online
Help	Allows you to search the online and offline Help system by keyword or table of contents, and access Microsoft Office Online
Search Results	Displays available Help topics related to entered keyword and enables you to initiate a new search
New	Allows you to create new files; name changes to New Document in Word, New Workbook in Excel, New File in Access, and New Presentation in PowerPoint
Clip Art	Allows you to search for all types of media clips (pictures, sound, video) and insert clips from the results
Clipboard	Allows you to paste some or all of the items that have been cut or copied from any Office program during the current work session
Research	Allows you to search a variety of reference material and other resources from within a file

No matter what their purpose, you use the same processes to open, close, and navigate between the task panes.

Opening and Closing Task Panes

When you first start any Office program, the Getting Started task pane opens by default along the right edge of the program window. You can resize or move the task pane to suit your work habits. You can also close the task pane to display the open file in the full available program window. For example, you might want to close the task pane when you are typing the body of a letter in Word or entering a lot of data in Excel.

You will open and close the task pane.

To open and close the task pane:

1. If necessary, click **View** on the menu bar, and then click **Task Pane**. The most recently viewed task pane opens on the right side of the screen. See Figure 11.

Getting Started task pane | **Figure 11**

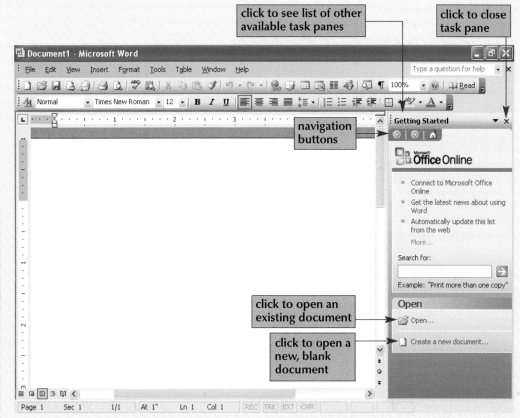

Trouble? If you do not see the task pane, you probably closed the open task pane in Step 1. Repeat Step 1 to reopen the task pane.

Trouble? If a different task pane than the Getting Started task pane opens, then another task pane was the most recently viewed task pane. You'll learn how to open different task panes in the next section; continue with Step 2.

2. Click the **Close** button ☒ on the task pane title bar. The task pane closes, leaving more room on the screen for the open file.

3. Click **View** on the menu bar, and then click **Task Pane**. The task pane reopens.

There are several ways to display different task panes.

Navigating Among Task Panes

Once the task pane is open, you can display different task panes to suit the task you are trying to complete. For example, you can display the New task pane when you want to create a new file from a template. The name of the New task pane varies, depending on the program you are using: Word has the New Document task pane, Excel has the New Workbook task pane, PowerPoint has the New Presentation task pane, and Access has the New File task pane.

One of the quickest ways to display a task pane is to use the Other Task Panes button. When you point to the name of the open task pane in the task pane title bar, it becomes the Other Task Panes button. When you click the Other Task Panes button, all the available task panes for that Office program are listed. Just click the name of the task pane you want to display to switch to that task pane.

There are three navigation buttons at the top of the task pane. The Back and Forward buttons enable you to scroll backward and forward through the task panes you have opened during your current work session. The Back button becomes available when you display two or more task panes. The Forward button becomes available after you click the Back button to return to a previously viewed task pane. The Home button returns you to the Getting Started task pane no matter which task pane is currently displayed.

You'll use each of these methods to navigate among the task panes.

To navigate among task panes:

1. Point to **Getting Started** in the task pane title bar. The title bar becomes the Other Task Panes button.

2. Click the **Other Task Panes** button. A list of the available task panes for Word is displayed. The check mark before Getting Started indicates that this is the currently displayed task pane.

3. Click **New Document**. The New Document task pane appears and the Back button is available.

4. Click the **Back** button 🔄 in the task pane. The Getting Started task pane reappears and the Forward button is available.

5. Click the **Forward** button 🔄 in the task pane. The New Document task pane reappears and the Back button is available.

6. Click the **Home** button 🏠 in the task pane. The Getting Started task pane reappears.

Using the Research Task Pane

The Research task pane allows you to search a variety of reference materials and other resources to find specific information while you are working on a file. You can insert the information you find directly into your open file. The thesaurus and language translation tools are installed with Office and therefore are stored locally on your computer. If you are connected to the Internet, you can also use the Research task pane to access a dictionary, an encyclopedia, research sites, as well as business and financial sources. Some of the sites that appear in the search results are fee-based, meaning that you'll need to pay to access information on that site.

To use the Research task pane, you type a keyword or phrase into the Search for text box and then select whether you want to search all the books, sites, and sources; one category; or a specific source. The search results appear in the Research task pane. Some of the results appear as links, which you can click to open your browser window and display that information. If you are using Internet Explorer 5.01 or later as your Web browser, the Research task pane is tiled (appears side by side) with your document. If you are using another Web browser, you'll need to return to the task pane in your open file to click another link.

The Research task pane functions independently in each file. So you can open multiple files and perform a different search in each. In addition, each Research task pane stores the results of up to 10 searches, so you can quickly return to the results from any of your most recent searches. To move among the saved searches, click the Back and Forward buttons in the task pane.

Using the Research Task Pane

- Type a keyword or phrase into the Search for text box.
- Select a search category, individual source, or all references.
- If necessary, click a link in the search results to display more information.
- Copy and paste selected content from the task pane into your file.

Jake plans to send a copy of the next quarter's sales report to the office in France. You'll use the bilingual dictionaries in the Research task pane to begin entering labels in French into an Excel workbook for the sales report.

To use the bilingual dictionaries in the Research task pane:

1. Click the **Microsoft Excel – Book1** button on the taskbar to switch to the Excel window.

2. Click the **Other Task Panes** button on the Getting Started task pane, and then click **Research**. The Research task pane opens.

3. Click in the **Search for** text box, and then type **paper**.

4. Click the **Search for** list arrow and then click **Translation**. The bilingual dictionary opens in the Research task pane. You can choose from among 12 languages to translate to and from, including Japanese, Russian, Spanish, Dutch, German, and French.

   Trouble? If a dialog box opens stating the translation feature is not installed, click the Yes button to install it.

5. If necessary, click the **To** list arrow, and then click **French (France)**. See Figure 12.

Research task pane | **Figure 12**

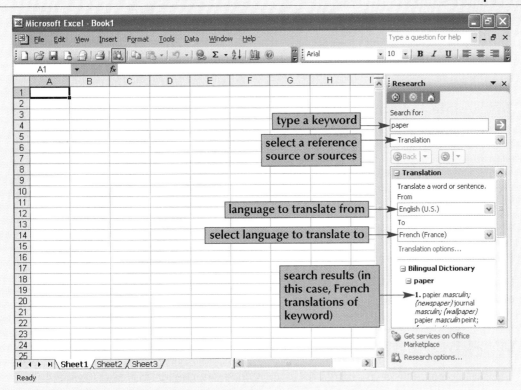

6. Scroll to read the different translations of "paper" in French.

After you locate specific information, you can quickly insert it into your open file. The information can be inserted by copying the selected content you want to insert, and then pasting it in the appropriate location in your file. In some instances, such as MSN Money Stock Quotes, a button appears enabling you to quickly insert the indicated information in your file at the location of the insertion point. Otherwise, you can use the standard Copy and Paste commands.

You'll copy the translation for "paper" into the Excel workbook.

To copy information from the Research task pane into a file:

1. Select **papier** in the Research task pane. This is the word you want to copy to the workbook.

2. Right-click the selected text, and then click **Copy** on the shortcut menu. The text is duplicated on the Office Clipboard.

3. Right-click cell **A1**, and then click **Paste**. The word "papier" is entered into the cell. See Figure 13.

Figure 13 **Translation copied into Excel**

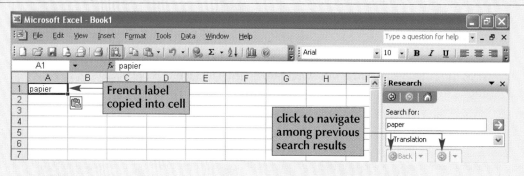

You'll repeat this process to look up the translation for "furniture" and copy it into cell A2.

To translate and copy another word into Excel:

1. Double-click **paper** in the Search for text box to select the text, type **furniture**, and then click the **Start searching** button → in the Research task pane.

2. Verify that you're translating from English (U.S) to French (France).

3. Select **meubles** in the translation results, right-click the selected text, and then click **Copy**.

4. Right-click cell **A2**, and then click **Paste**. The second label appears in the cell.

The Research task pane works similarly in all the Office programs. You'll use other task panes later in this tutorial to perform specific tasks, including opening a file and getting assistance.

Working with Files

The most common tasks you'll perform in any Office program are to create, open, save, and close files. The processes for each of these tasks are the same in all the Office programs. In addition, there are several methods for performing most tasks in Office. This flexibility enables you to use Office in a way that fits how you like to work.

Creating a File

To begin working in a program, you need to create a new file or open an existing file. When you start Word, Excel, or PowerPoint, the program opens along with a blank file—ready for you to begin working on a new document, workbook, or presentation. When you start Access, the Getting Started task pane opens, displaying options for opening a new database or an existing one.

Jake has asked you to start working on the agenda for the stockholder meeting, which he suggests you create using Word. You enter text in a Word document by typing.

To enter text in a document:

▶ **1.** Click the **Document1 – Microsoft Word** button on the taskbar to activate the Word program window.

▶ **2.** Type **Delmar Office Supplies**, and then press the **Enter** key. The text you typed appears on one line in the Word document.

   Trouble? If you make a typing error, press the Backspace key to delete the incorrect letters, and then retype the text.

▶ **3.** Type **Stockholder Meeting Agenda**, and then press the **Enter** key. The text you typed appears on the second line.

Next, you'll save the file.

Saving a File

As you create and modify Office files, your work is stored only in the computer's temporary memory, not on a hard disk. If you were to exit the programs, turn off your computer, or experience a power failure, your work would be lost. To prevent losing work, save your file to a disk frequently—at least every 10 minutes. You can save files to the hard disk located inside your computer or to portable storage disks, such as floppy disks, Zip disks, or read-write CD-ROMs.

The first time you save a file, you need to name it. This name is called a **filename**. When you choose a filename, select a descriptive one that accurately reflects the content of the document, workbook, presentation, or database, such as "Shipping Options Letter" or "Fourth Quarter Financial Analysis." Filenames can include a maximum of 255 letters, numbers, hyphens, and spaces in any combination. Office appends a **file extension** to the filename, which identifies the program in which that file was created. The file extensions are .doc for Word, .xls for Excel, .ppt for PowerPoint, and .mdb for Access. Whether you see file extensions depends on how Windows is set up on your computer.

You also need to decide where to save the file—on which disk and in what folder. A **folder** is a container for your files. Just as you organize paper documents within folders stored in a filing cabinet, you can organize your files within folders stored on your computer's hard disk or a removable disk. Store each file in a logical location that you will remember whenever you want to use the file again.

Reference Window | **Saving a File**

- Click the Save button on the Standard toolbar (*or* click File on the menu bar, and then click Save or Save As).
- In the Save As dialog box, click the Save in list arrow, and then navigate to the location where you want to save the file.
- Type a filename in the File name text box.
- Click the Save button.
- To resave the named file to the same location, click the Save button on the Standard toolbar (*or* click File on the menu bar, and then click Save).

The two lines of text you typed are not yet saved on disk. You'll do that now.

To save a file for the first time:

▶ **1.** Click the **Save** button 🔲 on the Standard toolbar. The Save As dialog box opens. The first few words of the first line appear in the File name text box, as a suggested filename. You'll replace this with a more descriptive filename.

▶ **2.** Click the **Save in** list arrow, and then click the location that contains your Data Files.

Trouble? If you don't have the Common Office Features Data Files, you need to get them before you can proceed. Your instructor will either give you the Data Files or ask you to obtain them from a specified location (such as a network drive). In either case, be sure that you make a backup copy of your Data Files before you start using them, so that the original files will be available on your copied disk in case you need to start over because of an error or problem. If you have any questions about the Data Files, see your instructor or technical support person for assistance.

▶ **3.** Double-click the **OFF** folder in the list box, and then double-click the **Tutorial** folder. This is the location where you want to save the document. See Figure 14.

▶ **4.** Type **Stockholder Meeting Agenda** in the File name text box.

Figure 14 | **Completed Save As dialog box**

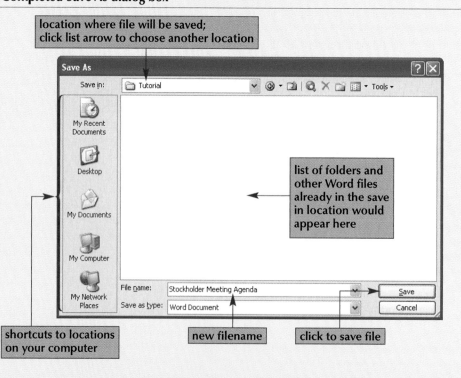

location where file will be saved;
click list arrow to choose another location

list of folders and other Word files already in the save in location would appear here

shortcuts to locations on your computer

new filename

click to save file

> **Trouble?** If the .doc file extension appears after the filename, then your computer is configured to show file extensions. Continue with Step 5.

▶ **5.** Click the **Save** button. The Save As dialog box closes, and the name of your file appears in the program window title bar.

The saved file includes everything in the document at the time you last saved it. Any edits or additions you then make to the document exist only in the computer's memory and are not saved in the file on the disk. As you work, remember to save frequently so that the file is updated to reflect the latest content of the document.

Because you already named the document and selected a storage location, the second and subsequent times you save, the Save As dialog box doesn't open. If you wanted to save a copy of the file with a different filename or to a different location, you would reopen the Save As dialog box by clicking File on the menu bar, and then clicking Save As. The previous version of the file remains on your disk as well.

You need to add your name to the agenda. Then you'll save your changes.

To modify and save a file:

▶ **1.** Type your name, and then press the **Enter** key. The text you typed appears on the next line.

▶ **2.** Click the **Save** button 🖫 on the Standard toolbar to save your changes.

When you're done with a file, you can close it.

Closing a File

Although you can keep multiple files open at one time, you should close any file you are no longer working on to conserve system resources as well as to ensure that you don't inadvertently make changes to the file. You can close a file by clicking the Close command on the File menu or by clicking the Close Window button in the upper-right corner of the menu bar.

As a standard practice, you should save your file before closing it. If you're unsure whether the file is saved, it cannot hurt to save it again. However, Office has an added safeguard: If you attempt to close a file or exit a program without saving your changes, a dialog box opens asking whether you want to save the file. Click the Yes button to save the changes to the file before closing the file and program. Click the No button to close the file and program without saving changes. Click the Cancel button to return to the program window without saving changes or closing the file and program. This feature helps to ensure that you always save the most current version of any file.

You'll add the date to the agenda. Then, you'll attempt to close the document without saving.

To modify and close a file:

▶ **1.** Type the date, and then press the **Enter** key. The text you typed appears under your name in the document.

▶ **2.** Click the **Close Window** button 🗙 on the Word menu bar to close the document. A dialog box opens, asking whether you want to save the changes you made to the document.

▶ **3.** Click the **Yes** button. The current version of the document is saved to the file, and then the document closes, and Word is still running.

Trouble? If Word is not running, then you closed the program in Step 2. Start Word, click the Close Window button on the menu bar to close the blank document.

Once you have a program open, you can create additional new files for the open program or you can open previously created and saved files.

Opening a File

When you want to open a blank document, workbook, presentation, or database, you create a new file. When you want to work on a previously created file, you must first open it. Opening a file transfers a copy of the file from the storage disk (either a hard disk or a portable disk) to the computer's memory and displays it on your screen. The file is then in your computer's memory and on the disk.

Reference Window | **Opening an Existing or a New File**

- Click the Open button on the Standard toolbar (or click File on the menu bar, and then click Open or click the More link in the Open section of the Getting Started task pane).
- In the Open dialog box, click the Look in list arrow, and then navigate to the storage location of the file you want to open.
- Click the filename of the file you want to open.
- Click the Open button.

or

- Click the New button on the Standard toolbar (or click File on the menu bar, click New, and then (depending on the program) click the Blank document, Blank workbook, Blank presentation, or Blank database link in the New task pane).

Jake asks you to print the agenda. To do that, you'll reopen the file. You'll use the Open button on the Standard toolbar.

To open an existing file:

▶ **1.** Click the **Open** button 📖 on the Standard toolbar. The Open dialog box, which works similarly to the Save As dialog box, opens.

▶ **2.** Click the **Look in** list arrow, and then navigate to the **OFF\Tutorial** folder included with your Data Files. This is the location where you saved the agenda document.

▶ **3.** Click **Stockholder Meeting Agenda** in the file list. See Figure 15.

Open dialog box ◄ Figure 15

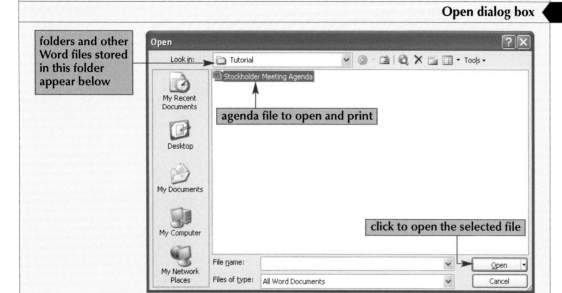

folders and other Word files stored in this folder appear below

agenda file to open and print

click to open the selected file

▶ **4.** Click the **Open** button. The file containing the agenda opens in the Word program window.

Next, you'll get information about printing files in Word.

Getting Help

If you don't know how to perform a task or want more information about a feature, you can turn to Office itself for information on how to use it. This information, referred to simply as **Help**, is like a huge encyclopedia available from your desktop. You can access Help in a variety of ways, including ScreenTips, the Type a question for help box, the Help task pane, and Microsoft Office Online.

Using ScreenTips

ScreenTips are a fast and simple method you can use to get help about objects you see on the screen. A **ScreenTip** is a yellow box with the button's name. Just position the mouse pointer over a toolbar button to view its ScreenTip.

Using the Type a Question for Help Box

For answers to specific questions, you can use the **Type a question for help box**, located on the menu bar of every Office program, to find information in the Help system. You simply type a question using everyday language about a task you want to perform or a topic you need help with, and then press the Enter key to search the Help system. The Search Results task pane opens with a list of Help topics related to your query. You click a topic to open a Help window with step-by-step instructions that guide you through a specific procedure and explanations of difficult concepts in clear, easy-to-understand language. For example, you might ask how to format a cell in an Excel worksheet; a list of Help topics related to the words you typed will appear.

Reference Window

Getting Help from the Type a Question for Help Box

- Click the Type a question for help box on the menu bar.
- Type your question, and then press the Enter key.
- Click a Help topic in the Search Results task pane.
- Read the information in the Help window. For more information, click other topics or links.
- Click the Close button on the Help window title bar.

You'll use the Type a question for help box to obtain more information about printing a document in Word.

To use the Type a question for help box:

▶ **1.** Click the **Type a question for help box** on the menu bar, and then type **How do I print a document?**

▶ **2.** Press the **Enter** key to retrieve a list of topics. The Search Results task pane opens with a list of topics related to your query. See Figure 16.

Figure 16 ▶ Search Results task pane displaying Help topics

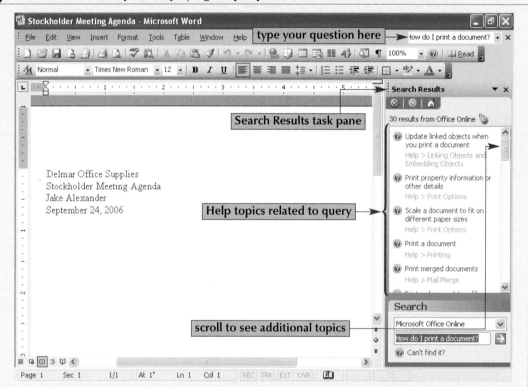

Trouble? If your search results list differs from the one shown in Figure 16, your computer is not connected to the Internet or Microsoft has updated the list of available Help topics since this book was published. Continue with Step 3.

▶ **3.** Scroll through the list to review the Help topics.

▶ **4.** Click **Print a document** to open the Help window and learn more about the various ways to print a document. See Figure 17.

Print a document Help window | **Figure 17**

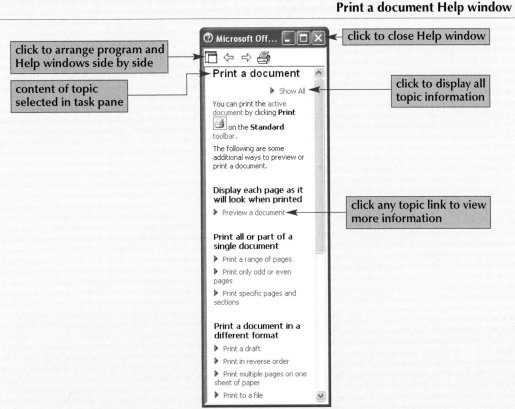

click to arrange program and Help windows side by side

content of topic selected in task pane

click to close Help window

click to display all topic information

click any topic link to view more information

Trouble? If the Word program window and the Help window do not appear side by side, then you need to tile the windows. Click the Auto Tile button on the toolbar in the Help window.

▶ **5.** Read the information, and then when you're done, click the **Close** button ⊠ on the Help window title bar to close the Help window.

The Help task pane works similarly.

Using the Help Task Pane

For more in-depth help, you can use the **Help task pane**, a task pane that enables you to search the Help system using keywords or phrases. You type a specific word or phrase in the Search for text box, and then click the Start searching button. The Search Results task pane opens with a list of topics related to the keyword or phrase you entered. If your computer is connected to the Internet, you might see more search results because some Help topics are stored only online and not locally on your computer. The task pane also has a Table of Contents link that organizes the Help system by subjects and topics, like in a book. You click main subject links to display related topic links.

Reference Window | **Getting Help from the Help Task Pane**

- Click the Other Task Panes button on the task pane title bar, and then click Help (*or* click Help on the menu bar, and then click Microsoft Word/Excel/PowerPoint/Access/ Outlook Help).
- Type a keyword or phrase in the Search for text box, and then click the Start searching button.
- Click a Help topic in the Search Results task pane.
- Read the information in the Help window. For more information, click other topics or links.
- Click the Close button on the Help window title bar.

You'll use the Help task pane to obtain more information about getting help in Office.

To use the Help task pane:

▶ 1. Click the **Other Task Panes** button on the task pane title bar, and then click **Help**.

▶ 2. Type **get help** in the Search for text box. See Figure 18.

Figure 18 ▶ | **Microsoft Word Help task pane with keyword**

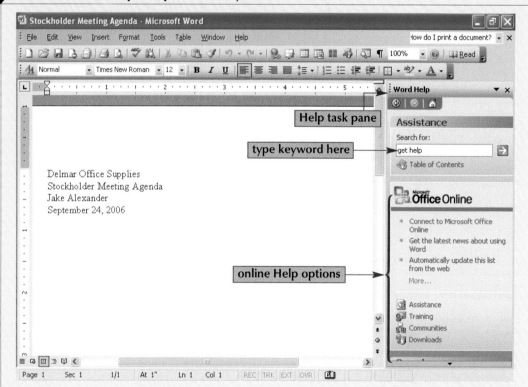

▶ 3. Click the **Start searching** button ⮕. The Search Results task pane opens with a list of topics related to your keywords.

▶ 4. Scroll through the list to review the Help topics.

▶ 5. Click **About getting help while you work** to open the Microsoft Word Help window and learn more about the various ways to obtain help in Word. See Figure 19.

About getting help while you work Help window ◄ **Figure 19**

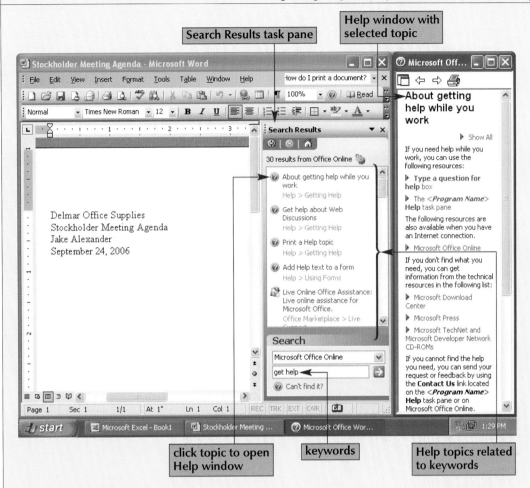

Search Results task pane

Help window with selected topic

click topic to open Help window

keywords

Help topics related to keywords

Trouble? If your search results list differs from the one shown in Figure 19, your computer is not connected to the Internet or Microsoft has updated the list of available Help topics since this book was published. Continue with Step 6.

Trouble? If the Word program window and the Help window do not appear side by side, then you need to tile the windows. Click the Auto Tile button on the toolbar in the Help window.

6. Click **Microsoft Office Online** in the right pane to display information about that topic. Read the information.

7. Click the other links about this feature and read the information.

8. When you're done, click the **Close** button ☒ on the Help window title bar to close the Help window. The task pane remains open.

If your computer has a connection to the Internet, you can get more help information from Microsoft Office Online.

Using Microsoft Office Online

Microsoft Office Online is a Web site maintained by Microsoft that provides access to additional Help resources. For example, you can access current Help topics, read how-to articles, and find tips for using Office. You can search all or part of a site to find information about tasks you want to perform, features you want to use, or anything else you want more help with. You can connect to Microsoft Office Online from the Getting Started task pane, the Help task pane, or the Help menu.

To connect to Microsoft Office Online, you'll need Internet access and a Web browser such as Internet Explorer.

To connect to Microsoft Office Online:

1. Click the **Back** button in the Search Results task pane. The Word Help task pane reappears.

2. Click the **Connect to Microsoft Office Online** link in the task pane. Internet Explorer starts and the Microsoft Office Online home page opens. See Figure 20. This Web page offers links to Web pages focusing on getting help and for accessing additional Office resources, such as additional galleries of clip art, software downloads, and training opportunities.

Figure 20 ▶ **Microsoft Office Online home page**

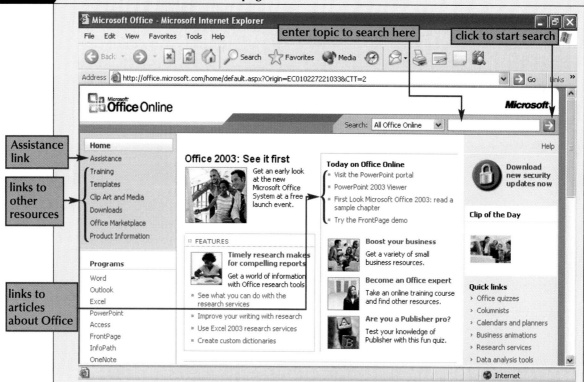

Trouble? If the content you see on the Microsoft Office Online home page differs from the figure, the site has been updated since this book was published. Continue with Step 3.

3. Click the **Assistance** link. The Assistance page opens. From this page, you browse for help in each of the different Office programs. You can also enter a keyword or phrase pertaining to a particular topic you wish to search for information on using the Search box in the upper-right corner of the window.

4. Click the **Close** button on the Internet Explorer title bar to close the browser.

The Help features enable the staff at Delmar Office Supplies to get answers to questions they have about any task or procedure when they need it. The more you practice getting information from the Help system, the more effective you will be at using Office to its full potential.

Printing a File

At times, you'll want a paper copy of your Office file. The first time you print during each session at the computer, you should use the Print menu command to open the Print dialog box so you can verify or adjust the printing settings. You can select a printer, the number of copies to print, the portion of the file to print, and so forth; the printing settings vary slightly from program to program. For subsequent print jobs, you can use the Print button to print without opening the dialog box, if you want to use the same default settings.

Printing a File

Reference Window

- Click File on the menu bar, and then click Print.
- Verify the print settings in the Print dialog box.
- Click the OK button.

or

- Click the Print button on the Standard toolbar.

Now that you know how to print, you'll print the agenda for Jake.

To print a file:

1. Make sure your printer is turned on and contains paper.
2. Click **File** on the menu bar, and then click **Print**. The Print dialog box opens. See Figure 21.

Print dialog box　　**Figure 21**

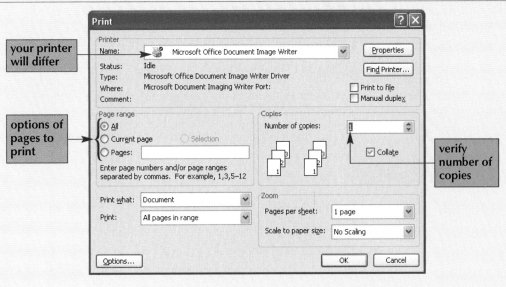

▶ **3.** Verify that the correct printer appears in the Name list box in the Printer area. If the wrong printer appears, click the **Name** list arrow, and then click the correct printer from the list of available printers.

▶ **4.** Verify that **1** appears in the Number of copies text box.

▶ **5.** Click the **OK** button to print the document.

   Trouble? If the document does not print, see your instructor or technical support person for help.

Now that you have printed the agenda, you can close Word and Excel.

Exiting Programs

Whenever you finish working with a program, you should exit it. As with many other aspects of Office, you can exit programs with a button or from a menu. You'll use both methods to close Word and Excel. You can use the Exit command to exit a program and close an open file in one step. If you haven't saved the final version of the open file, a dialog box opens, asking whether you want to save your changes. Clicking the Yes button saves the open file, closes the file, and then exits the program.

To exit a program:

▶ **1.** Click the **Close** button ⊠ on the Word title bar to exit Word. The Word document closes and the Word program exits. The Excel window is visible again on your screen.

   Trouble? If a dialog box opens, asking whether you want to save the document, you may have inadvertently made a change to the document. Click the No button.

▶ **2.** Click **File** on the Excel menu bar, and then click **Exit**. A dialog box opens asking whether you want to save the changes you made to the workbook.

▶ **3.** Click the **Yes** button. The Save As dialog box opens.

▶ **4.** Save the workbook in the **OFF\Tutorial** folder with the filename **French Sales Report**. The workbook closes, saving a copy to the location you specified, and the Excel program exits.

Exiting programs after you are done using them keeps your Windows desktop uncluttered for the next person using the computer, frees up your system's resources, and prevents data from being lost accidentally.

Review

Quick Check

1. List the five programs included in Office.
2. How do you start an Office program?
3. Explain the difference between Save As and Save.
4. What is one method for opening an existing Office file?
5. What happens if you attempt to close a file or exit a program without saving the current version of the open file?
6. What are four ways to get help?

Review

Tutorial Summary

You have learned how to use features common to all the programs included in Microsoft Office 2003, including starting and exiting programs; resizing windows; using menus and toolbars; working with task panes; saving, opening, closing, and printing files; and getting help.

Key Terms

Access	menu	Outlook
database	menu bar	PowerPoint
document	menu command	presentation
Excel	Microsoft Access 2003	ScreenTip
file extension	Microsoft Excel 2003	task pane
filename	Microsoft Office 2003	toolbar
folder	Microsoft Office Online	Type a question for help box
Help	Microsoft Outlook 2003	Word
Help task pane	Microsoft PowerPoint 2003	workbook
integration	Microsoft Word 2003	
keyboard shortcut	Office	

Practice

Practice the skills you learned in the tutorial using the same case scenario.

Review Assignments

Data Files needed for the Review Assignments: Finances.xls, Letter.doc

Before the stockholders meeting at Delmar Office Supplies, you'll open and print documents for the upcoming presentation. Complete the following steps:

1. Start PowerPoint.
2. Use the Help task pane to learn how to change the toolbar buttons from small to large, and then do it. Use the same procedure to change the buttons back to regular size. Close the Help window when you're done.
3. Start Excel.
4. Switch to the PowerPoint window using the taskbar, and then close the presentation but leave open the PowerPoint program. (*Hint:* Click the Close Window button on the menu bar.)
5. Open a new, blank PowerPoint presentation from the Getting Started task pane. (*Hint:* Click Create a new presentation in the Open section of the Getting Started task pane.)
6. Close the PowerPoint presentation and program using the Close button on the PowerPoint title bar; do not save changes if asked.

7. Open the **Finances** workbook located in the **OFF\Review** folder included with your Data Files using the Open button on the Standard toolbar in Excel.
8. Use the Save As command to save the workbook as **Delmar Finances** in the **OFF\Review** folder.
9. Type your name, press the Enter key to insert your name at the top of the worksheet, and then save the workbook.
10. Print one copy of the worksheet using the Print command on the File menu.
11. Exit Excel using the File menu.
12. Start Word, and then use the Getting Started task pane to open the **Letter** document located in the **OFF\Review** folder included with your Data Files. (*Hint:* Click the More link in the Getting Started task pane to open the Open dialog box.)
13. Use the Save As command to save the document with the filename **Delmar Letter** in the **OFF\Review** folder.
14. Press and hold the Ctrl key, press the End key, and then release both keys to move the insertion point to the end of the letter, and then type your name.
15. Use the Save button on the Standard toolbar to save the change to the Delmar Letter document.
16. Print one copy of the document, and then close the document.
17. Exit the Word program using the Close button on the title bar.

Review

Quick Check Answers

1. Word, Excel, PowerPoint, Access, Outlook
2. Click the Start button on the taskbar, point to All Programs, point to Microsoft Office, and then click the name of the program you want to open.
3. Save As enables you to change the filename and storage location of a file. Save updates a file to reflect its latest contents using its current filename and location.
4. Either click the Open button on the Standard toolbar or click the More link in the Getting Started task pane to open the Open dialog box.
5. A dialog box opens asking whether you want to save the changes to the file.
6. ScreenTips, Type a question for help box, Help task pane, Microsoft Office Online

New Perspectives on
Microsoft® Office
Excel 2003

Read This Before You Begin: Tutorials 1–4

To the Student

Data Files

To complete the Level I Excel Tutorials (Tutorials 1 through 4), you need the starting student Data Files. Your instructor will either provide you with these Data Files or ask you to obtain them yourself.

The Level I Excel tutorials require the folders shown in the next column to complete the Tutorials, Review Assignments, and Case Problems. You will need to copy these folders from a file server, a standalone computer, or the Web to the drive and folder where you will be storing your Data Files. Your instructor will tell you which computer, drive letter, and folder(s) contain the files you need. You can also download the files by going to www.course.com; see the inside back or front cover for more information on downloading the files, or ask your instructor or technical support person for assistance.

If you are storing your Data Files on floppy disks, you will need **two** blank, formatted, high-density disks for these tutorials. Label your disks as shown, and place on them the folders indicated.

▼ **Excel 2003: Data Disk 1**
  Tutorial.01 folder
  Tutorial.02 folder

▼ **Excel 2003: Data Disk 2**
  Tutorial.03 folder
  Tutorial.04 folder

When you begin a tutorial, refer to the Student Data Files section at the bottom of the tutorial opener page, which indicates which folders and files you need for the tutorial. Each end-of-tutorial exercise also indicates the files you need to complete that exercise.

Course Labs

The Level I Excel tutorials feature an interactive Course Lab to help you understand spreadsheet concepts. There are Lab Assignments at the end of Tutorial 1 that relate to this lab. Contact your instructor or technical support person for assistance in accessing the lab.

To the Instructor

The Data Files and Course Labs are available on the Instructor Resources CD for this title. Follow the instructions in the Help file on the CD to install the programs to your network or standalone computer. See the "To the Student" section above for information on how to set up the Data Files that accompany this text.

You are granted a license to copy the Data Files and Course Labs to any computer or computer network used by students who have purchased this book.

System Requirements

If you are going to work through this book using your own computer, you need:

• **Computer System** Microsoft Windows 2000, Windows XP or higher must be installed on your computer. These tutorials assume a typical installation of Microsoft Excel 2003.

• **Data Files** You will not be able to complete the tutorials or exercises in this book using your own computer until you have the necessary starting Data Files.

• **Course Labs** See your instructor or technical support person to obtain the Course Lab software for use on your own computer.

www.course.com/NewPerspectives

Objectives

Lab

Spreadsheets

Student Data Files

Using Excel to Manage Data

Creating a Sales Order Report

Case

Dalton Food Co-op

Sandra Dalton and her husband, Kevin, own a farm in northern Florida. Recently, Sandra has been selling produce to local families to earn extra income. When she started, Sandra kept a paper record of customer orders, and all of the data was entered into a paper ledger with the calculations done on a tabletop calculator. Several months ago, Sandra and Kevin purchased a computer for the co-op. Bundled with the other software installed on the computer was a copy of **Microsoft Office Excel 2003** (or simply **Excel**), a computer program used to enter, analyze, and present quantitative data.

Sandra, who handles most of the financial aspects of the business, has been using Excel for several months, but as the business continues to grow and its busy season approaches, she has asked you to help. She wants you to use an Excel workbook to keep track of orders recently made at the Dalton Food Co-op.

Session 1.1

Spreadsheets

Introducing Excel

Before you begin working with the recent orders at the co-op, you need to understand some of the key terms and concepts associated with a program such as Excel.

Understanding Spreadsheets

Excel is a computerized spreadsheet. A **spreadsheet** is an important tool used for analyzing and reporting information. Spreadsheets are often used in business for budgeting, inventory management, and decision making. For example, an accountant might use a paper-based spreadsheet like the one shown in Figure 1-1 to record a company's estimated and actual monthly cash flow.

| Figure 1-1 | A sample spreadsheet |

Cash Flow Comparison
Actual versus Budget

	Estimated	Actual
		Jan-06
Cash balance(start of month)	$ 1,500.00	$ 1,500.00
Receipts		
Cash sales	1700.00	1852.00
Cash expenditures		
Advertising	200.00	211.00
Wages	900.00	900.00
Supplies	100.00	81.00
Total cash expenditures	1200.00	1192.00
Net cash flow	500.00	660.00
Cash balance(end of month)	$ 2,000.00	$ 2,160.00

In this spreadsheet, the accountant has recorded the estimated and actual cash flow for the month of January. Each line, or row, in this spreadsheet displays a different cash flow value. Each column contains the predicted or actual values, or text that describes those values. The accountant has also entered the total cash expenditures, net cash flow, and closing cash balance for the month, perhaps having used a calculator to do the calculations.

Figure 1-2 shows the same spreadsheet in Excel. The spreadsheet is now laid out in a grid in which the rows and columns are easily apparent. As you will see later, calculations are also part of this electronic spreadsheet, so that total cash expenditures, net cash flow, and cash balances are calculated automatically rather than entered manually. When you change an entry in the electronic spreadsheet, the spreadsheet automatically updates any calculated values based on the entry. You can also use an electronic spreadsheet to perform a **what-if analysis** in which you change one or more of the values in the worksheet and then examine the recalculated values to determine the effect of the change. (You will have a chance to explore this feature at the end of the tutorial.) So, an electronic spreadsheet provides more flexibility in entering and analyzing your data than the paper version.

The same spreadsheet in Excel | **Figure 1-2**

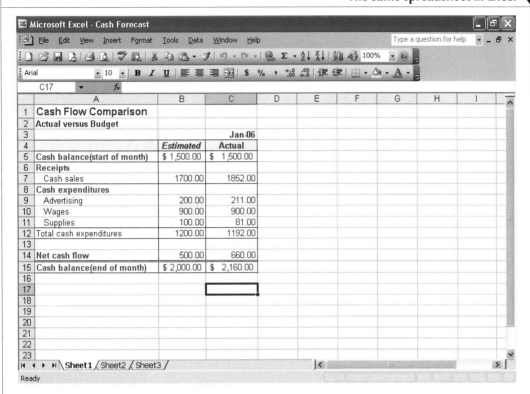

Excel stores electronic spreadsheets in files called **workbooks**. Each workbook is made up of individual **worksheets**, or **sheets**, just as a spiral-bound ledger, which an accountant would use, is made up of sheets of paper. You will learn more about multiple worksheets later in the tutorial. For now, keep in mind that the terms *worksheet* and *sheet* are often used interchangeably.

Parts of the Excel Window

Excel displays workbooks within a window that contains many tools for entering, editing, and viewing data. You will learn about some of these tools after starting Excel. By default, Excel opens with a blank workbook.

To start Excel:

1. Click the **Start** button on the taskbar, point to **All Programs**, point to **Microsoft Office**, and then click **Microsoft Office Excel 2003**. The Excel window opens. See Figure 1-3.

Figure 1-3 | **Parts of the Excel window**

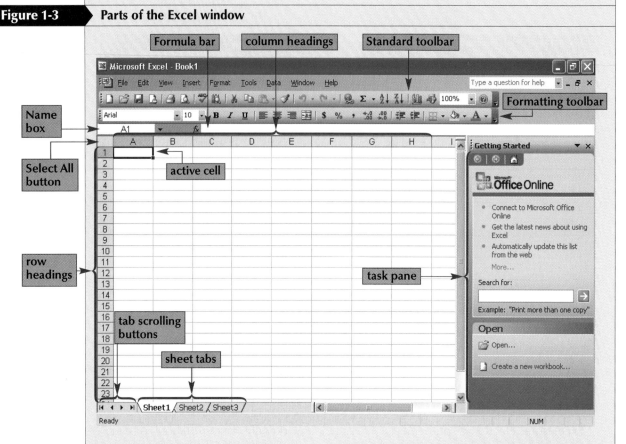

Trouble? If you don't see the Microsoft Office Excel 2003 option on the Microsoft Office submenu, look for it in a different submenu or as an option on the All Programs menu. If you still cannot find the Microsoft Office Excel 2003 option, ask your instructor or technical support person for help.

The Excel window contains many of the components that you find in other Windows programs, including a title bar, a menu bar, scroll bars, and a status bar. The Excel window also contains features that are unique to Excel. Within the Excel program window is another window, referred to as the **workbook window** or **worksheet window**. The worksheet window provides a grid of **columns** and **rows**, and the intersection of a column and row is called a **cell**. Each cell is identified by a **cell reference**, which is its column and row location. For example, the cell reference B6 indicates that the cell is located where column B and row 6 intersect. The column letter is always first in the cell reference: B6 is a correct reference; 6B is not. The cell in which you are working is called the **active cell**. Excel identifies the active cell by outlining it with a dark border. In Figure 1-3, cell A1 is the active cell. Notice that the cell reference for the active cell appears in the **Name box** next to the **Formula bar**. You can change the active cell by selecting another cell in the worksheet. As you review the layout of the Excel window shown in Figure 1-3, refer to Figure 1-4 for a description of each component.

Excel window components | **Figure 1-4**

Feature	Description
Active cell	The cell in which you are currently working. A dark border outlining the cell identifies the active cell.
Column headings	The letters that appear along the top of the worksheet window. Columns are listed alphabetically from A to IV (a total of 256 possible columns).
Formula bar	The bar located immediately below the toolbars that displays the contents of the active cell. As you type or edit data, the changes appear in the Formula bar.
Name box	The box that displays the cell reference, or column and row location, of the active cell in the workbook window.
Row headings	The numbers that appear along the left side of the worksheet window. Rows are numbered consecutively from 1 to 65,536.
Select All button	Square button located at the intersection of the column and row headings that you click to select the entire contents of the worksheet.
Sheet tabs	Tabs located at the bottom of each worksheet in the workbook that display the names of the sheets. To move between worksheets, click the appropriate sheet tab.
Task pane	The pane that provides access to frequently used tasks. When you start Excel, the Getting Started task pane appears. The task pane disappears once you open a workbook. There are several task-specific panes available in Excel.
Tab scrolling buttons	Series of buttons located to the left of the sheet tabs that you can click to move between worksheets in the workbook.
Toolbars	Toolbars that provide quick access to commonly used commands. The Standard toolbar contains buttons for the most frequently used program commands, such as Save and Print. The Formatting toolbar contains buttons used to format the appearance of the workbook, such as Bold and Italics. Additional toolbars are available.

Now that you are familiar with the basic layout of an Excel window, you can try moving around within the workbook.

Navigating a Worksheet

Excel provides several ways of moving around within a worksheet. You can use your mouse to click a cell to make it the active cell, or you can use the vertical and horizontal scroll bars to display the area of the worksheet containing the cell you want to make active. You can also navigate a worksheet by using your keyboard. Figure 1-5 describes some of these keyboard shortcuts that Excel provides so you can move from cell to cell within the worksheet quickly and easily.

Shortcut keys for navigating a worksheet | **Figure 1-5**

Keystroke	Action
↑ , ↓ , ←, →	Moves the active cell up, down, left, or right one cell
Ctrl + Home	Moves the active cell to cell A1
Ctrl + End	Moves to the last cell in the worksheet that contains data
Enter	Moves the active cell down one cell, or moves to the start of the next row in the selected range of cells
F5	Opens the Go To dialog box, in which you specify the cell you want to move to
Home	Moves the active cell to column A of the current row
Page Up, Page Down	Moves the active cell up or down one full screen
Tab, Shift + Tab	Moves the active cell to the right or left one cell

Try navigating the worksheet now.

To move around in the worksheet:

▶ **1.** Click the **Close** button 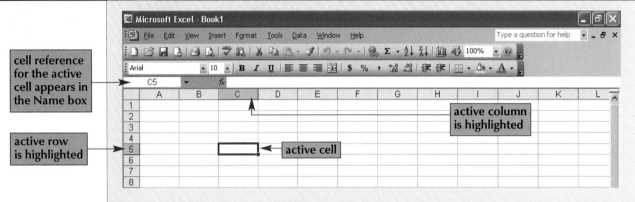 in the task pane to close it because you will not be using it in this session. The active cell is A1. The cell A1 is surrounded by a black border, indicating it is the active cell, and the Name box displays the cell reference A1.

▶ **2.** With cell A1 the active cell, press the ↓ key on your keyboard four times to move to cell A5, and then press the → key twice to make cell C5 the active cell, as shown in Figure 1-6. Note that the column and row headings are highlighted and the cell reference appears in the Name box.

Figure 1-6 | **Making cell C5 the active cell**

▶ **3.** Press the **Enter** key to move down one cell, and the press the **Tab** key to move to the right one cell. The active cell is now D6.

▶ **4.** Press the **Page Down** key to move the display down one screen. The active cell should now be cell D29. If the actual number of columns and rows displayed on your screen differs from that shown in Figure 1-2, the active cell on your screen might not be cell D29. You will learn more about working with the number of columns and rows on your screen later in this tutorial; for now the active cell on your screen should be a screen full of rows down the worksheet.

▶ **5.** Press the **Page Up** key to move the display back up one screen, making cell D6 the active cell again.

▶ **6.** Press the **Home** key to move to the first cell in the current row, and then press the **Ctrl + Home** keys to make cell A1 active.

You will probably use the keyboard keys to navigate a worksheet the most frequently, but there will also be situations in which you will want to go directly to a cell on your worksheet. Although you can use the Page Up and Page Down keys or use the scroll bars, you have two other options: the Name box and the Go To dialog box. You can just click in the Name box and type the cell reference you want to go to, or you can open the Go To dialog box from any location in the worksheet by pressing the F5 function key. Try using these methods to navigate the worksheet.

To use the Go To dialog box and Name box:

▶ **1.** Press the **F5** key to open the Go To dialog box, type **K55** in the Reference text box, and then click the **OK** button to make cell K55 the active cell.

▶ **2.** Click in the **Name** box, type **E6**, and then press the **Enter** key to make cell E6 the active cell.

Navigating Between Worksheets

By default, a new Excel workbook contains three worksheets, labeled Sheet1, Sheet2, and Sheet3. Each sheet can be used to display different information. To move from one sheet to another, click the sheet tabs at the bottom of each sheet.

To move between worksheets:

1. Click the **Sheet2** tab. Sheet2, which is blank, appears in the workbook window. Notice that the Sheet2 tab is now white with the name "Sheet2" in a bold font. This is a visual indicator that Sheet2 is the active worksheet.
2. Click the **Sheet3** tab to move to the next worksheet in the workbook.
3. Click the **Sheet1** tab to make it the active worksheet.

Now that you have some basic skills navigating through a worksheet and a workbook, you can begin work on Sandra's worksheet.

Developing a Worksheet

Before you begin to enter data in a worksheet, you should think about the purpose of the worksheet and what will be needed to meet the challenge of that purpose. Effective worksheets are well planned and carefully designed. A well-designed worksheet should clearly identify its overall goal. It should present information in a clear, well-organized format and include all the data necessary to produce results that address the goal of the application. The process of developing a good worksheet includes the following planning and execution steps:

- Determine the worksheet's purpose, what it will include, and how it will be organized.
- Enter the data and formulas into the worksheet.
- Test the worksheet, and then edit the worksheet to correct any errors or to make modifications.
- Document the worksheet and format the worksheet's appearance.
- Save and print the complete worksheet.

To develop a worksheet that records orders made at the co-op, Sandra wants to develop a planning analysis sheet that will help her answer the following questions:

1. What is the goal of the worksheet? This helps to define its purpose or, in other words, the problem to solve.
2. What are the desired results? This information describes the output—the information required to help solve the problem.
3. What data is needed to calculate the results you want to see? This information is the input—data that must be entered.
4. What calculations are needed to produce the desired output? These calculations specify the formulas used in the worksheet.

After careful consideration of these questions, Sandra has developed the planning analysis sheet shown in Figure 1-7.

Figure 1-7 ▶ **Planning analysis sheet**

Planning Analysis Sheet
Author: Sandra Dalton, Dalton Food Co-op
Date: 4/26/2006

My goal
To develop a worksheet in which I can enter food co-op orders, calculating the total
quantity of the items ordered and the revenue generated.

What results do I need to see?
- A listing of each order made by customers
- The total amount of each order
- The total quantity of items ordered by all of the customers
- The total revenue generated by all of the orders

What data do I need?
- The customer's name and address
- The date of the order
- The item purchased by the customer
- The price of each item
- The quantity of items ordered by the customer

What calculations must be performed by the worksheet?
- The total amount of each order (= price of the item x the quantity ordered)
- The total quantity of items ordered (= sum of the order quantities)
- The total revenue generated by all of the orders (= sum of the total amount of each order)

Sandra also knows the information that needs to go into the worksheet, including titles,
column headings, row labels, and data values. Figure 1-8 shows how Sandra wants the
sales data laid out, based on a sampling of customer orders.

Figure 1-8 ▶ **Sales data for co-op worksheet**

Name	Address	Date	Item	Price	Qty	Total
Alison Wilkes	45 Lincoln Street Midtown, FL 80481	4/16/2006	Red Grapefruit	$14	2	
David Wu	315 Oak Lane Midtown, FL 80422	4/16/2006	Navel Oranges	$17	1	
Carl Ramirez	900 South Street Crawford, FL 81891	4/17/2006	Navel Oranges	$17	2	
Jerry Dawson	781 Tree Lane Midtown, FL 80313	4/18/2006	Deluxe Combo	$21	4	
TOTAL						

The first two columns contain the name and address of the person ordering items from
the co-op. The Date and Item columns indicate the date that the order was placed and the
item ordered. The Price column displays the price of the item. The Qty column indicates
the quantity of each item ordered by the customer. The Total column will display the total

amount of each order. The TOTAL row will display the total quantity of items ordered and the total revenue generated by all of the sales. With this information in hand, you are now ready to create Sandra's worksheet in Excel.

Entering Data into a Worksheet

A worksheet can contain the following types of data: text, numeric values, dates, and calculated values. A text entry is simply any combination of words, letters, and numbers, typically used to label key features of the worksheet. Numeric values are numbers on which calculations can be made. Numeric values do not contain alphabetic characters, but may contain characters such as commas, dollar signs, and percent signs. Dates are special numeric values recognized by Excel and can be used to determine date-related calculations. The power of Excel lies in the formulas that you can enter into the worksheet cells, whose calculated values are based on the text, dates, and numeric values entered into other cells in the workbook (or in more complicated cases, other workbooks). If those values are changed, the calculated values will also be changed.

Worksheet cells in Excel can also be formatted to improve or enhance the appearance of the cell contents or an entire worksheet. You'll learn about formatting later in Tutorial 3.

Entering Text

To insert text into a worksheet cell, you first make the cell active by using one of the navigation techniques discussed earlier, and then you type the text you want the cell to contain. Excel automatically aligns the text with the left edge of the cell.

First, you'll enter the column headings that Sandra wants across the top row of her worksheet.

To enter the column headings in row 1:

► 1. Press the **Ctrl + Home** keys to make cell A1 the active cell on the Sheet1 worksheet.

► 2. Type **Name** and then press the **Tab** key. Pressing the Tab key enters the text in the cell and moves the insertion point to the right to cell B1, making it the active cell.

► 3. Type **Address** in cell B1, and then press the **Tab** key again. Cell C1 becomes the active cell.

► 4. Enter the remaining column headings **Date**, **Item**, **Price**, **Qty**, and **Total** in cells C1 through G1. Press the **Enter** key after you type the text for cell G1. Figure 1-9 shows the column headings for the worksheet.

Entering text into the worksheet ◄ **Figure 1-9**

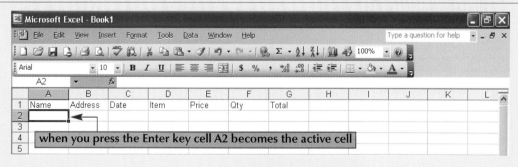

Trouble? If you make a mistake as you type, you can correct the error by clicking the cell and retyping the entry.

Note that when you press the Enter key, the active cell becomes cell A2, not cell G2. Excel recognizes that when you enter a row of data and then press the Enter key, you have completed the task of entering data in the current row, so the insertion point moves to the start of the next row. If you had started entering data in cell C1 rather than A1, pressing the Enter key would have made cell C2 the active cell.

Entering Several Lines of Text Within a Cell

In the next row, you'll enter actual sales information. One cell in this row contains the customer's address. In Sandra's records, this information is presented on two separate lines, with the street address on one line and the city, state, and ZIP code on the other. To place text on separate lines within the same cell, you press and hold the Alt key on the keyboard while pressing the Enter key.

Reference Window

Entering Multiple Lines of Text Within a Cell

- Click the cell in which you want to enter the text.
- Enter a line of text.
- Press and hold the Alt key, and then press the Enter key to move the insertion point to a new line within the cell.
- Enter the next line of text.
- Press the Alt + Enter keys for each new line of text you need to enter within the cell.

Try this technique now by entering the first customer's name and address.

To enter the address on two lines within a cell:

1. Verify that cell **A2** is the active cell, type **Alison Wilkes**, and then press the **Tab** key to move to column B, where you will enter the two-line address.

2. Type **45 Lincoln Street** in cell B2, but do *not* press the Tab or Enter key.

3. Press and hold the **Alt** key, and then press the **Enter** key to insert a line break, moving the insertion point to a new line within the cell.

4. Type **Midtown, FL 80481** on the second line of the cell, and then press the **Tab** key. Figure 1-10 shows the worksheet with the text you have entered so far.

Figure 1-10 > Entering the customer name and address

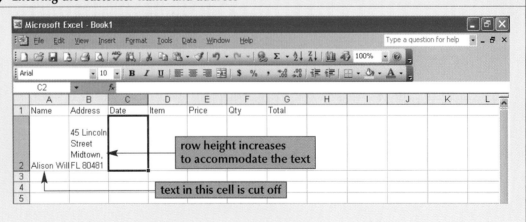

Excel has done a couple of things that you need to understand before entering more data. First, the name of the customer in cell A2 has been cut off, or truncated. When you enter more text than can be displayed within a cell, Excel will display the additional text in the cell or cells to the right as long as they are empty. If the cells to the right are not empty, Excel will truncate the display of the text when it encounters the first non-empty cell. The text itself is not affected. The complete name of the first customer is still entered in cell A2; it's just not displayed.

Second, the customer address in cell B2 does not extend into cell C2, even though that cell is empty. Instead, the height of row 2 has been increased to accommodate this text. If a cell contains multiple lines of text, Excel increases the height of the row to display all of the text entry. Note that the text in cell B2 "appears" to be on four lines, even though you entered the address on two lines. Excel wrapped the text in this way so that it would fit within the existing column width. Later in this session, you will learn how to adjust column widths and row heights to improve the worksheet's appearance.

Entering Dates

In Excel, dates are treated as numeric values, not text. This allows you to perform calculations with dates, such as determining the number of days between two dates. You'll learn how to work with date values in the next tutorial. For now, you need to know how to enter a date. You can enter a date using any of the following date formats, which are recognized by Excel:

- 4/16/2006
- 4/16/06
- 4-16-2006
- April 16, 2006
- 16-Apr-06

The appearance of a date, regardless of how you enter it in a cell, depends on the date format that has been set as the default in your version of Excel. For example, if you enter the date as the text string "April 26, 2006," Excel will automatically convert the entry to "26-Apr-2006" if the DD-MMM-YYYY format has been set as the default. You will learn about cell formats and date formats in Tutorial 3.

Sandra wants the date "4/16/2006" to appear in cell C2, so you will enter that next.

To insert the date in cell C2:

▶ **1.** Verify that cell **C2** is the active cell.

▶ **2.** Type **4/16/2006** and then press the **Tab** key.

Trouble? If your computer is set up to display dates using a different date format, do not worry about their appearance at this time.

▶ **3.** Type **Red Grapefruit** in cell D2, and then press the **Tab** key. Note that the text in cell D2 is completely displayed because, at this point, the cells to the right of D2 are still empty.

Entering Values

Values are numbers that represent a quantity of some type: the number of units in an inventory, stock prices, an exam score, and so on. Values can be numbers such as 378 and 25.275 or negative numbers such as –55.208. Values can also be expressed as currency such as $14.95 or as percentages such as 95%. Not all numbers are treated as values. For example, Excel treats a telephone number (1-800-555-8010) or a Social Security number (372-70-9654) as a text entry. As you type information into a cell, Excel determines whether the entry can be treated as a value, and if so, automatically right-aligns the value within the cell.

Next, you'll enter the price and quantity of the first order into cells E2 and F2.

To enter the price and quantity values:

1. Type **$14** in cell E2, and then press the **Tab** key.

2. Type **2** in cell F2, and then press the **Tab** key. Figure 1-11 shows the data for the first order. The last cell in the row is empty, but next you will enter a calculation that will give Sandra the total amount of the order.

| Figure 1-11 | Entering the price and quantity values |

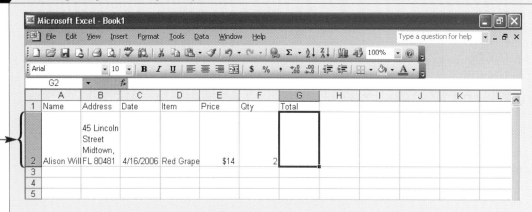

data for the first order entered

The remaining cell in this row will contain the total price of the order, which is equal to the price of the red grapefruit item multiplied by the quantity ordered. The total price of the first order is $14 multiplied by 2, or $28. Rather than entering this value into the cell, you'll let Excel calculate it for you by entering a formula.

Entering Formulas

The single most important reason for using a spreadsheet is to perform calculations on data. To accomplish that goal, you need to enter formulas. A **formula** is a mathematical expression that calculates a value. Excel formulas always begin with an equal sign (=) followed by an expression that describes the calculation to be done. A formula can contain one or more **arithmetic operators**, such as +, –, *, or /. For example, the formula =A1+A2 calculates the sum by adding the values of cells A1 and A2. Figure 1-12 gives examples of some other Excel formulas. Note that, by convention, cell references appear in uppercase letters, but this is not a requirement for Excel formulas. You can type the formula using either upper- or lowercase letters, and Excel will automatically convert the cell references to uppercase.

Sample Excel formulas using arithmetic operators ◄ **Figure 1-12**

Operation	Operator	Example	Description
Addition	+	=10+A5	Adds 10 to the value in cell A5
		=B1+B2+B3	Adds the values of cells B1, B2, and B3
Subtraction	−	=C9–B2	Subtracts the value in cell B2 from the value in cell C9
		=1–D2	Subtracts the value in cell D2 from 1
Multiplication	*	=C9*B9	Multiplies the value in cell C9 by the value in cell B9
		=E5*0.06	Multiplies the value in cell E5 by 0.06
Division	/	=C9/B9	Divides the value in cell C9 by the value in cell B9
		=D15/12	Divides the value in cell D15 by 12
Exponentiation	^	=B5^3	Raises the value in cell B5 to the third power
		=3^B5	Raises 3 to the power specified in cell B5

Entering a Formula

- Click the cell where you want the formula result to appear.
- Type = and then type the expression that calculates the value you want.
- For a formula that includes cell references, such as B2 or D78, type the cell reference, or use the mouse or arrow keys to select each cell.
- When the formula is complete, press the Enter key (or press the Tab key or click the Enter button on the Formula bar).

If an expression contains more than one arithmetic operator, Excel performs the calculation in the order of precedence. The **order of precedence** is a set of predefined rules that Excel follows to calculate a formula by determining which operator is applied first, which operator is applied second, and so forth. First, Excel performs exponentiation (^). Second, Excel performs multiplication (*) or division (/). Third, Excel performs addition (+) or subtraction (−).

For example, because multiplication has precedence over addition, the formula =3+4*5 results in the value 23. If the expression contains two or more operators with the same level of precedence, Excel applies them from left to right in the expression. In the formula =4*10/8, Excel first multiplies 4 by 10 and then divides the result by 8 to produce the value 5.

When building a formula, you must add parentheses to change the order of operations. Excel will calculate any expression contained within the parentheses before any other part of the formula. The formula =(3+4)*5 first calculates the value of 3+4 and then multiplies the total by 5, resulting in the value 35. (Note that without the parentheses, Excel would produce a value of 23, as noted in the previous paragraph.) Figure 1-13 shows other examples of Excel formulas using the order of precedence rules.

Figure 1-13 | **Examples illustrating order of precedence rules**

Formula (A1=50, B1=10, C1=5)	Order of precedence rule	Result
=A1+B1*C1	Multiplication before addition	100
=(A1+B1)*C1	Expression inside parentheses executed before expression outside	300
=A1/B1–C1	Division before subtraction	0
=A1/(B1–C1)	Expression inside parentheses executed before expression outside	10
=A1/B1*C1	Two operators at same precedence level, leftmost operator evaluated first	25
=A1/(B1*C1)	Expression inside parentheses executed before expression outside	1

Using what you know about formulas, you'll enter a formula in cell G2 to calculate the total amount of Alison Wilke's order.

To enter a formula to calculate the total amount of the first order:

1. Verify that cell **G2** is the active cell.

2. Type **=E2*F2** (the price of the item multiplied by the quantity ordered). Note that as you type the cell reference, Excel surrounds each cell with a different colored border that matches the color of the cell reference in the formula. As shown in Figure 1-14, Excel surrounds cell E2 with a blue border, matching the blue used for the cell reference. Green is used for the F2 cell border and cell reference.

Figure 1-14 | **Typing a formula into the active cell**

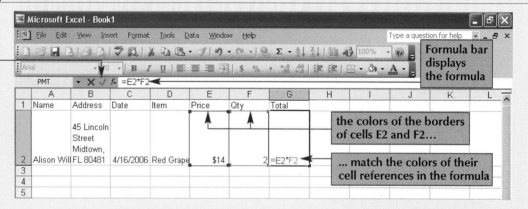

3. Press the **Enter** key. The total amount of the first order displayed in cell G2 is $28. Note that the value is displayed as currency because one of the components of the formula (cell E2) is a currency value. As you can see, the result of the formula is displayed in the worksheet. To see the formula itself, you need to select the cell and examine the formula in the Formula bar.

You can also enter formulas interactively by clicking each cell. In this technique, you type = (an equal sign) to begin the formula, and then click each cell that needs to be entered in the formula. Using this point-and-click method reduces the possibility of error caused by typing an incorrect cell reference.

Next, you'll enter the data for the second order, and then enter the formula =E3*F3 (the price of the item multiplied by the quantity ordered) using the point-and-click method.

To enter the same formula using the point-and-click method:

▶ 1. Enter **David Wu** in cell A3, **315 Oak Lane** on one line in cell B3 and **Midtown, FL 80422** on a second line in the cell, **4/16/2006** in cell C3, **Navel Oranges** in cell D3, **$17** in cell E3, and **1** in cell F3. Be sure to press the Alt + Enter keys to enter the address information on two separate lines as you did for the address in cell B2.

▶ 2. Make sure cell **G3** is the active cell, and then type **=** (but do *not* press the Enter or Tab key). When you type the equal sign, Excel knows that you are entering a formula. Any cell that you click from now on will cause Excel to insert the reference of the selected cell into the formula until you complete the formula by pressing the Enter or Tab key or by clicking the Enter button on the Formula bar (refer to Figure 1-14).

▶ 3. Click cell **E3**. Note that the cell is highlighted in the same color as the cell reference that now appears in the formula in cell G3.

▶ 4. Type ***** to enter the multiplication operator.

▶ 5. Click cell **F3** to enter this cell reference, and then press the **Enter** key. Cell G3 now contains the formula =E3*F3 and displays the value $17, which is the total amount of the second order.

Using AutoComplete

As you continue to work with Excel, you may find yourself entering the same text in different rows in the worksheet. To help make entering repetitive text easier, Excel provides the **AutoComplete** feature. Once you enter text in a worksheet, Excel tries to anticipate the text you are about to enter by displaying text that begins with the same letter as a previous entry. For example, two people—David Wu and Carl Ramirez—have ordered a box of navel oranges. You have already entered the data for David Wu's order. When you enter the data for Carl Ramirez's order, you will see how AutoComplete works.

To enter text using AutoComplete:

▶ 1. Enter **Carl Ramirez** in cell A4, **900 South Street Crawford**, **FL 81891** in cell B4 on two separate lines within the cell, and **4/17/2006** in cell C4. Do *not* enter the item for Carl's order yet.

▶ 2. Make sure cell **D4** is the active cell, and then type **N**. Note that Excel anticipates the entry by displaying "Navel Oranges," which is text you have already entered beginning with the letter N. See Figure 1-15. At this point, you can accept Excel's suggestion by pressing the Enter or Tab key to complete the text entry and to exit the cell. To override Excel's suggestion, you simply keep typing the text you want to enter into the cell.

Figure 1-15 **Entering text with the AutoComplete feature**

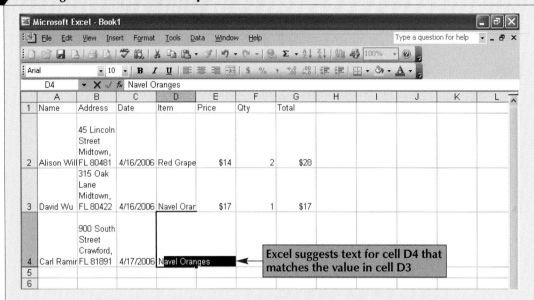

Trouble? If your version of Excel is not set up to use AutoComplete, you will not see the suggested text; therefore you must type "Navel Oranges".

3. Press the **Tab** key to accept Excel's AutoComplete suggestion and to move to cell E4.

4. Type **$17** in cell E4, press the **Tab** key, type **2** in cell F4, and then press the **Tab** key to move to cell G4.

5. Enter **=E4*F4** in cell G4 by typing the formula or by using the point-and-click method. Note that from now on in this text, when you are instructed to "enter" something versus "type" it, use the method that you most prefer; that is, press the Enter key, press the Tab key, or click the Enter button on the Formula bar. Clicking the Enter button not only enters the value in the cell, but also keeps that cell as the active cell.

Excel does not apply AutoComplete to dates or values. However, you can use another feature, AutoFill, to automatically fill in formulas. You'll learn more about AutoFill in the next tutorial.

Now you'll enter the last co-op order into the worksheet.

To enter the last order into the worksheet:

1. Enter **Jerry Dawson** in cell A5, **781 Tree Lane Midtown, FL 80313** in cell B5, **4/18/2006** in cell C5, **Deluxe Combo** in cell D5, **$21** in cell E5, and **4** in cell F5. (Remember to enter the address on two lines.)

2. In cell G5, enter the formula **=E5*F5**. Figure 1-16 shows the completed worksheet.

Four co-op orders entered ◄ **Figure 1-16**

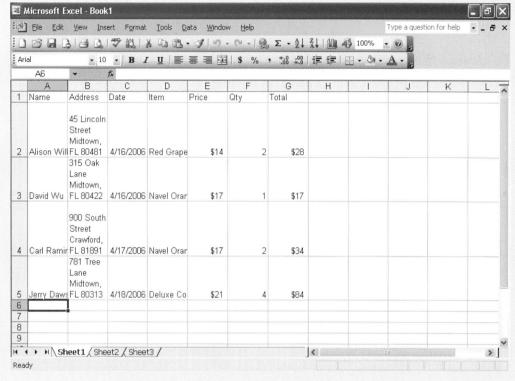

Changing the Size of a Column or Row

The default sizes of the columns and rows in an Excel worksheet may not always accommodate the information you need to enter. You can change the width of one column or multiple columns or the height of one row or multiple rows. Excel provides several methods for changing the width of a column or the height of a row. You can click the dividing line of the column or row, or you can drag the dividing line to change the width of the column or the height of the row. Heights and widths are expressed in terms of the number of characters that can be displayed in the cell, as well as the number of screen pixels, which are small units of measurement that appear as tiny dots on the screen.

Changing the Column Width or Row Height

Reference Window

- Click the column or row heading whose width or height you want to change.
- Click Format on the menu bar, point to Column or Row, and then click Width or Height (or click AutoFit or AutoFit Selection to make the column or row as large as the longest entry of the cells).
- In the Column Width or Row Height dialog box, enter the new column width or row height, and then click the OK button.

or

- Drag the column or row heading dividing line to the right or up to increase the column width or row height, or drag the dividing line to the left or down to decrease the column width or row height.

or

- Double-click the column or row heading dividing line to make the column or row as large as the longest entry of the cells in the column or row.

You'll use the drag technique to increase the width of the columns in which the data display has been truncated. As you drag the dividing line, a ScreenTip appears and displays the column width in characters and pixels.

To change the width of columns in the worksheet:

▸ 1. Move the mouse pointer to the dividing line between the column A and column B headings until the pointer changes to ↔.

▸ 2. Click and drag the pointer to the right to a length of about **20** characters (or **145 pixels**). See Figure 1-17.

Figure 1-17 **Increasing the width of column A**

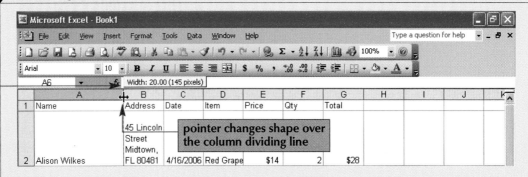

ScreenTip showing the width in characters and pixels

▸ 3. Release the mouse button. All the names in column A should now be visible.

Trouble? If the text in column A is still truncated, drag the dividing line further to the right.

▸ 4. Move the mouse pointer to the dividing line between column B and column C until the pointer changes to ↔, and then increase the width of column B to **25** characters (or **180** pixels).

▸ 5. Use your mouse to increase the width of column D to **15** characters (or **110** pixels).

Changing the width of the columns does not affect the height of the rows. However, now that column A is wider and the rows are taller, there is a great deal of empty space. To remove the empty space, you'll resize the rows. Rather than choosing a size for the rows, you'll let Excel make the adjustment automatically. If you double-click the dividing line of a column or row heading, the column width or row height adjusts to match the length of the longest entry in that column or row. You'll use this technique now to modify the height of the second row in the worksheet.

To change the height of the second row:

▸ 1. Move the mouse pointer to the dividing line between the second and third rows until the pointer changes to ⤬.

▸ 2. Double-click the dividing line between the second and third rows. See Figure 1-18.

Changing the height of the second row | **Figure 1-18**

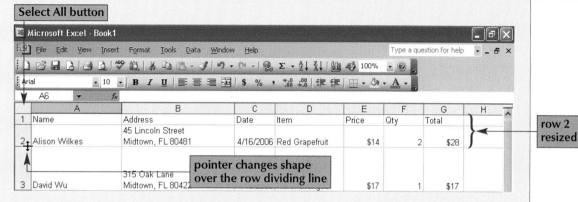

You can continue modifying the height of the remaining rows using this technique, but, for a worksheet containing a large amount of data, that would be extremely time-consuming. Another approach is to select the entire worksheet and then double-click the dividing line between any two row headings. When you do that, Excel changes the height of the rows to accommodate the data in them and reduces the amount of empty space. You can use this approach to resize columns, too.

You can select the entire worksheet by clicking the Select All button. You'll use this approach now to change the height of the remaining rows in the co-op order worksheet.

To change the height of the remaining rows:

1. Click the **Select All** button located at the junction of the row and column headings (see Figure 1-18). The row and column headings are displayed in black or dark blue, and all of the worksheet cells are displayed in light blue, indicating that the entire worksheet has been selected.

2. Move the mouse pointer to a dividing line between any two rows until the pointer changes to ✛.

3. Double-click the dividing line. Excel resizes the height of all the rows.

4. Click cell **A1** to make it the active cell and to remove the blue highlighting from the worksheet. Figure 1-19 shows the revised layout of the sheet.

Adjusting the height of the worksheet rows | **Figure 1-19**

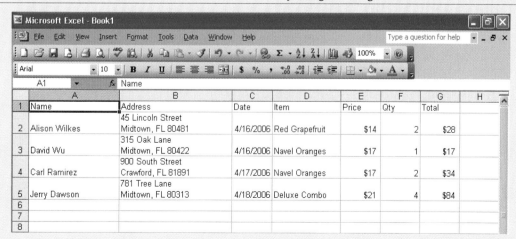

You've entered the data that Sandra wanted in the worksheet. Before proceeding further, she suggests that you save the file with the name "Dalton".

To save the workbook:

1. Click **File** on the menu bar, and then click **Save**. The Save As dialog box opens with the current workbook name, which is "Book1," in the File name text box.

2. Navigate to the Tutorial.01\Tutorial folder included with your Data Files.

   Trouble? If you don't have the Excel 2003 Data Files, you need to get them before you can proceed. Your instructor will either give you the Data Files or ask you to obtain them from a specified location (such as a network drive). In either case, be sure that you make a backup copy of your Data Files before you start using them, so that the original files will be available on your copied disk in case you need to start over because of an error or problem. If you have any questions about the Data Files, see your instructor or technical support person for assistance.

3. Replace the default filename with **Dalton**, make sure that **Microsoft Office Excel Workbook** is displayed in the Save as type list box, and then click the **Save** button. Excel saves the workbook with the name "Dalton" and closes the Save As dialog box. The new workbook name appears in the title bar of the Excel window.

   Trouble? If your computer has been set up to display file extensions, the filename "Dalton.xls" will appear in the title bar.

By default, Excel saves the workbook in Microsoft Excel Workbook format, and for most of the work you will do in this text, you will use this file format. If you are creating a workbook that will be read by applications other than Excel (or earlier versions of Excel), you can save your workbook in a different file format by following these steps:

1. Open the Save or Save As dialog box.
2. Display the location in which you want to save the file, and enter a filename, if necessary.
3. Click the Save as type list arrow, and then select the file format you want to apply.
4. Click the Save button.

Figure 1-20 describes some of the file formats in which you can save your workbooks.

Figure 1-20   **Some of the formats supported by Excel**

Format	Description
Microsoft Excel 4.0, 5.0, 97, 2000, 2002 Workbook	Saves the workbook in an earlier version of Excel
Single File Web Page	Saves the workbook as a single Web page file (MHTML file) that can be read by Internet Explorer 4.0 or later
Template	Saves the workbook as a template to be used for creating other Excel workbooks
Web Page	Saves the workbook in separate files that are used as the basis for a Web site, in a format that is readable by most browsers
XML Spreadsheet	Saves the workbook as an XML document

Sandra has some other changes to the workbook that she wants you to make. You'll continue working with the worksheet in the next session.

Session 1.1 Quick Check

1. A(n) _____ is the place on the worksheet where a column and row intersect.
2. Cell _____ refers to the intersection of the fourth column and second row.
3. What combination of keys can you press to make A1 the active cell in the worksheet?
4. To make Sheet2 the active worksheet, you _____.
5. Indicate whether Excel treats the following cell entries as text, a value, or a formula.
   a. 11/09/2006
   b. Net Income
   c. 321
   d. C11*225
   e. 201-19-1121
   f. =D1-D9
   g. 44 Evans Avenue
6. How do you enter multiple lines of text within a cell?
7. What formula would you enter to divide the value in cell E5 by the value in cell E6?

Session 1.2

Working with Ranges

Sandra has had a chance to study your work from the previous session. She likes the layout of her data, but she wants to have a title at the top of the worksheet that displays information about the sheet's contents. To make room for the title, you have to move the contents of the worksheet down a few rows. Before you attempt that, you have to first understand how Excel works with groups of cells.

A group of worksheet cells is called a **cell range**, or just **range**. Ranges can be either adjacent or nonadjacent. An **adjacent range** is a single rectangular block, such as all of the data entered in cells A1 through G5 of the Dalton workbook. A **nonadjacent range** consists of two or more separate adjacent ranges. For example, a nonadjacent range might be composed of the names of the customers in the cell range A1 through A5 and the total price of their orders in the cell range G1 through G5.

Just as a cell reference indicates the location of a cell on the worksheet, a **range reference** indicates the location and size of a cell range. For adjacent ranges, the range reference identifies the cells in the upper-left and lower-right corners of the rectangle, with the individual cell references separated by a colon. For example, the range reference for the order data you entered in the last session was A1:G5 because it included the range of cells from A1 through G5. If the range is nonadjacent, a semicolon separates the rectangular blocks A1:A5 and G1:G5, as in A1:A5;G1:G5. This nonadjacent range references the customer names in the range A1:A5 and the total amounts of their orders in the range G1:G5.

Selecting Ranges

Once you know how to select ranges of cells, you can move and copy the data anywhere in the worksheet or workbook.

Reference Window

Selecting Adjacent or Nonadjacent Ranges of Cells

To select an adjacent range of cells:
- Click a cell in the upper-left corner of the rectangle that comprises the adjacent range.
- Press and hold the left mouse button, and then drag the pointer through the cells you want selected.
- Release the mouse button.

To select a nonadjacent range of cells:
- Select an adjacent range of cells.
- Press and hold the Ctrl key, and then select another adjacent cell range.
- With the Ctrl key still pressed, continue to select other cell ranges until all of the ranges are selected.
- Release the mouse button and the Ctrl key.

To see how to select ranges, you'll start by selecting all of the cells containing order information.

To select the order data:

1. If you took a break at the end of the previous session, make sure that Excel is running and that the Dalton workbook is open.

2. Click cell **A1** on the Sheet1 worksheet, press and hold the left mouse button, and then drag the pointer to cell **G5**.

3. Release the mouse button. All the cells in the range A1:G5 are now highlighted, indicating that they are selected. See Figure 1-21.

Figure 1-21 Selecting the range A1:G5

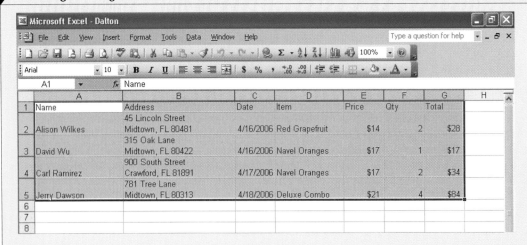

4. Click any cell in the worksheet to deselect the range.

Now try selecting the nonadjacent range A1:A5;G1:G5.

To select the nonadjacent range A1:A5;G1:G5:

▶ **1.** Select the range **A1:A5**, press and hold the **Ctrl** key, select the range **G1:G5**, and then release the mouse button and the Ctrl key. See Figure 1-22 for the selected nonadjacent range.

Selecting the nonadjacent range A1:A5;G1:G5 ◀ **Figure 1-22**

▶ **2.** Click any cell in the worksheet to deselect the range.

Other Selection Techniques

You can also select large cell ranges that extend beyond the borders of the workbook window. When this situation occurs, Excel automatically scrolls the workbook window horizontally or vertically to display additional cells in the worksheet. Selecting a large cell range using the mouse drag technique can be slow and frustrating. For this reason, Excel provides keyboard shortcuts that enable you to quickly select large blocks of data without having to drag through the worksheet to select the necessary cells. Figure 1-23 describes some of these selection techniques.

Other range selection techniques ◀ **Figure 1-23**

To Select...	Action
A large range of cells	Click the first cell in the range, press and hold down the Shift key, and then click the last cell in the range. All of the cells between the first and last cell are selected.
All cells on the worksheet	Click the Select All button, the gray rectangle in the upper-left corner of the worksheet where the row and column headings meet.
All cells in an entire row or column	Click the row or column heading.
A range of cells containing data	Click the cell where you want to begin the selection of the range, press and hold down the Shift key, and then double-click the side of the cell in the direction that you want to extend the selection. Excel selects all adjacent cells that contain data, extending the selection of the range to the first empty cell.

Try some of the techniques described to select ranges of cells in the Dalton workbook.

To select a range of cells using keyboard shortcuts:

▶ 1. Click cell **A1** to make it the active cell.

▶ 2. Press and hold the **Shift** key, click cell **A5**, and then release the Shift key. Note that all of the cells between A1 and A5 are selected.

   Trouble? If the range A1:A5 is not selected, try again, but make sure you hold the Shift key while you click cell A5.

▶ 3. Click cell **A1** to make it the active cell again. Note that you don't have to deselect one range before clicking another cell.

▶ 4. Press and hold the **Shift** key, move the pointer to the bottom edge of cell A1 until the mouse pointer changes to ⬚, and then double-click the bottom edge of cell **A1**. The selection extends to cell A5, the last cell before the empty cell A6.

▶ 5. With the Shift key still pressed, move the pointer to the right edge of the selection until, once again, the pointer changes to ⬚, double-click the right edge of the selection, and then release the Shift key. The selection extends to the last nonblank column in the worksheet, selecting the range A1:G5.

▶ 6. Click the **A** column heading. All of the cells in column A are selected. Note that you didn't have to deselect the range A1:G5.

▶ 7. Click the **1** row heading. All of the cells in the first row are selected.

Moving a Selection of Cells

Now that you know various ways to select a range of cells, you can move the co-op data down a few rows in the worksheet. To move a cell range, you first select it; then you position the pointer over the selection border, and drag the selection to a new location. Try this technique to move the order data from the cell range A1:G5 to the cell range A5:G9.

To move the order data:

▶ 1. Select the range **A1:G5**, and then move the pointer over the bottom border of the selection until the pointer changes to ⬚.

▶ 2. Press and hold the left mouse button, changing the pointer to ⬚, and then drag the selection down four rows. A ScreenTip appears indicating the new range reference of the selection. See Figure 1-24.

Moving the selection to the range A5:G9 | **Figure 1-24**

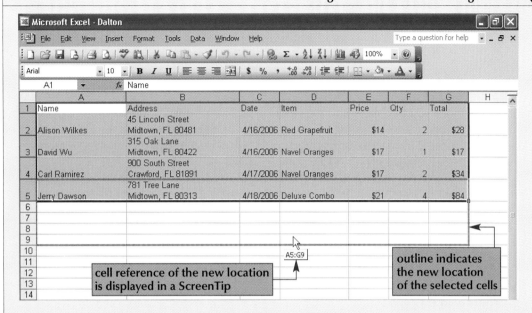

3. When the ScreenTip displays "A5:G9," release the left mouse button. The order data is now moved to range A5:G9.

Trouble? If you selected the wrong range or moved the selection to the wrong location, click the Undo button 🔄 on the Standard toolbar, and then repeat Steps 1 through 3.

4. Click cell **A1** to remove the selection and to make cell A1 the active cell so you can enter the new titles in the worksheet.

5. Type **Dalton Food Co-op** in cell A1, **List of Orders** in cell A2, **April, 2006** in cell A3, and then press the **Enter** key. Note that moving the cell range had no impact on the values in the worksheet; the values shown by the formulas in column G are also unchanged. This is because Excel automatically updated the cell references in the formulas to reflect the new location of the data. To confirm this, you'll examine the formula in cell G6.

6. Click cell **G6** and observe what is displayed in the Formula bar. The formula in cell G6 is now =E6*F6. Recall that when you originally entered Alison Wilke's order, the formula for this cell was =E2*G2 because the order was originally placed in the second row of the worksheet. When you moved the data, Excel automatically updated the formula to reflect the new location of Alison Wilke's order.

The technique you used to move the cell range is called "drag and drop." You can also use the drag-and-drop technique to copy a cell range. Copying a range of cells is similar to moving a range, except that you must press the Ctrl key while you drag the selection to its new location. A copy of the original data will then appear at the location of the pointer when you release the mouse button. You'll learn more about copying and pasting in the next two tutorials.

A cell range can also be moved from one worksheet in the workbook to another. To do this, press and hold the Alt key and then drag the selection over the sheet tab of the new worksheet. Excel will automatically make that worksheet the active sheet, so you can drag the selection into its new location on the worksheet.

Calculating Sums with AutoSum

Sandra reminds you that she wants the worksheet to also display summary information about the co-op orders, including the total number of items ordered and the amount of revenue generated from those orders. You could calculate the total quantity and total revenue using the formulas =F6+F7+F8+F9 and =G6+G7+G8+G9.

One problem with this approach is that as Sandra adds new orders to the worksheet, you will have to constantly update these formulas, adding cell references for the new orders. As you add more orders, the length of these two expressions will increase dramatically, increasing the possibility of making errors in the formulas.

One way to solve this problem is to use a **function**, which is a predefined formula that performs calculations using specific values. You will learn about and work with functions in more detail in the next tutorial. In this case, you'll insert one of Excel's most commonly used Financial functions, the SUM function, using the AutoSum button on the Standard toolbar. The **AutoSum** feature is a quick and convenient way to enter the SUM function. You use the **SUM function** to calculate the sum of values in a cell range. In this case, you want to calculate the sum of the values in the range F6:F9 and in the range G6:G9.

Now, you'll use AutoSum to calculate the total quantity and total revenue of the ordered items, putting these values in cells F10 and G10.

To calculate the total order quantity and revenue:

1. Click cell **A10**, type **TOTAL**, and then press the **Tab** key five times to move to cell F10.

2. With cell F10 as the active cell, click the **AutoSum** button Σ on the Standard toolbar. Excel automatically inserts the SUM function in the active cell and selects a cell range that it anticipates is the range of cells to be summed. See Figure 1-25. A ScreenTip also appears, showing the form of the SUM function. The mode indicator in the status bar changes to Point, indicating that you can point to the cell references. In this case, the range that Excel has selected for you is the correct range of cells, so all you need to do is indicate that you accept the range. You can complete the function and move to the next cell by pressing the Tab key.

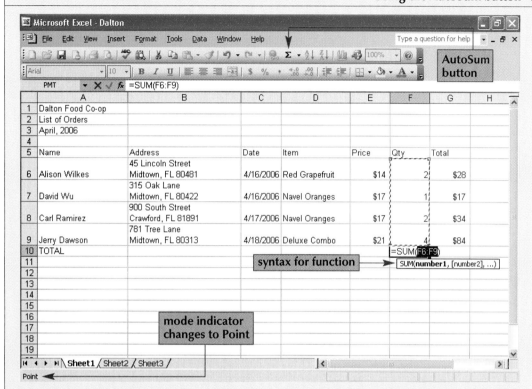

3. Press the **Tab** key to move to cell G10. The result of the formula =SUM(F6:F9) appears in cell F10, and you are in position to calculate the next set of values.

4. Click the **AutoSum** button Σ on the Standard toolbar to enter the SUM function in cell G10, and then press the **Enter** key to complete the formula =SUM(G6:G9), accepting the range that Excel highlighted. See Figure 1-26. Nine items were sold, for a total of $163.

Calculating the total quantity and total income for the co-op ◀ Figure 1-26

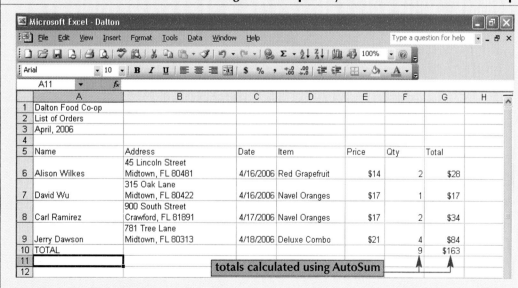

You can use AutoSum to calculate other summary values, such as the average, minimum, maximum, and total number of items in a cell range. You will learn more about using AutoSum to summarize values in Tutorial 2.

Working with Rows and Columns

Sandra has received a new order that she wants you to add to her worksheet. She wants to insert the new order right after Jerry Dawson's order, but wants to make sure the row containing the total values is still the last row. To do this, you need to insert a new row into the worksheet between row 9 and row 10.

Inserting a Row or Column

You can insert rows and columns in a worksheet, or you can insert individual cells within a row or column. When you insert rows, Excel shifts the existing rows down. When you insert columns, Excel shifts the existing columns to the right. If you insert cells within a row, Excel shifts the existing cells down; if you insert cells within a column, Excel shifts the existing cells to the right. Figure 1-27 illustrates what happens when you insert a row, a column, and cells within a row and within a column.

Figure 1-27 | **Inserting new rows and columns**

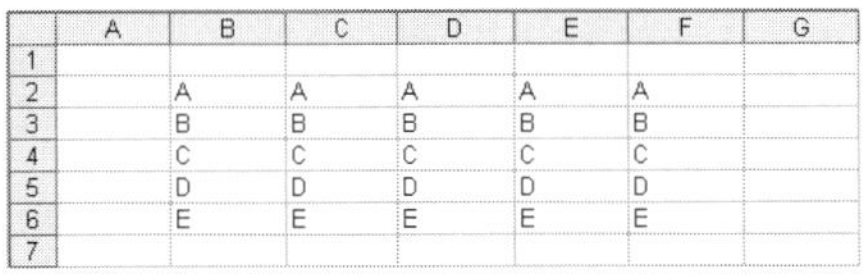

original layout of cells

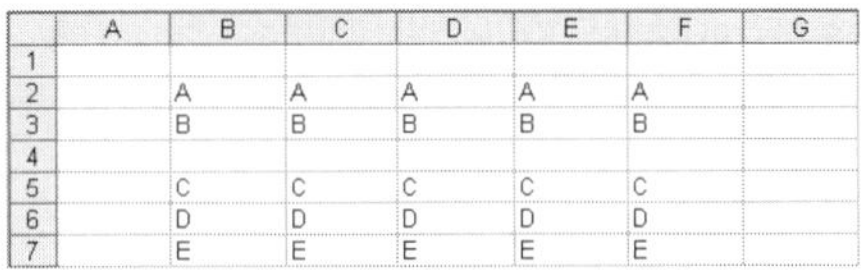

inserting a new row 4

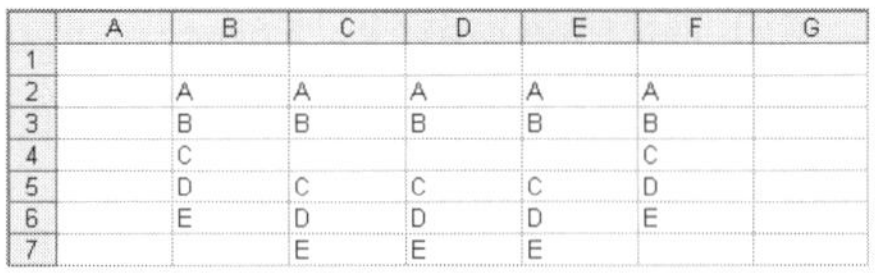

inserting new cells in row 4

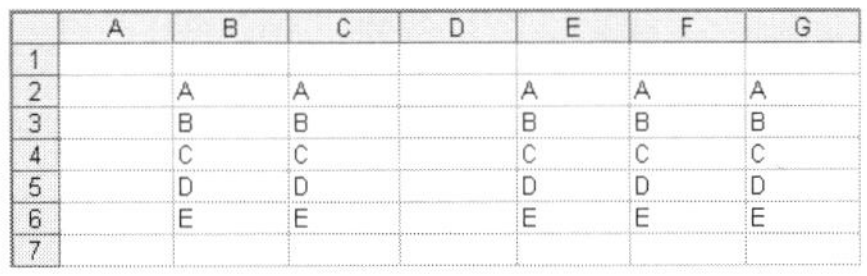

inserting a new column D

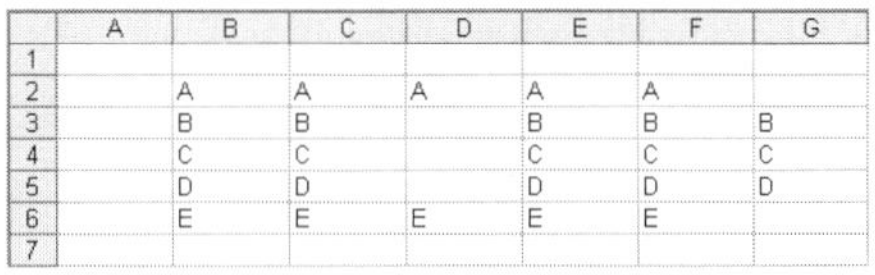

inserting new cells in column D

You can use the Insert menu to insert cells, rows, and columns. You can also use the right-click method to display a shortcut menu that provides the Insert command, which opens the Insert dialog box.

Inserting a Row or Column into a Worksheet

- Select a cell where you want to insert the new row or column.
- Click Insert on the menu bar, and then click Rows or Columns.

or

- Right-click a cell where you want to insert a new row or column, and then click Insert on the shortcut menu.
- In the Insert dialog box, click the Entire row or Entire column option button, and then click the OK button.

To insert multiple rows or columns, you select a cell range that contains multiple rows or columns before applying the Insert command. For example, to insert two new blank rows, select two rows or any portion of two rows. To insert three blank columns, select three columns or any portion of three columns.

Sometimes you might need to insert individual cells, rather than an entire row or column, into a worksheet. To insert cells into a row or column, you must select the number of cells you want to insert, and then open the Insert dialog box. In this dialog box you indicate how Excel should shift the existing cells to accommodate the cells you want to insert.

Inserting Cells into a Worksheet

- Select a cell range equal to the number of cells you want to insert.
- Click Insert on the menu bar, and then click Cells; or right-click the selected range, and then click Insert on the shortcut menu.
- Click the Shift cells right option button to insert the new cells into the row, or click the Shift cells down button to insert the new cells into the column.

Sandra wants the data for the new order to be entered above the TOTAL row, row 10. You'll use the right-click method to insert a new row 10, and then you'll enter the data.

To insert a new row 10:

▶ **1.** Right-click cell **A10**, which is where you want to insert the new row.

▶ **2.** Click **Insert** on the shortcut menu. The Insert dialog box opens. See Figure 1-28.

Insert dialog box ◀ **Figure 1-28**

▶ **3.** Click the **Entire row** option button, and then click the **OK** button. Excel inserts a new row 10 and shifts the calculations of the total values down one row.

▶ **4.** Enter the data for Karen Paulson's order into row 10, as shown in Figure 1-29. Make sure that you press the Tab key to move from cell to cell and press the Alt + Enter keys to enter the address on two lines within cell B10.

Figure 1-29	Data entered in the new row 10

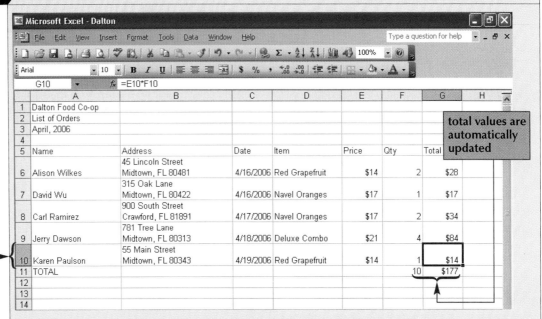

Note that Excel automatically inserts the formula *=E10*F10* into cell G10 for you. Excel recognizes that you are inserting a new set of values into a list of values and assumes that you intend to use the same formulas for the new order that you used for the previous ones. Also note that the calculations of the total quantity of items ordered and the total revenue from those orders have been updated. The functions now calculate the sums in the cell ranges F6:F10 and G6:G10. You'll learn more about how such formulas are automatically adjusted by Excel in the next tutorial.

Deleting a Row or Column

Sandra has also learned that David Wu has canceled his co-op order. You have two options for removing data from a worksheet. If you simply want to erase the contents of a cell, you can **clear** the cell, without actually removing the cell from the worksheet. If you want to remove not only the contents of the cells from the worksheet, but also the cells themselves, you can **delete** a cell range, and Excel then shifts the contents of the adjacent cells into the location of the deleted cells.

To clear the contents of a cell or range of cells, you select the range and then select the Clear command on the Edit menu or on the shortcut menu that you display by right-clicking the selection. Pressing the Delete key on the keyboard also clears the contents of the selected cells, without removing the cells themselves. To delete cells and their contents, you select the range and then choose the Delete command on the Edit menu, or right-click the selected cells, and click Delete on the shortcut menu. To adjust the adjacent cells, Excel opens the Delete Cells dialog box, which you can select to shift the remaining cells left or up, or choose to delete the entire row.

Because David Wu has canceled his order, you'll delete it from the worksheet.

To delete the row that contains David Wu's order:

▶ **1.** Click the row heading for row **7**, which contains the data you want to delete.

▶ **2.** Click **Edit** on the menu bar, and then click **Delete**. Excel deletes the row and shifts the next row up. See Figure 1-30. The total calculations in cells F10 and G10 are automatically updated to reflect the fact that David Wu's order has been deleted.

Deleting a row from the worksheet ◀ **Figure 1-30**

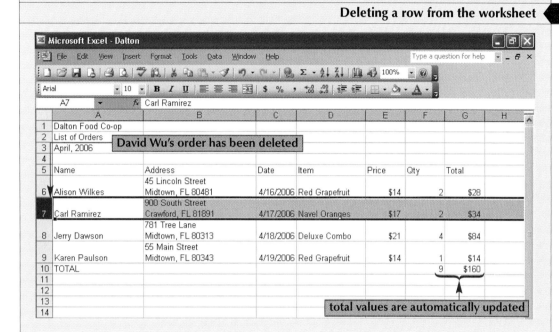

Editing Your Worksheet

When you work in Excel, you might make mistakes that you want to correct or undo. Sandra has noticed such a mistake in the Dalton workbook. The price for the Deluxe Combo box should be $23, not $21. You could simply clear the value in cell E8 and then type the correct value. However, there may be times when you will not want to change the entire contents of a cell, but merely edit a portion of the entry, especially if the cell contains a large block of text or a complicated formula. To edit the cell contents, you need to work in **edit mode**.

When you are working in edit mode, some of the keyboard shortcuts you've been using perform differently. For example, the Home, Delete, Backspace, and End keys do not move the insertion point to different cells in the worksheet; rather they move the insertion point to different locations within the cell. The Home key, for example, moves the insertion point to the beginning of whatever content has been entered into the cell. The End key moves the insertion point to the end of the cell's content. The left and right arrow keys move the insertion point backward and forward through the cell's content. The Backspace key deletes the character immediately to the left of the insertion point, and the Delete key deletes the character to the right of the insertion point.

Editing a Cell

- Switch to edit mode by double-clicking the cell, clicking the cell and pressing the F2 key, or clicking the cell and then clicking in the Formula bar.
- Use the Home, End, ←, or → keys to move the insertion point within the cell's content, or use the Delete and Backspace keys to erase characters.
- Press the Enter key when finished, or if you are working in the Formula bar, click the Enter button.

You'll switch to edit mode and then change the value in cell E8.

To edit the value in cell E8:

1. Double-click cell **E8**. Note that the mode indicator in the status bar switches from Ready to Edit. Also note that the value 21 appears in the cell, not $21. This is because the cell contains a numeric value, not a text string. The dollar sign ($) is used to format the value. You'll learn more about formats in Tutorial 3.

2. Press the **End** key to move the blinking insertion point to the end of the cell.

3. Press the **Backspace** key once to delete the 1 character, type **3** to update the value, and then press the **Enter** key to accept the change. The value $23 appears in cell E8, and the total amount of this order in cell G8 changes to $92. Note that the mode indicator on the status bar switches back to Ready.

If you make a mistake as you type in edit mode, you can press the Esc key or click the Cancel button on the Formula bar to cancel all changes you made while in edit mode.

Undoing an Action

As you revise your worksheet, you may find that you need to undo one of your changes. To undo an action, click the Undo button on the Standard toolbar. As you work, Excel maintains a list of your actions, so you can undo most of the actions you perform in your workbook during the current session. To reverse more than one action, click the list arrow next to the Undo button and click the action you want to undo from the list. To see how this works, you'll use the Undo button to remove the edit you just made to cell E8.

To undo your last action:

1. Click the **Undo** button 🔄 on the Standard toolbar. The value $21 appears again in cell E8, indicating that your last action, editing the value in this cell, has been undone.

If you find that you have gone too far in undoing your previous actions, you can go forward in the action list and redo those actions. To redo an action, you click the Redo button on the Standard toolbar. Now you'll use the Redo button to return the value in cell E8 to $23.

To redo your last action:

1. Click the **Redo** button 🔄 on the Standard toolbar. The value in cell E8 changes back to $23.

Through the use of edit mode and the Undo and Redo buttons, you should be able to correct almost any mistake you make in your Excel workbook. The Undo and Redo commands are also available on the Edit menu or by using the shortcut keys Ctrl + Z, to undo an action, and Ctrl + Y, to redo an action.

Working with Worksheets

By default, Excel workbooks contain three worksheets, labeled Sheet1, Sheet2, and Sheet3. You can add new worksheets or remove old ones. You can also give your worksheets more descriptive names. In the Dalton workbook, there is no data entered in the Sheet2 or Sheet3 worksheets. Sandra suggests that you remove these sheets from the workbook.

Adding and Removing Worksheets

To delete a worksheet, you first select its sheet tab to make the worksheet the active sheet; then right-click the sheet tab and choose Delete from the shortcut menu. Try this now by deleting the Sheet2 and Sheet3 worksheets.

To delete the Sheet2 and Sheet3 worksheets:

1. Click the **Sheet2** tab to make Sheet2 the active sheet.

2. Right-click the sheet tab, and then click **Delete** on the shortcut menu. Sheet2 is deleted and Sheet3 becomes the active sheet.

3. Right-click the **Sheet3** tab, and then click **Delete**. There is now only one worksheet in the workbook.

After you delete the two unused sheets, Sandra informs you that she wants to include a description of the workbook's content and purpose. In other words, Sandra wants to include a **documentation sheet**, a worksheet that provides information about the content and purpose of the workbook. A documentation sheet can be any information that you feel is important, for example, the name of the person who created the workbook or instructions on how to use the workbook. A documentation sheet is a valuable element if you intend to share the workbook with others. The documentation sheet is often the first worksheet in the workbook, though in this case, Sandra wants to place it at the end of the workbook.

To insert a new worksheet, you can either use the Worksheet command on the Insert menu or the right-click method. Both methods insert a new worksheet *before* the active sheet.

To insert a new worksheet in the workbook:

1. Click **Insert** on the menu bar, and then click **Worksheet**. A new worksheet with the name "Sheet4" is placed at the beginning of your workbook. Your worksheet might be named Sheet2 or another name.

Sandra wants the documentation sheet to include the following information:

- The name of the co-op
- The date that this workbook was originally created
- The person who created the workbook
- The purpose of the workbook

You'll add this information to the new sheet in the Dalton workbook.

To insert the documentation information in the new worksheet:

▶ 1. Click cell **A1**, if necessary, type **Dalton Food Co-op**, and then press the **Enter** key twice.

▶ 2. Type **Date:** in cell A3, and then press the **Tab** key.

▶ 3. Enter the *current date* in cell B3, and then press the **Enter** key.

▶ 4. Type **Created By:** in cell A4, and then press the **Tab** key.

▶ 5. Enter *your name* in cell B4, and then press the **Enter** key.

▶ 6. Type **Purpose:** in cell A5, and then press the **Tab** key.

▶ 7. Type **To enter orders for the Dalton Food Co-op** in cell B5, and then press the **Enter** key.

▶ 8. Increase the width of column A to **15** characters (**110** pixels). Figure 1-31 shows the completed documentation sheet.

Figure 1-31 ▶ **Completed documentation sheet**

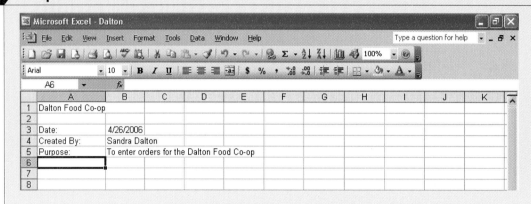

Renaming a Worksheet

The current sheet names, "Sheet4" and "Sheet1," are not very descriptive. Sandra suggests that you rename Sheet4 "Documentation" and Sheet1 "Orders." To rename a worksheet, you double-click the sheet tab to select the sheet name, and then you type a new name for the sheet. Sheet names cannot exceed 31 characters in length, including blank spaces.

To rename the worksheets:

▶ 1. Double-click the **Sheet4** tab. Note that the name of the sheet is selected.

▶ 2. Type **Documentation** and then press the **Enter** key. The width of the sheet tab adjusts to the length of the name you type.

▶ 3. Double-click the **Sheet1** tab.

▶ 4. Type **Orders** and then press the **Enter** key. Both worksheets are renamed.

Moving a Worksheet

You can change the placement of the worksheets in the workbook. To move the position of a worksheet in the workbook, click the sheet tab and then drag and drop it to a new location relative to the other worksheets. You can also make a copy of a worksheet using a similar drag-and-drop technique. To create a copy of a worksheet, press the Ctrl key as you drag and drop the sheet tab of the worksheet you want duplicated.

Reference Window

Moving or Copying a Worksheet

- Click the sheet tab of the worksheet you want to move (or copy).
- Drag the sheet tab along the row of sheet tabs until the small arrow appears in the new location. To create a copy of the worksheet, press and hold the Ctrl key as you drag the sheet tab to the new location.
- Release the mouse button. Release the Ctrl key if necessary.

Try this now by switching the location of the Documentation and Orders worksheets.

To reposition the worksheets:

▶ **1.** Click the **Orders** tab, and then press and hold the left mouse button so the pointer changes to ⇗ and a small arrow appears in the upper-left corner of the tab.

▶ **2.** Drag the pointer to the left of the sheet tab for the Documentation sheet, and then release the mouse button. The Documentation sheet is now the second sheet in the workbook, but Sandra would prefer that the documentation sheet be the first sheet.

▶ **3.** Click the **Orders** tab, and then drag the sheet tab to the right of the Documentation sheet tab to place it back in its original location.

When you create a copy of a worksheet, you move the copy of the original worksheet to a new location, while the original sheet remains at its initial position.

Using the Spell Checker

One of Excel's editing tools is the **Spell Checker**. This feature checks the words in the workbook against the program's internal dictionary. If the Spell Checker comes across a word not in its dictionary, it displays the word in a dialog box along with a list of suggested replacements. You can replace the word with one from the list, or you can choose to ignore the word and go to the next word that might be misspelled. You can also add the word to the dictionary to prevent it from being flagged in the future. There are words that are not included in the online dictionary (for example, some uncommon personal names or last names). The Spell Checker will stop at these words. You can then choose to ignore all occurrences of the word, change the word, or add the word to the dictionary. Excel checks the spelling on the current worksheet only.

To see how the Spell Checker works, you'll make an intentional spelling error in the Orders worksheet.

To check the spelling in the Orders sheet:

▶ 1. Make sure the Orders sheet is the active sheet, and then click cell **G5**. You will enter the error in this cell.

▶ 2. Type **Totale** and then click cell **A1**. The Spell Checker always starts at the active cell in the worksheet. You can start from other cells, and the Spell Checker will cycle back to the first cell in the worksheet to continue checking each cell for spelling errors. However, you will find it helpful and more efficient to begin spell checking with the first cell in the sheet, cell A1.

▶ 3. Click the **Spelling** button on the Standard toolbar. The Spelling dialog box opens, with the first word that the spell checker does not recognize, "Totale." See Figure 1-32.

Figure 1-32	Spelling dialog box

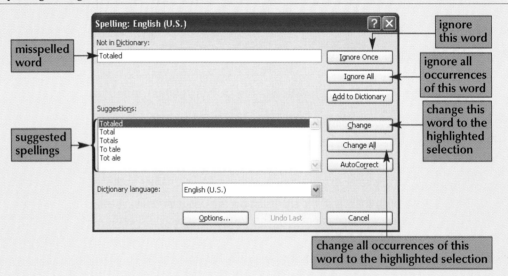

▶ 4. Click **Total** in the list of suggestions, and then click the **Change** button. The word "Totale" changes to "Total," and then Spell Checker continues to look for other potential spelling errors. There shouldn't be any other errors in this workbook.

Trouble? If there are any other errors (you may have misspelled a name, address, or item), fix them before continuing to the next step.

▶ 5. Click the **OK** button to close the Spell Checker.

Previewing and Printing a Worksheet

Sandra would like a printed hard copy of the Dalton workbook for her records. You can print the contents of your workbook either by using the Print command on the File menu or by clicking the Print button on the Standard toolbar. If you use the Print command, Excel opens the Print dialog box in which you can specify which worksheets you want to print, the number of copies, and the print quality. If you click the Print button, your worksheet will print using the options already set in the Print dialog box. If you want to change a setting, you must open the Print dialog box using the File menu.

Before sending a worksheet to the printer, you should preview how the worksheet will appear as a printed page. You can display the worksheet in the Print Preview window either by selecting the Print Preview command on the File menu or by clicking the Print Preview button on the Standard toolbar. You can also click the Preview button in the Print dialog box. Previewing the printout is a helpful way to avoid printing errors.

If you are printing to a shared printer on a network, other people might be sending print jobs at the same time you do. To avoid confusion, you will print the contents of both the Documentation sheet and the Orders sheet. You will use the Print command on the File menu because you need to print the entire workbook and not just the active worksheet (which is the default print setting).

To open the Print dialog box:

▶ **1.** Click **File** on the menu bar, and then click **Print** to open the Print dialog box.

▶ **2.** Click the **Name** list box, and then select the printer to which you want to print, if it is not already selected.

Now you need to select what to print. To print the complete workbook, select the Entire workbook option button. To print the active worksheet, select the Active sheet(s) option button. To print the selected cells on the active sheet, click the Selection option button.

▶ **3.** Click the **Entire workbook** option button.

▶ **4.** Make sure **1** appears in the Number of copies list box, since you only need to print one copy of the workbook. Figure 1-33 shows the Print dialog box.

Print dialog box ◀ **Figure 1-33**

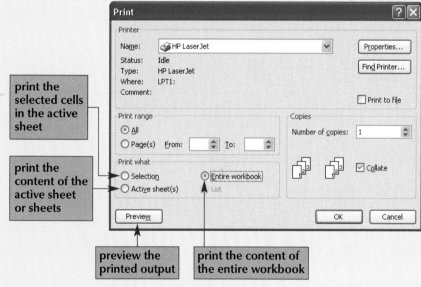

print the selected cells in the active sheet

print the content of the active sheet or sheets

preview the printed output

print the content of the entire workbook

Next you will preview the worksheet to ensure that it looks correct before printing it.

To preview the workbook before printing it:

▶ **1.** Click the **Preview** button in the Print dialog box. Excel displays a preview of the first full page of the worksheet, in this case the Documentation sheet, as it will appear printed. As you can see from the status bar in Figure 1-34, this is the first of three pages.

Trouble? If the status bar on your screen indicates that there are just two pages, you can still complete the steps.

Figure 1-34 Print Preview window

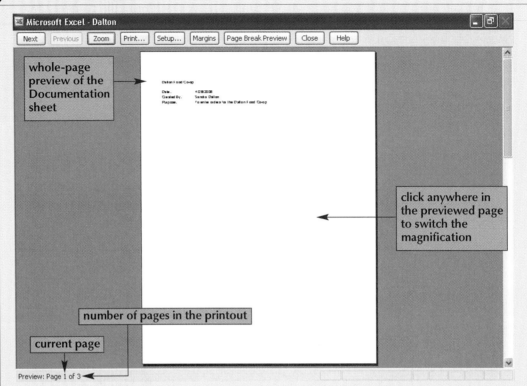

2. Click the **Next** button on the Print Preview toolbar to move to the next page in the preview. On this page you see part of the Orders worksheet, but it is difficult to read because the text is so small. To better see the content of the printed page, you can click the preview page to switch between a magnified view and a whole-page view.

3. Click anywhere within the previewed page with the 🔍 pointer to increase the magnification, and click again to reduce the magnification.

Working with Portrait and Landscape Orientation

Not all of the Orders worksheet is displayed in the Print Preview window. The last column in the sheet, which displays the total amount of each order, has been cut off and is displayed on the third page of the printout. Naturally Sandra wants all of the information on a single sheet, but the problem is that the page is not wide enough to display all of this information. One way of solving this problem is to change the orientation of the page. There are two types of page orientations: portrait and landscape. In **portrait orientation** the page is taller than it is wide. In **landscape orientation** the page is wider than it is tall. In many cases, you will want to print your worksheets in landscape orientation. You'll choose this option for the Orders worksheet.

To print in landscape orientation:

1. Click the **Setup** button on the Print Preview toolbar. The Page Setup dialog box opens.

2. Verify that the Page tab is selected in the dialog box, and then click the **Landscape** option button. See Figure 1-35.

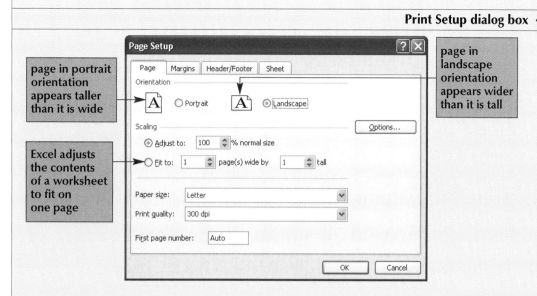

page in portrait orientation appears taller than it is wide

page in landscape orientation appears wider than it is tall

Excel adjusts the contents of a worksheet to fit on one page

3. Click the **OK** button to close the Page Setup dialog box.

4. If necessary, click anywhere within the previewed page to switch the magnification back to a whole-page view. As shown in Figure 1-36, the entire Orders worksheet is now displayed on the second (and last) page of this printout.

Orders sheet in landscape orientation ◄ **Figure 1-36**

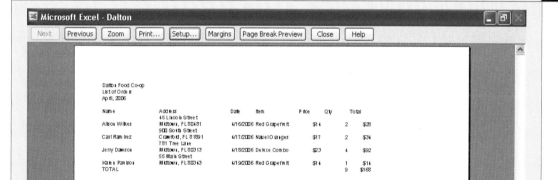

5. Click the **Print** button on the Print Preview toolbar to print the workbook and close the Print Preview window.

Note that the Documentation sheet is printed in portrait orientation, whereas the Orders worksheet is printed in landscape orientation. Changing the orientation only affects the worksheet currently displayed in the Print Preview window; it does not apply to other sheets in the workbook.

Printing the Worksheet Formulas

Sandra examines the printout and notices that none of the formulas are displayed. This is to be expected since most of the time you're only interested in the final results and not the formulas used to calculate those results. In some cases, you will want to view the formulas used in developing your workbook. This is particularly useful in situations where the results were not what you expected, and you want to examine the formulas to see if a mistake has been made. To switch to **Formula view** in your workbook, you can press the keyboard shortcut Ctrl + grave accent (`). Try this now for the Orders worksheet.

To view the worksheet formulas:

1. With the Orders worksheet active, press the **Ctrl + `** (grave accent) keys and then scroll the worksheet to the left so columns F and G are visible. (Make sure you press the grave accent key (`) and not the single quotation mark key ('). The grave accent key is usually located above the Tab key on your keyboard.) Excel displays the formulas in columns F and G. See Figure 1-37.

Figure 1-37 **Viewing the worksheet formulas**

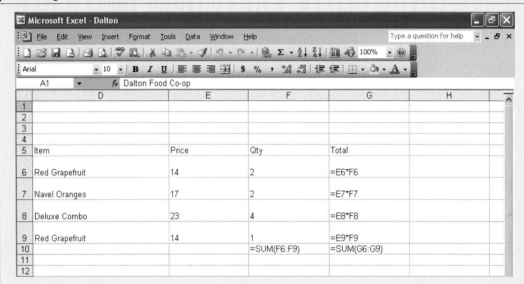

Trouble? If the Formula Auditing toolbar appears, close the toolbar.

Note that the column widths have been changed. Excel does this automatically to ensure that the entire formula can be displayed within each cell. These changed column widths will not affect the normal view of your worksheet as long as you don't change the column widths while in Formula view.

Sandra asks you to print a copy of the worksheet with the formulas displayed. First, you'll preview the worksheet.

2. Click the **Print Preview** button 🔍 on the Standard toolbar. Excel displays a preview of the Orders worksheet in Formula view. Not all of the contents of the worksheet in this view are displayed on a single page. To fit the printout to a single page, you will change the setup of the page using the Page Setup dialog box.

3. Click the **Setup** button on the Print Preview toolbar. The Page Setup dialog box opens.

4. Click the **Fit to** option button to fit the Orders worksheet on one page, and then click the **OK** button. The Formula view of the Orders worksheet should now fit on a single page.

5. Click the **Print** button on the Print Preview toolbar to print the worksheet and close the Print Preview window.

   Trouble? If the Print Preview window closes and the Print dialog box opens, click the OK button to print the worksheet.

As you may have noticed while you were working in Print Preview and the Page Setup dialog box, there are a lot of options for choosing what to print and how to print. You'll examine more of these options in Tutorial 3. For now, you can switch the Orders worksheet back to Normal view and save and then close the file.

To complete your work:

▶ **1.** Press the **Ctrl +`** (grave accent) keys to switch the worksheet back to Normal view. The keyboard shortcut Ctrl + ` (grave accent) works as a toggle, so you can display or hide the formulas by pressing this combination of keys.

▶ **2.** Save your changes to the Dalton workbook, and then close it.

You give Sandra the hard copy of the Dalton workbook. If she needs to add new information to the workbook or if she needs you to make further changes to the structure of the workbook, she'll contact you.

Session 1.2 Quick Check

Review

1. Describe the two types of cell ranges in Excel.
2. How do you write the cell reference for the rectangular group of cells that extends from cell A5 through cell F8?
3. The _____ button provides a quick way to enter the SUM function.
4. When you insert a new row into a worksheet, the existing rows are shifted

   _____.
5. When you insert a new column into a worksheet, the existing columns are shifted

   _____.
6. How do you change the name of a worksheet?
7. How does clearing a cell differ from deleting a cell?
8. What keyboard shortcut do you press to display the worksheet formulas?

Tutorial Summary

Review

In this tutorial, you learned the basics of spreadsheets and Excel. You learned about the major components of the Excel window. You also learned how to navigate within a worksheet and between worksheets in an Excel workbook. You learned how to enter text, dates, values, and formulas into a worksheet and were introduced to functions using the AutoSum button. Within the workbook, you practiced selecting and moving cell ranges. You saw how to insert new rows and columns into a workbook and how to modify the size of a column or row. You learned how to create new worksheets, rename them, and move them around the workbook. You learned how to check the spelling in a workbook, and finally, you learned how to print the contents of a workbook in different orientations and how to print the formulas in that workbook.

Key Terms

active cell	edit mode	sheet
adjacent range	formula	sheet tab
argument	Formula bar	Spell Checker
arithmetic operator	Formula view	spreadsheet
AutoComplete	function	SUM function
AutoSum	landscape orientation	tab scrolling buttons
cell	Name box	value
cell range	nonadjacent range	what-if analysis
cell reference	order of precedence	workbook
clear	portrait orientation	workbook window
column	range	worksheet
delete	range reference	worksheet window
documentation sheet	row	

Practice

Practice the skills you learned in the tutorial using the same case scenario.

Review Assignments

There are no Data Files needed for the Review Assignments.

Sandra has another set of orders she wants you to enter into a new Excel workbook. The data is shown in Figure 1-38.

Figure 1-38

Name	Address	Date	Item	Price	Qty
Wendy Battle	313 Oak Street Midtown, FL 80481 (833) 555-1284	5/1/2006	Deluxe Combo	$23	2
Eugene Burch	25 Fourth Street Cabot, FL 81121 (833) 555-3331	5/1/2006	Red Grapefruit	$14	4
Nicole Sweeny	312 Olive Street Midtown, FL 81241 (833) 555-9811	5/3/2006	Deluxe Combo	$23	1
Amy Yang	315 Maple Street Midtown, FL 80440 (833) 555-3881	5/4/2006	Navel Oranges	$17	3

Note that Sandra has added the phone numbers of the customers to her data. She wants the phone numbers entered into the customer address cell, but on a different line within that cell. To complete this task:

1. Start Excel and open a blank workbook. In the range A1:F5, enter the labels and data from Figure 1-38. Make sure that the address information is inserted with the street address on the first line; the city, state, and ZIP code on the second line; and the phone number on the third line.
2. In cell G1, enter the label "Total."
3. In the cells below G1, enter formulas to calculate the total amount of each order.
4. In cell A6, enter the label "TOTAL."

5. In cell F6, use the AutoSum button to calculate the total quantity of items ordered, and in cell G6, use the AutoSum button to calculate the total revenue generated by these orders.

6. Move sales data from the range A1:G6 to the range A5:G10.

7. In cell A1, enter the text "Dalton Food Co-op." In cell A2, enter the text "List of Orders." In cell A3, enter the text "May, 2006."

8. Change the width of columns A and B to 20 characters (or 145 pixels) each. Change the width of column D to 15 characters (or 110 pixels). Change the width of column G to 10 characters (or 75 pixels).

9. Select all of the cells in the worksheet, and then reduce the amount of empty space in the rows by reducing the row height to the height of the data contained in the rows.

10. Change the name of the worksheet to "Orders".

11. Create a worksheet named "Documentation" at the beginning of the workbook and, in the Documentation sheet, enter the following:
    - Cell A1: Dalton Food Co-op
    - Cell A3: Date:
    - Cell B3: *current date*
    - Cell A4: Created By:
    - Cell B4: *your name*
    - Cell A5: Purpose:
    - Cell B5: To enter May orders for the Dalton Food Co-op

12. Increase the width of column A in the Documentation worksheet to 20 characters.

13. Check the spelling on both worksheets, correcting any errors found.

14. Delete any empty worksheets from the workbook.

15. Print the contents of the workbook with the Documentation sheet in portrait orientation and the Orders worksheet in landscape orientation.

16. Display the formulas in the Orders worksheet. Preview the worksheet before printing it, and set up the worksheet to print as a single page.

17. Save the workbook as **Dalton2** in the Tutorial.01\Review folder included with your Data Files.

18. Insert the following new order in the Orders worksheet directly below Amy Yang's order:
    - Name: Chad Reynolds
    - Address: 100 School Lane
      Midtown, FL 80411
      (833) 555-4425
    - Date: 5/5/2006
    - Item: Navel Oranges
    - Price: $17
    - Qty: 2

19. Remove Amy Yang's order from the worksheet, and change the quantity ordered by Eugene Burch from 4 to 3.

20. Check the spelling in the Orders worksheet again, correcting any errors found.

21. Print the contents and formulas of the Orders worksheet again.

22. Save the workbook as **Dalton3** in the Tutorial.01\Review folder, and then close the workbook.

Apply

Use the skills you have learned to create a cash flow analysis worksheet for a working couple.

Case Problem 1

Data File needed for this Case Problem: CFlow1.xls

Madison Federal   Lisa Wu is a financial consultant at Madison Federal. She is working on a financial plan for Tom and Carolyn Watkins. Lisa has a cash flow analysis for the couple, and she wants you to record this information for her. Here are the relevant financial figures:

Receipts
- Employment Income: 95,000
- Other Income: 5,000

Disbursements
- Insurance: 940
- Savings/Retirement: 8,400
- Mortgage Payments: 18,000
- Children's Tuition: 10,000
- Groceries: 14,000
- Utilities: 6,000
- Other: 15,000
- Taxes: 16,300

Lisa wants you to calculate the total receipts and total disbursements and then calculate the cash surplus (receipts minus disbursements) in an Excel workbook that she has already started. To complete this task:

1. Open the **CFlow1** workbook located in the Tutorial.01\Cases folder included with your Data Files, and then save the workbook as **CFlow2** in the same folder.
2. Move the contents of the range A1:C16 to the range A5:C20.
3. Insert the text "Tom and Carolyn Watkins" in cell A1. In cell A2, insert the text "Cash Flow Analysis." In cell A3, insert the text "For the year 2006."
4. Increase the width of column A to 130 pixels, the width of column B to 160 pixels, and the width of column C to 130 pixels.
5. Insert the financial numbers listed earlier into the appropriate cells in column C.
6. Use the AutoSum button to calculate the total receipts and total disbursements, placing these values in cells C8 and C18, respectively.
7. Insert a formula to calculate the surplus in cell C20 (total receipts minus total disbursements).
8. Rename Sheet1 as "Cash Flow."
9. Insert a worksheet at the beginning of the workbook named "Documentation," and then enter the following information on the sheet:
   - Cell A1:   Cash Flow Report
   - Cell A3:   Date:
   - Cell B3:   *current date*
   - Cell A4:   Created By:
   - Cell B4:   *your name*
   - Cell A5:   Purpose:
   - Cell B5:   Cash flow analysis for Tom and Carolyn Watkins
10. Increase the width of column A in the Documentation worksheet to 20 characters.
11. Delete any empty sheets in the workbook.
12. Use the Spell Checker to correct any spelling errors in the workbook.
13. Print the contents of the entire workbook in portrait orientation, and then save your changes to the workbook.

14. Change the couple's taxes to 18,500, and then print the Cash Flow worksheet with the recalculated values.
15. Save the workbook as **CFlow3** in the Tutorial.01\Cases folder, and then close the workbook.

Case Problem 2

Data File needed for this Case Problem: Balance1.xls

EMS Industries Lee Evans is an agent at New Haven Financial Services. His job is to maintain financial information on investments for client companies. He has the balance sheet data for a company named EMS Industries in an Excel workbook and needs your help in finishing the workbook layout and contents. To complete this task:

1. Open the **Balance1** workbook located in the Tutorial.01\Cases folder included with your Data Files, and then save the workbook as **Balance2** in the same folder.
2. Select the range A1:C4, and then insert four new rows into the worksheet, shifting the selected cells down.
3. Enter the text "EMS Industries" in cell A1 and "Balance Sheet" in cell A2. In cell A3, enter the date "4/30/2006".
4. Increase the width of column A to 110 pixels.

5. Move the contents of the range A22:C32 to the range E5:G15, and then move the range A34:C38 to the range E20:G24.
6. Change the width of column B to 150 pixels, the width of column D to 20 pixels, and the width of column F to 240 pixels.
7. Use the AutoSum button to calculate the total current assets in cell C12; to calculate the total property, plant, and equipment assets in cell C18; to calculate the total current liabilities in cell G9; and to calculate the total long-term liabilities (only one value) in cell G13.
8. In cell C20, insert a formula to calculate the total of the current assets (cell C12) plus the noncurrent assets (cell C18). In cell G15, insert a formula to calculate the total of the current liabilities (cell G9) plus the long-term liabilities (cell G13).
9. In cell G23, enter a formula to calculate the total shareholders' equity, which is equal to the value of the common stock (cell G21) plus the value of retained earnings (cell G22). In cell G24, calculate the value of the total liabilities (cell G15) plus the shareholders' equity (cell G23).
10. Rename Sheet1 as "Balance Sheet," and then delete Sheet2 and Sheet3.
11. Insert a worksheet named "Documentation" at the front of the workbook, and then enter the following information into the sheet:
    - Cell A1: Balance Sheet
    - Cell A3: Company:
    - Cell B3: EMS Industries
    - Cell A4: Date:
    - Cell B4: *current date*
    - Cell A5: Recorded By:
    - Cell B5: *your name*
    - Cell A6: Purpose:
    - Cell B6: Balance Sheet
12. Increase the width of column A in the Documentation worksheet to 20 characters.
13. Use the Spell Checker to correct any spelling mistakes in the workbook.
14. Print the entire contents of the workbook in landscape orientation.
15. Save your changes to the workbook, and then close it.

Challenge

Challenge yourself by going beyond what you've learned to create a worksheet that calculates the weighted scores of four possible locations for a new shoe factory.

Case Problem 3

Data File needed for this Case Problem: Site1.xls

Kips Shoes Kips Shoes is planning to build a new factory. The company has narrowed the site down to four possible cities. Each city has been graded on a 1-to-10 scale for four categories: the size of the local market, the quality of the labor pool, the local tax base, and the local operating expenses. Each of these four factors is given a weight, with the most important factor given the highest weight. After the sites are analyzed, the scores for each factor will be multiplied by their weights, and then a total weighted score will be calculated.

Gwen Sanchez, the senior planning manager overseeing this project, has entered the weights and the scores for each city into an Excel workbook. She needs you to finish the workbook by inserting the formulas to calculate the weighted scores and the total overall score for each city. To complete this task:

1. Open the **Site1** workbook located in the Tutorial.01\Cases folder included with your Data Files, and then save the workbook as **Site2** in the same folder.
2. Switch to the Site Analysis sheet.
3. In cell B14, calculate the weighted Market Size score for Waukegan by inserting a formula that multiplies the value in cell B7 by the weight value in cell G7.
4. Insert formulas to calculate the weighted scores for the rest of the cells in the range B14:E17.

Explore

5. Select the range B18:E18, and then click the AutoSum button to calculate the sum of the weighted scores for all four of the cities. Note that you can apply the AutoSum button to more than one cell at a time. Which city has the highest weighted score?
6. Switch to the Documentation sheet, and enter your name and the date in the appropriate locations on the sheet.
7. Spell check the workbook, print the entire workbook in portrait orientation, and then save your changes to the workbook.

Explore

8. Gwen has another set of weighted scores she wants you to try. However, she doesn't want you to enter the new values in the Site Analysis worksheet, so you need to make a copy of the worksheet. To learn how to copy a worksheet, open the Excel Help task pane, and then enter "copy a worksheet" in the Search for text box. Scroll the list of topics in the Search Results task pane to locate the topic "Move or copy sheets." Open the topic, read the information about copying a sheet, and then close the Microsoft Excel Help window and the Search Results task pane.

Explore

9. Using what you learned in Step 8, create a copy of the Site Analysis worksheet, placing the new worksheet at the end of the workbook. Rename the new sheet "Site Analysis 2".
10. In the Site Analysis 2 worksheet, change the weighted scores of Market Size to 0.2 and Labor Pool to 0.4. Which city has the highest weighted score now?
11. Print the contents of the Site Analysis 2 worksheet.
12. Save the workbook as **Site3** in the Tutorial.01\Cases folder, and then close the workbook.

Create

Use Figure 1-39, which shows the "end results," to create a workbook containing monthly budget figures over a three-month period for a college student.

Case Problem 4

There are no Data Files needed for this Case Problem.

Monthly Budget Alice Drake is a first-year student at MidWest University and has a part-time job in the admissions department. Her college-related expenses, such as tuition, books, and fees, are covered through grants and scholarships, so the money Alice makes goes towards her personal expenses. Being on her own for the first time, Alice is finding it difficult to keep within a budget. She has asked you to look at her finances and help her figure out how her money is being spent. Figure 1-39 shows the worksheet that you will create to help Alice analyze her budget.

Figure 1-39

enter formulas to calculate the ending cash balance and the net cash flows

use the AutoSum button to calculate these totals

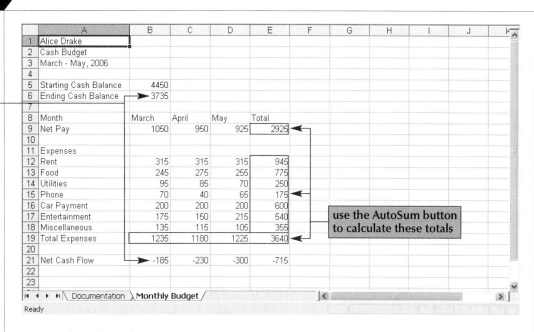

To complete this task:

1. Start Excel and save a new workbook with the name **Budget** in the Tutorial.01\Cases folder included with your Data Files.
2. On the Sheet1 worksheet, enter the labels and values as indicated in Figure 1-39. Note that the cells in which totals will be calculated have been marked. Do not enter the values shown; you will enter appropriate formulas next.
3. Using the AutoSum button, calculate the values for the total net pay, the total monthly expenses, and the total of each expense for the three months.
4. Enter formulas to calculate the net cash flow for each month and for all three months.
5. Enter a formula to calculate the ending cash balance, which is based on the value of the starting cash balance minus the total net cash flow over the three months. (*Hint:* Because two negatives make a positive, you need to *add* the total net cash flow to the starting cash balance.)
6. Rename Sheet1 as "Monthly Budget."
7. Create a worksheet named "Documentation" at the front of the workbook containing your name, the date, and the purpose of the workbook.
8. Delete any blank worksheets in the workbook.
9. Check the spelling on both worksheets, correcting any errors found.
10. Print the entire workbook in portrait orientation.
11. Save your changes to the workbook, and then close it.

Research

Use the Internet to find and work with data related to the topics presented in this tutorial.

Internet Assignments

The purpose of the Internet Assignments is to challenge you to find information on the Internet that you can use to work effectively with this software. The actual assignments are updated and maintained on the Course Technology Web site. Log on to the Internet and use your Web browser to go to the Student Online Companion for New Perspectives Office 2003 at **www.course.com/np/office2003**. Click the Internet Assignments link, and then navigate to the assignments for this tutorial.

Assess

SAM Assessment and Training

If you have a SAM user profile, you may have access to hands-on instruction, practice, and assessment of the skills covered in this tutorial. Log in to your SAM account and go to your assignments page to see what your instructor has assigned.

Reinforce

Lab Assignments

The New Perspectives Labs are designed to help you master some of the key concepts and skills presented in this text. The steps for completing this Lab are located on the Course Technology Web site. Log on to the Internet and use your Web browser to go to the Student Online Companion for New Perspectives Office 2003 at **www.course.com/np/office2003**. Click the Lab Assignments link, and then navigate to the assignments for this tutorial.

Review

Quick Check Answers

Session 1.1

1. cell
2. D2
3. Ctrl + Home
4. click the Sheet2 tab
5. a. value
   b. text
   c. value
   d. text (there is no equal sign indicating a formula)
   e. text
   f. formula
   g. text
6. Press the Alt + Enter keys to enter text on a new line within a cell.
7. =E5/E6

Session 1.2

1. An adjacent cell range is a rectangular block of cells. A non-adjacent cell range consists of two or more separate adjacent ranges.
2. A5:F8
3. AutoSum
4. down
5. to the right
6. Double-click the sheet tab and then type the new name to replace the highlighted sheet tab name.
7. Clearing a cell deletes the cell's contents but does not affect the position of other cells in the workbook. Deleting a cell removes the cell from the worksheet, and other cells are shifted in the direction of the deleted cell.
8. Ctrl + ` (grave accent)

Objectives

Working with Formulas and Functions

Developing a Family Budget

Case

Tyler Family Budget

As a newly married couple, Amanda and Joseph Tyler are trying to balance career, school, and family life. Amanda works full time as a legal assistant, and Joseph is in a graduate program at a nearby university. He recently was hired as a teaching assistant. In the summer, he is able to take on other jobs that bring additional income to the family. The couple also just moved into a new apartment. Although Joseph's and Amanda's salaries for the past year were greater than the years before, the couple seemed to have less cash on hand. This financial shortage has prompted them to take a closer look at their finances and figure out how to best manage them.

Because Amanda has agreed to take the lead role in the management of the family finances, she has set up an Excel workbook. Amanda has entered their salary amounts, which are their only income, and she has identified and entered several expenses that the family pays on a monthly basis, such as the rent and Joseph's tuition. She wants to calculate how much money they bring in and how much money they spend. She also wants to figure out their average monthly expenses and identify their greatest financial burden.

Amanda has asked for your help in completing the workbook. She wants you to insert formulas to perform the calculations she needs to get a better overall picture of the family's finances, which, in turn, should help the couple manage their money more effectively. Because the values entered cover a 12-month span, you will be able to copy and paste the formulas from one month to another and fill in series of data, such as the months of the year, rather than retyping formulas or entering each month individually. Finally, Amanda also wants the current date in her workbook, which you can enter using one of Excel's Date functions.

Student Data Files

Once she has a better handle on the family's finances, Amanda might want to evaluate whether buying a house would be possible in the near future, especially in light of the low interest rates that are available.

Session 2.1

Working with Excel Functions

In her budget worksheet, Amanda has already entered the couple's take-home salaries (that is, the amount of money in their paychecks minus taxes and other work-related deductions) and their expenses from the past year. You'll begin by opening her workbook so you can see what Amanda has done so far.

To open Amanda's workbook:

1. Start Excel and then open the **Budget1** workbook located in the Tutorial.02\Tutorial folder included with your Data Files.

2. On the Documentation sheet, enter *your name* in cell B3 and the *current date* in cell B4.

3. Save the workbook as **Budget2** in the Tutorial.02\Tutorial folder, and then click the **Budget** tab to make this sheet the active worksheet. See Figure 2-1. Amanda has recorded the couple's take-home salaries as income and has listed a variety of expenses in columns for each month. January's income and expenses are shown in column B, February's income and expenses are shown in column C, and so forth.

Figure 2-1 ▶ **Budget worksheet**

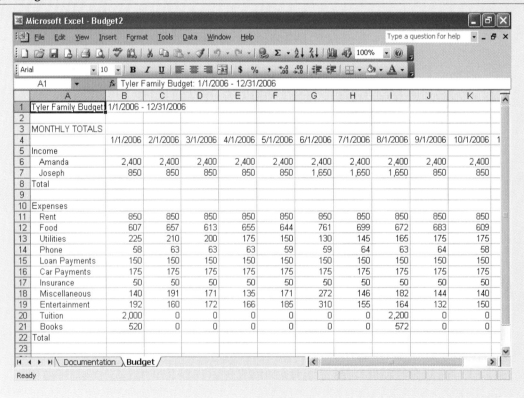

Amanda would like the worksheet to calculate the family's total income and expenses for each month. She would also like to see a year-end summary that displays the family's total income and expenses for the entire year. This summary should also display the average income and expenses so that Amanda can get a picture of what a typical month looks like for her family. Amanda realizes that some expenses increase and decrease during certain months, so she would like to calculate the minimum and maximum values for each expense category, which will give her an idea of the range of these values throughout the year. All of this information will help Amanda and Joseph budget for the upcoming year.

To perform these calculations, you'll have to add several formulas to the workbook. As discussed in the previous tutorial, formulas are one of the most useful features in Excel because they enable you to calculate values based on data entered into the workbook. For more complex calculations, you can enter formulas that contain one or more functions. Recall that a function is a predefined formula that performs calculations using specific values. Each Excel function has a name and syntax. The **syntax** is the rule specifying how the function should be written. The general syntax of all Excel functions is

FUNCTION(argument1, argument2, ...)

where FUNCTION is the name of the Excel function and argument1, argument2, and so forth are **arguments** specifying the numbers, text, or cell references used by the function to calculate a value. An argument can also be an **optional argument** that is not necessary for the function to calculate a value. If an optional argument is not included, Excel assumes a default value for it. Each argument entered in a function is separated by a comma. The convention used in this text shows optional arguments within square brackets along with the argument's default value, as follows:

FUNCTION(argument1, [argument2=value2])

where argument2 is an optional argument and value2 is the default value for this argument. As you learn more about individual functions, you will also learn which arguments are required and which are optional.

Another convention followed in this text is to write function names in uppercase letters, but Excel recognizes the function names entered in either uppercase or lowercase letters, converting the lowercase letters to uppercase automatically.

There are 350 different Excel functions organized into the following 10 categories:

- Database functions
- Date and Time functions
- Engineering functions
- Financial functions
- Information functions
- Logical functions
- Lookup and Reference functions
- Math and Trigonometry functions
- Statistical functions
- Text and Data functions

You can learn about each function using Excel's online Help. Figure 2-2 describes some of the more important Math and Statistical functions that you may often use in your workbooks.

Figure 2-2	Math and Statistical functions

Function	Description
AVERAGE(number1, [number2, number3, ...])	Calculates the average of a collection of numbers, where number1, number2, and so forth are numeric values or cell references
COUNT(value1, [value2, value3, ...])	Calculates the total number of values, where value1, value2, and so forth are numeric values, text entries, or cell references
MAX(number1, [number2, number3, ...])	Calculates the maximum of a collection of numbers, where number1, number2, and so forth are either numeric values or cell references
MEDIAN(number1, [number2, number3, ...])	Calculates the median, or the number in the middle, of a collection of numbers, where number1, number2, and so forth are either numeric values or cell references
MIN(number1, [number2, number3, ...])	Calculates the minimum of a collection of numbers, where number1, number2, and so forth are either numeric values or cell references
ROUND(number, num_digits)	Rounds a number to a specified number of digits, where number is the number you want to round and num_digits specifies the number of digits to which you want to round the number
SUM(number1, [number2, number3, ...])	Calculates the sum of a collection of numbers, where number1, number2, and so forth are either numeric values or cell references

For example, the **AVERAGE function** calculates the average value of a collection of numbers. The syntax of this function is AVERAGE(number1, [number2, ...]). When you enter the arguments (number1, number2), you can enter these numbers directly into the function, as in AVERAGE(3, 2, 5, 8), or you can enter the references to the worksheet cells that contain those numbers, as in AVERAGE(A1:A4). You can also enter a function as part of a larger formula. For example, the formula =MAX(A1:A100)/100 calculates the maximum value in the cell range A1:A100 and then divides that number by 100. You can include, or "nest," one function within another. For example, in the formula =ROUND(AVERAGE(A1:A100),1), the first argument in the ROUND function uses the value calculated by the AVERAGE function; the second argument is a constant. The result is a formula that calculates the average value of the numbers in the range A1:A100, rounding that value to the first decimal place.

In the previous tutorial, you calculated totals using the AutoSum button on the Standard toolbar. Although using the AutoSum feature is a quick and convenient way to calculate a value, it is only one way to perform this calculation in Excel. To determine the totals Amanda wants, you can also use the **SUM function**, which calculates the sum of a collection of numbers. The syntax of the SUM function is SUM(number1, [number2, ...]), which is similar to that of the AVERAGE function.

You'll use the SUM function now to begin calculating the values Amanda needs, starting with the values for the month of January.

To calculate the total income and expenses for January using the SUM function:

▶ 1. Click cell **B8** on the Budget worksheet, type **=SUM(B6:B7)** and then press the **Enter** key. Excel displays the value 3,250 in cell B8, indicating that the total income for the month of January is $3,250.

You can also enter the cell range for a function by selecting the cell range rather than typing it. You'll use this method to determine the total expenses for January.

▶ 2. Click cell **B22** and then type **=SUM(** to begin the function.

▶ 3. Select the range **B11:B21** using your mouse. As you drag to select the range, its cell reference is automatically entered into the SUM function, as shown in Figure 2-3.

Entering the SUM function ◀ **Figure 2-3**

▶ 4. Press the **Enter** key to complete the formula. Note that you didn't have to type the closing parenthesis. When you press the Enter key, the closing parenthesis is inserted automatically. The value 4,967 is displayed in cell B22, indicating that the total expenses for January are $4,967.

Amanda wants to know how much money is left over at the end of each month or, in other words, the family's *net income* each month. To determine this amount, you need to enter a formula that subtracts the total monthly expenses from the total monthly income. You'll begin by calculating the net income for the month of January.

To calculate the net income for the first month:

▶ 1. Click cell **A24**, type **Net Income**, and then press the **Tab** key to move to cell B24, where you will enter the formula.

▶ 2. Type **=B8-B22** and then press the **Enter** key. Excel displays the value –1,717, which indicates that the family's net income for the month of January is a negative $1,717. Amanda and Joseph's expenses are greater than their income for that month.

Now that you've entered the formulas to calculate the total income, total expenses, and net income for January, you need to enter the same formulas for the other 11 months of the year. Entering the formulas for each of the remaining months individually would be time-consuming, but there is a quicker way.

Copying and Pasting Formulas

To use the same formula in different cells on the worksheet, you can copy the formula and paste it to a new location or locations. The cell (or range of cells) that contains the formula you copy is referred to as the **source cell** (or **source range**). The new location is the **destination cell** (or **destination range**). When you paste your selection, Excel automatically adjusts the cell references contained in the formulas. For example, if you copy cell B8, which contains the formula =SUM(B6:B7), and paste the contents of the copied cell into cell C8 (the destination cell), Excel automatically changes the formula in cell C8 to =SUM(C6:C7).

In effect, Excel recognizes that the intent of the function is to calculate the sum of the values in the two cells above the active cell. The new location does not even have to be in the same row as the copied cell. If you copy the formula in cell B8 to cell C10, the pasted formula would be =SUM(C8:C9). You can copy the formula in one cell to a whole range of cells, and Excel will correctly adjust the cell references in the formula for each cell in the range.

Reference Window | **Copying and Pasting a Cell or Range**

- Select the cell or range that you want to copy, and then click the Copy button on the Standard toolbar.
- Select the cell or range into which you want to copy the selection, and then click the Paste button on the Standard toolbar.

Next, you'll copy the formula in cell B8 to the range C8:M8 to calculate the total income for the remaining months.

To copy and paste the formula from cell B8 to the range C8:M8:

▶ 1. Click cell **B8** on the Budget worksheet, and then click the **Copy** button 🖺 on the Standard toolbar. Note that the copied cell has a moving border. This border is a visual reminder that the range has been copied and is ready to be pasted.

▶ 2. Select the range **C8:M8**, and then click the **Paste** button 🖺 on the Standard toolbar. Excel copies the formula in cell B8 into each of the cells in the range C8:M8, changing the cell references to match the location of each cell in the range. See Figure 2-4. Note that when you paste a selection, Excel automatically displays the Paste Options button. This button provides options that give you control over the paste process. You will learn more about this button in the next tutorial.

Copying the SUM function for the monthly income | **Figure 2-4**

Trouble? If your screen does not match the one shown in the figure, you may have scrolled the worksheet further to the right so column B is no longer visible. You can click the left scroll button on the horizontal scroll bar to reposition the worksheet in the workbook window to better match the one in the figure.

3. Press the **Ctrl +** ` (grave accent) keys to display the formulas in the range B8:M8. Notice that the cell references in each formula refer to the income values for that particular month.

4. Press the **Ctrl +** ` (grave accent) keys to return to Normal view.

You are not limited to copying a single formula from one cell. You can also copy a range of formulas. When you copy a range of cells, each of which contains a formula, and then paste the selection into a new location, Excel pastes the formulas in each cell to their corresponding locations in the new cell range. You don't have to select a range that is the same size as the range being copied. You just need to select the first, or upper leftmost, cell in the destination range, and Excel will paste the selection in a range that accommodates all the cells. Any existing text or values in the destination range will be overwritten. So, be sure you paste the selection in an area of the worksheet that can accommodate the selection without deleting existing data.

Next, you need to copy the formulas for January's total expenses and net income, which are in cells B22 and B24, to the ranges C22:M22 and C24:M24. Then Amanda will be able to see each month's total expenses and net income values. Although there is no formula in cell B23, you will select the range B22:B24 and paste the selection to range C22:M24, simplifying the process. No values will appear in row 23.

To copy and paste the formulas in the range B22:B24 to the range C22:M24:

1. Scroll the worksheet to the left, if necessary, so column B is visible, select the range **B22:B24**, and then click the **Copy** button 🖹 on the Standard toolbar.

   Trouble? If the Clipboard task pane opens, close it. You will not need to use it in this tutorial.

> **2.** Select the range **C22:M24**, and then click the **Paste** button 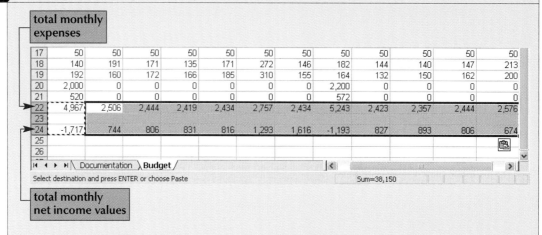 on the Standard toolbar. Figure 2-5 shows the total expenses and net income values for each month in the Budget worksheet. Note that Excel has duplicated the two formulas from the first month in each succeeding month.

Figure 2-5   **Copying and pasting a cell range**

> **3.** Press the **Esc** key to remove the moving border from the selected range.

As you can see, Excel's ability to adjust cell references when copying and pasting formulas makes it easy to create columns or rows of formulas that share a common structure.

Using Relative and Absolute References

The type of cell reference that you just worked with is called a relative reference. A **relative reference** is a cell reference that changes when it is copied and pasted in a new location. Excel interprets the reference *relative* to the position of the active cell. For example, when you copied the formula =SUM(B6:B7) from the source cell, B8, and pasted it in the destination range, C8:M8, Excel adjusted the cell references in each pasted formula relative to the new location of the formula itself. The formula in cell C8 became =SUM(C6:C7), the formula in cell D8 became =SUM(D6:D7), and so on.

A second type of cell reference is an absolute reference. An **absolute reference** is a cell reference that doesn't change when it is copied. Excel does not adjust the cell reference because the cell reference points to a fixed, or *absolute,* location in the worksheet, and it remains fixed when the copied formula is pasted. In Excel, an absolute reference appears with a dollar sign ($) before each column and row designation. For example, $B$8 is an absolute reference, and when it is used in a formula, Excel will always point to the cell located at the intersection of column B and row 8.

Figure 2-6 provides an example in which an absolute reference is necessary to a formula. In this example, a sales worksheet records the units sold for each region as well as the overall total. If you want to calculate the percent of units sold for each region, you divide the units sold for each region by the overall total. If you use only relative references, copying the formula from the first region to the second will produce an incorrect result, because Excel shifts the location of the total sales cell down one row. To correct this problem, you use an absolute cell reference, fixing the location of the total sales cell at cell B8. In the example, this means changing the formula in cell C4 from =B4/B8 to =B4/$B$8.

Using relative and absolute references ◀ **Figure 2-6**

Formulas Using Relative References

	A	B	C	D
1	Sales			
2				
3	Regions	Units Sold	Percent	
4	Region 1	2,238	=B4/B8	
5	Region 2	1,321		
6	Region 3	3,093		
7	Region 4	1,905		
8	Total	8,557		
9				
10				

	A	B	C	D
1	Sales			
2				
3	Regions	Units Sold	Percent	
4	Region 1	2,238	0.26154026	
5	Region 2	1,321	=B5/B9	
6	Region 3	3,093		
7	Region 4	1,905		
8	Total	8,557		
9				
10				

When the formula is copied, the relative reference to the cell (B8) is shifted down and now points to an incorrect cell (B9).

Formulas Using Absolute References

	A	B	C	D
1	Sales			
2				
3	Regions	Units Sold	Percent	
4	Region 1	2,238	=B4/$B$8	
5	Region 2	1,321		
6	Region 3	3,093		
7	Region 4	1,905		
8	Total	8,557		
9				
10				

	A	B	C	D
1	Sales			
2				
3	Regions	Units Sold	Percent	
4	Region 1	2,238	0.26154026	
5	Region 2	1,321	=B5/$B$8	
6	Region 3	3,093		
7	Region 4	1,905		
8	Total	8,557		
9				
10				

When the formula is copied, the absolute reference to the cell ($B$8) continues to point to that cell.

Another type of reference supported by Excel is the mixed reference. A **mixed reference** contains both relative and absolute cell references. A mixed reference for cell B8 is either $B8 or B$8. In the case of the mixed reference $B8, the column portion of the reference remains fixed, but the row number adjusts as the formula is copied to a new location. In the B$8 reference, the row number remains fixed, whereas the column portion adjusts to each new cell location.

As you enter a formula that requires an absolute reference or a mixed reference, you can type the dollar sign for the column and row references as needed. If you have already entered a formula and need to change the type of cell reference used, you can switch to edit mode and then press the **F4** key. As you press this function key, Excel cycles through the different references for the cell in the formula at the location of the insertion point. Pressing the F4 key changes a relative reference to an absolute reference, then to a mixed reference for the row, then to a mixed reference for the column, and then back to a relative reference.

In Amanda's family budget, monthly expenses vary greatly throughout the year. For example, tuition is a major expense, and that bill must be paid once in January and once in August. Amanda knows that the family has more entertainment and miscellaneous expenses during the month of December than at other times. The family's monthly income also fluctuates as Joseph brings in more income during the summer months than at other times. Amanda would like her budget worksheet to keep a running total of the family's net income as it progresses through the year. For example, she knows that the family will start the year with less money because of the tuition bill in January. Amanda wonders how many months pass before they recover from that major expense and begin saving money again.

One way to calculate the running total is to add the net income values of consecutive months. For example, to figure out how much money the family has saved or lost after two months, you add the net income for January to the net income for February, using the formula =SUM(B24:C24). To figure out the total net income for the first three months, you use the formula =SUM(B24:D24); through the first four months the formula will be =SUM(B24:E24), and so on.

The starting point of the range in the formula needs to be fixed at the cell that contains the net income for January, cell B24. To be sure that the formula points to cell B24, you need to use the absolute reference $B$24. The ending cell of the range will shift as you copy the formula to the other months in the worksheet. You need to use a relative reference for the ending cell in the range so that Excel will adjust the reference as the formula is copied. The formula for the running total through the first two months will be =SUM($B$24:C24). When you paste this formula to the other months of the year, Excel will adjust the cell range to calculate the total for all of the months up to that point.

To calculate the running total using an absolute reference to cell B24:

1. Click cell **A25**, type **Running Total**, and then press the **Tab** key twice to move to column C.

2. Type **=SUM(B24:C24)** in cell C25, and then press the **Enter** key. Excel displays the value –973, showing that the family's expenses exceed their income by $973 through the first two months of the year.

   Now you'll change the formula to use an absolute reference for cell B24 by selecting it in the formula and pressing the F4 key.

3. Double-click cell **C25** to switch to edit mode, and then double-click **B24** within the formula to select the cell reference.

4. Press the **F4** key to change the cell reference from B24 to $B$24. See Figure 2-7.

Figure 2-7   **Entering an absolute reference**

17	Insurance	50	50	50	50	50	50	50	50	50	50
18	Miscellaneous	140	191	171	135	171	272	146	182	144	140
19	Entertainment	192	160	172	166	185	310	155	164	132	150
20	Tuition	2,000	0	0	0	0	0	0	2,200	0	0
21	Books	520	0	0	0	0	0	0	572	0	0
22	Total	4,967	2,506	2,444	2,419	2,434	2,757	2,434	5,243	2,423	2,357
23											
24	Net Income	-1,717	744	806	831	816	1,293	1,616	-1,193	827	893
25	Running Total		=SUM($B$24:C24)								
26			SUM(**number1**, [number2], ...)								
27											
28				absolute reference entered by pressing the F4 key							
29											

◄ ◄ ► ►I \ Documentation \ Budget /

Edit

Trouble? If you pressed the F4 key too many times and passed the absolute reference, continue pressing the F4 key to cycle through the options until $B$24 is displayed in the formula.

5. Press the **Enter** key when the correct reference is displayed. Excel displays the value –973.

   Now you can copy this formula to the remaining months of the year.

6. Click cell **C25**, and then click the **Copy** button on the Standard toolbar. The moving border indicates that cell C25 has been copied.

7. Select the range **D25:M25**, and then click the **Paste** button on the Standard toolbar. Excel copies the formula to the remaining cells, as shown in Figure 2-8. The amount shown for each month represents the cash on hand that the family accumulated during the year, up to and including that month. So, for example, at the end of the year, after paying all expenses, they have a total of $6,396.

Running total of the family's net income ◀ **Figure 2-8**

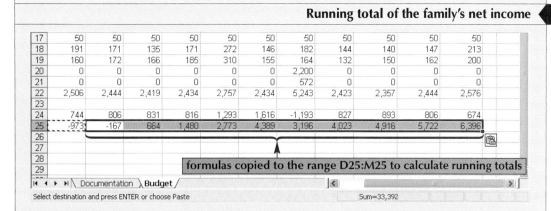

17	50	50	50	50	50	50	50	50	50	50	50
18	191	171	135	171	272	146	182	144	140	147	213
19	160	172	166	185	310	155	164	132	150	162	200
20	0	0	0	0	0	0	2,200	0	0	0	0
21	0	0	0	0	0	0	572	0	0	0	0
22	2,506	2,444	2,419	2,434	2,757	2,434	5,243	2,423	2,357	2,444	2,576
23											
24	744	806	831	816	1,293	1,616	-1,193	827	893	806	674
25	-973	-167	664	1,480	2,773	4,389	3,196	4,023	4,916	5,722	6,396
26											
27											
28											
29											

formulas copied to the range D25:M25 to calculate running totals

|◄ ◄ ► ►|\ Documentation \ **Budget** /

Select destination and press ENTER or choose Paste   Sum=33,392

▶ **8.** Press the **Ctrl + `** (grave accent) keys to examine the pasted formulas in the range D25:M25. The use of absolute and relative references ensures the integrity of the formula copied in each cell used to calculate the running net income total.

▶ **9.** Press the **Ctrl + `** (grave accent) keys to return to Normal view.

Working with Other Paste Options

So far you've used the Paste button to paste formulas from a source cell or range to a destination cell or range. When Excel pastes the contents of a selected cell or range, it also pastes any formatting applied to the source cell (you'll learn about formatting in the next tutorial). If you want more control over how Excel pastes the data from the source cell, you can click the list arrow next to the Paste button and choose one of the available paste options. Figure 2-9 describes each of these options.

Paste options ◀ **Figure 2-9**

Option	Description
Formulas	Pastes the formula(s), but not the formatting, of the source cell range
Values	Pastes the value(s), but not the formula(s) or formatting, of the source cell range
No Borders	Pastes the formula(s) and formatting of the source cell range, but not the format of the cell range's borders
Transpose	Pastes the formula(s) and formatting of the source cell range, except changes the orientation so that rows in the source cell range become columns, and columns become rows
Paste Link	Pastes a link to the cell(s) in the source cell range, including the formatting used
Paste Special	Opens a dialog box displaying more paste options

For example, if you want to paste the value calculated by the formula in a cell but not the formula itself, you use the Values option. This is useful in situations in which you want to "freeze" a calculated value and remove the risk of it being changed by inadvertently changing another value in the worksheet. For even more control over the paste feature, you can select the Paste Special option. When you select this option, the Paste Special dialog box opens, as shown in Figure 2-10.

Figure 2-10	Paste Special dialog box

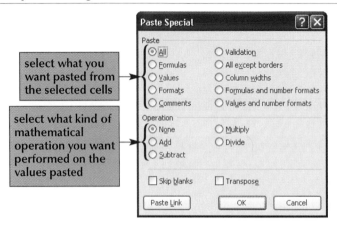

Using this dialog box, you can not only specify exactly which parts of the source cell or range—formulas, values, or formats—you want to paste, but also specify a mathematical operation you want performed as part of the paste action. For example, you can copy the value of one cell and add that value to cells in the destination range.

Another method that gives you control over the paste process is provided by the Paste Options button, which appears each time you paste a selection. By clicking this icon, you can choose from a variety of options that determine how the pasted data should be formatted. You'll explore this feature more in the next tutorial.

Changing the Magnification of a Worksheet

As you learned in Tutorial 1, an Excel worksheet can have 256 columns and more than 65,000 rows of data. You also learned that you can freeze columns and rows, so as you scroll through the data in the worksheet, the column and row headings remain visible. The number of columns and rows displayed in the workbook window depends on the zoom magnification set for the worksheet. The default zoom magnification setting is 100%. You can change this setting using the Zoom command on the View menu or the Zoom button on the Standard toolbar. Changing the zoom magnification setting allows you to see more or less of the worksheet at one time. If you decrease the magnification, you will see more of the data in the worksheet, but the data will be smaller and may be more difficult to read. If you increase the magnification, you will see less of the data in the worksheet, but the data will be larger and easier to read.

Reference Window | **Changing the Zoom Magnification of the Workbook Window**

- Click View on the menu bar, and then click Zoom.
- Click the option button for the percent magnification you want to apply, and then click the OK button.

or

- Click the Zoom list arrow on the Standard toolbar, and then click the percent option you want to apply.

You can change the magnification of the workbook window from 10% up to 400% or enter a percent not offered, for example, 65%, to further customize the display of your workbook window. You can also select a zoom magnification specific to the content of your worksheet. To do this, you select the worksheet's content and then choose the Selection option in the Zoom dialog box or on the Zoom list. Excel displays the content of the selection at a magnification that fills the entire workbook window.

Before continuing, Amanda wants to review the work done so far. Try changing the magnification so more of the worksheet is displayed at one time.

To change the zoom setting for the workbook window:

▶ **1.** Press the **Ctrl + Home** keys to make cell A1 the active cell.

▶ **2.** Click **View** on the menu bar, and then click **Zoom** to open the Zoom dialog box.

▶ **3.** Click the **75%** option button in the list of options, and then click the **OK** button. At this setting, all the data in the worksheet is displayed in the workbook window, as shown in Figure 2-11.

Budget worksheet at 75 percent magnification

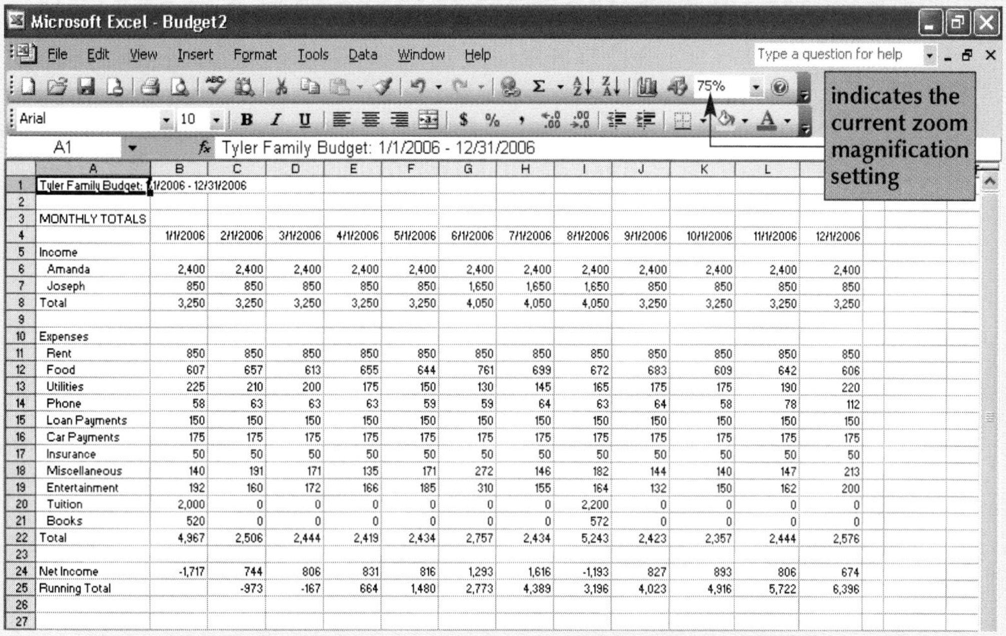

Figure 2-11

indicates the current zoom magnification setting

More of the worksheet is visible; however, reading the individual cell values is more difficult, so you will change the magnification back to 100%.

▶ **4.** Click the **Zoom** list arrow `100%` on the Standard toolbar, and then click **100%** to return to this higher magnification. Although the overall appearance of your screen may differ from the figures in this text, the data is not affected.

From examining the running totals, Amanda has learned several important facts. One of the family's largest expenses is Joseph's tuition, which is paid in January and August. She has also learned that the family does not recover from this January expense and show a positive overall net income until the month of April, when the total savings amount for the year up to that point is $664. Therefore, with their current income and expenses, it takes four months to "catch up" with the tuition expenditure in January, which leaves the family short on cash during February and March. The good news is that the total net income at the end of 12 months is $6,396, which represents the amount of money the family is able to save for the entire year.

Amanda now wants to know the family's total income and its total yearly expenses. You'll place these calculations in a table below the monthly figures. First, you will copy the income and expense categories to a new cell range.

To copy the income and expense categories:

1. Click cell **A27**, type **YEAR-END SUMMARY**, and then press the **Enter** key.

2. Copy the range **A5:A24** and paste it into the range **A29:A48**. If you want to remove the selection border from the copied range, you can press the Esc key. The selection border will disappear as soon as you select another range.

   Now you will enter the formula to calculate the total income for the family over the entire year.

3. Click cell **B28**, type **Total**, and then press the **Enter** key twice. You will enter the formula to calculate Amanda's salary for the year.

4. Type **=SUM(B6:M6)** in cell B30, and then press the **Enter** key. The amount 28,800 appears in the cell.

   Now you will copy this formula to calculate Joseph's yearly income, the couple's combined income, and the yearly totals for the expense categories.

5. Click cell **B30** to select this cell again, and then click the **Copy** button 🖹 on the Standard toolbar.

6. Select the range **B31:B32**, press and hold the **Ctrl** key, select the range **B35:B46**, click cell **B48**, and then release the mouse button and the Ctrl key. The nonadjacent range B31:B32;B35:B46;B48 should now be selected.

7. Click the **Paste** button 🖹 on the Standard toolbar. As shown in Figure 2-12, the total values for all income and expense categories should now be pasted in the worksheet.

Figure 2-12 | **Year-end totals for income and expenses**

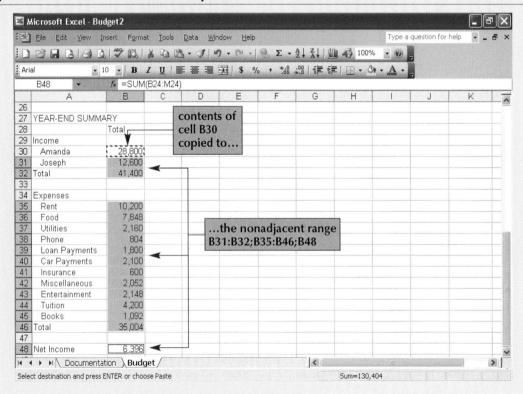

From these calculations, Amanda can quickly see that her family's yearly income is $41,400, whereas their yearly expenses total $35,004. Their largest expense is rent—a total of $10,200 per year.

Using the Insert Function Dialog Box

It's easier for Amanda to plan a budget if she knows approximately how much the family makes and spends each month. So your next task is to add a column that calculates the monthly averages for each of the income and expense categories. Rather than typing the function directly into the cell, you may find it helpful to use the Insert Function button on the Formula bar. Clicking this button displays a dialog box from which you can choose the function you want to enter. Once you choose a function, another dialog box opens, which displays the function's syntax. In this way, Excel makes it easy for you to avoid making mistakes. Try this now by entering the AVERAGE function using the Insert Function dialog box.

To insert the AVERAGE function:

▶ 1. Click cell **C28**, type **Average**, and then press the **Enter** key.

▶ 2. Click cell **C30** and then click the **Insert Function** button ƒ𝑥 on the Formula bar. The Insert Function dialog box opens. See Figure 2-13.

Insert Function dialog box ◀ **Figure 2-13**

The Insert Function dialog box shows a list of the most recently used functions. As you can see from Figure 2-13, one of these is the AVERAGE function. However, your list may be different and might not include the AVERAGE function. You can display a different function list using the category list box. Try this now to display a list of the Statistical functions supported by Excel.

▶ 3. Click the **Or select a category** list arrow, and then click **Statistical**. Excel displays a list of Statistical functions. See Figure 2-14.

Figure 2-14   **Excel's Statistical functions**

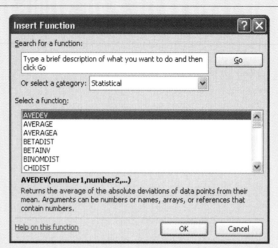

4. Click **AVERAGE** in the list, and then click the **OK** button. The Function Arguments dialog box opens.

The Function Arguments dialog box provides the syntax of the selected function in an easy-to-use form. You can enter the values needed for the arguments in the reference boxes by typing them or by selecting the cell range from the worksheet. To select a cell range in the worksheet, you can click the Collapse Dialog Box button located to the right of each argument reference. Clicking this button reduces the size of the dialog box so you can see more of the worksheet. The Collapse Dialog Box button is a toggle button and, when clicked, changes to the Expand Dialog box button, which you click to restore the dialog box to its original size.

Although Amanda's salary did not change during the past year, she wants to use this workbook as a model for the next couple of years. If her salary changes in the future, the formula to calculate the average income will be in place.

You will use the Insert Function dialog box to enter the formula to calculate the average value of the cells in the range B6:M6, which contains Amanda's monthly salary amount.

To insert values into the AVERAGE function:

1. Click the **Collapse Dialog Box** button located to the right of the Number1 argument reference box. The Function Arguments dialog box reduces in size to let you see more of the worksheet, and the Collapse Dialog Box button changes to the Expand Dialog Box button.

Trouble? If the collapsed dialog box is still in the way of the range you need to select, drag the dialog box to another location on the worksheet.

2. Select the range **B6:M6** on the worksheet, and then click the **Expand Dialog Box** button to restore the Function Arguments dialog box to its original size, as shown in Figure 2-15.

Function Arguments dialog box ◀ **Figure 2-15**

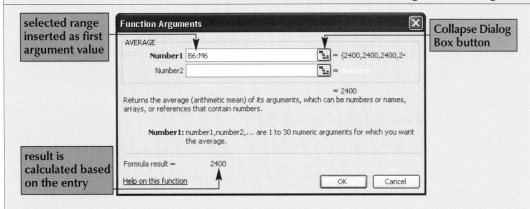

3. Click the **OK** button. The value 2,400 appears in C30.

Now you will copy the formula to calculate the average of other income and expense categories.

To copy the AVERAGE function into the remaining cells:

▶ **1.** Click cell **C30**, if necessary, and then click the **Copy** button 🖹 on the Standard toolbar.

▶ **2.** Select the nonadjacent range **C31:C32;C35:C46;C48**, and then click the **Paste** button 🖹 on the Standard toolbar. Figure 2-16 shows the monthly averages in Amanda's budget.

Year-end average values ◀ **Figure 2-16**

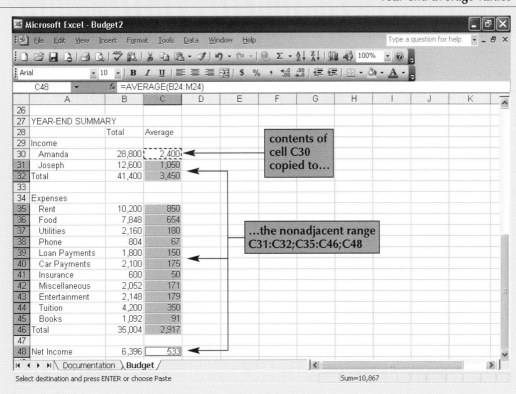

On average, the couple makes $3,450 per month and spends $2,917. Their net income is about $533 a month on average; this is the amount that Amanda can expect the family to save. It is obvious that expenses for some months will be higher than expected. Amanda wonders how much higher? She would like to calculate the maximum and minimum amounts for each of the income and expense categories. She knows that this will give her a better picture of the range of values for her family's income and expenses.

Filling in Formulas and Series

Up to now you've used the Copy and Paste buttons to enter the same formula into multiple cells. Another approach you can use is to fill in the values. You may have noticed a small black square in the lower-right corner of a selected cell or cell range. That small black square is called the **fill handle**. This Excel tool enables you to copy the contents of the selected cells simply by dragging the fill handle over another adjacent cell or range of cells rather than going through the two-step process of clicking the Copy and Paste buttons. This technique is also referred to as **Auto Fill**.

Reference Window	**Copying Formulas Using the Fill Handle**

- Select the cell or range that contains the formula or formulas you want to copy.
- Drag the fill handle in the direction you want to copy the formula(s), and then release the mouse button.
- To select a specific fill option, click the Auto Fill Options button, and then select the option you want to apply to the selected range.

To calculate the maximum and minimum amounts for each of the income and expense categories, you will enter the **MIN** and **MAX functions**, which have a similar syntax as the AVERAGE and SUM functions. Once you enter the formulas using the MIN and MAX functions for Amanda's income, you can use Auto Fill to fill in the formulas for Joseph's income and for the expense categories.

To calculate the year-end minimum and maximum amounts:

1. Click cell **D28**, type **Minimum**, and then press the **Tab** key.

2. Type **Maximum** in cell E28, and then press the **Enter** key twice to move back to column D where you will enter the formula to calculate minimum values.

3. Type **=MIN(B6:M6)** in cell D30, and then press the **Tab** key to move to column E where you will enter the formula to calculate maximum values.

4. Type **=MAX(B6:M6)** in cell E30, and then press the **Enter** key. Excel displays the value 2,400 in both cell D30 and cell E30 because Amanda's monthly salary is $2,400 and does not vary throughout the year.

   You will use the fill handle to copy the formulas with the MIN and MAX functions into the remaining income and expense categories.

5. Select the range **D30:E30**. The fill handle appears in the lower-right corner of the selection.

6. Position the pointer over the fill handle until the pointer changes to ╋, and then drag the fill handle down the worksheet until the selection border encloses the range **D30:E48**.

7. Release the mouse button. The Auto Fill Options button appears, and by default Excel copies the formulas and formats found in the source range, D30:E30, into the destination range. Note that rows 33, 34, and 47 contain zeros. This is because those rows correspond to empty cells in the monthly table. You can delete the MIN and MAX functions in those cells.

8. Select the nonadjacent range **D33:E34;D47:E47**, and then press the **Delete** key to clear the contents of the selected cells. Figure 2-17 shows the minimum and maximum values for each income and expense category.

Year-end minimum and maximum values ◄ Figure 2-17

These calculations provide Amanda with an idea of the range of possible values in her budget. From these figures she can see that the maximum amount the family earned in a single month was $4,050 (cell E32), while the maximum amount the family spent in a single month was $5,243 (cell E46). How frugal can the family be? Based on her calculations, the lowest amount the family spent in a given month was $2,357 (cell D46). Amanda has also discovered that the most the family was able to save in a month was $1,616 (cell E48), while their largest deficit was $1,717—which occurred in the month of January, when a tuition payment was due. If the average values in column C give Amanda a picture of what a "typical" month looks like, the values in columns D and E give her an idea of the extremes in the family budget.

If you have a large selection to fill, you may find it difficult to use the fill handle feature of Auto Fill. If you don't want to use the fill handle, you can select the cell range that you want to fill and then use the Fill command on the Edit menu. Excel provides a list of Fill commands that you can use to fill in the selected range.

Auto Fill Options

When you use Auto Fill with formulas, Excel copies not only the formulas but also the formatting applied to the copied cell or range. However, there may be times when you only want the values in a cell copied, or maybe just the formatting. You can control what Excel does when you use the fill handle to copy formulas. When you release the mouse button, a button appears at the lower-right corner of the cell range. This is the Auto Fill Options button. Clicking this button provides a list of available options that you can choose to specify how Excel should handle the pasted selection.

The Auto Fill default option is to copy both the formulas and the formats of selected cells into the cell range. To copy only the formulas or just the formats, you can choose one of the other Auto Fill options, as shown in Figure 2-18.

Figure 2-18 ▶ **Auto Fill options**

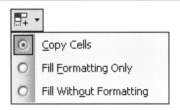

Filling a Series

The Auto Fill feature can also be used to continue a series of values, dates, or text based on an established pattern. As shown in Figure 2-19, to create a list of sequential numbers, you enter the first few numbers of the sequence and then drag the fill handle, completing the sequence. In this case, a list of numbers from 1 to 10 is quickly generated.

Figure 2-19 ▶ **Using Auto Fill to complete a series of numbers**

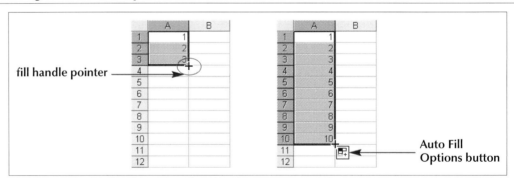

The series does not have to be numeric. It can also contain text and dates. Figure 2-20 shows a few examples of other series that can be completed using the Auto Fill feature.

Applying Auto Fill to different series | **Figure 2-20**

Type	Initial Selection	Extended Series
Values	1, 2, 3	4, 5, 6, ...
	2, 4, 6	8, 10, 12, ...
Dates and Times	Jan	Feb, Mar, Apr, ...
	January	February, March, April, ...
	Jan, Apr	Jul, Oct, Jan, ...
	15-Jan, 15-Feb	15-Mar, 15-Apr, 15-May, ...
	12/30/2005	12/31/2005, 1/1/2006, 1/2/2006, ...
	12/31/2005, 1/31/2006	2/28/2006, 3/31/2006, 4/30/2006, ...
	Mon	Tue, Wed, Thu, ...
	Monday	Tuesday, Wednesday, Thursday, ...
	11:00 AM	12:00 PM, 1:00 PM, 2:00 PM, ...
Patterned Text	1st period	2nd period, 3rd period, 4th period, ...
	Region 1	Region 2, Region 3, Region 4, ...
	Quarter 3	Quarter 4, Quarter 1, Quarter 2, ...
	Qtr3	Qtr4, Qtr1, Qtr2, ...

Amanda would like to replace dates in the Budget worksheet with the abbreviations of each month. Rather than directly typing this text, you will insert the abbreviations using the fill handle.

To fill in the abbreviations for the months of the year:

1. Press the **Ctrl + Home** keys to make the columns on the left and the top rows visible.

2. Click cell **B4**, type **Jan**, and then click the **Enter** button ✔ on the Formula bar. Because "Jan" is a commonly used abbreviation for January, Excel will recognize it as a month without your having to type in "Feb" for the next month in the series.

3. Position the pointer over the fill handle in the lower-right corner of cell B4 until the pointer changes to ✚.

4. Drag the fill handle over the range **B4:M4**, and then release the mouse button. Excel fills in the abbreviation for each month in the range of cells, as shown in Figure 2-21. As you drag the fill handle, ScreenTips for the month abbreviations appear.

Filling in the month abbreviations | **Figure 2-21**

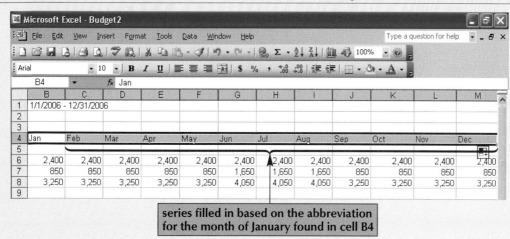

series filled in based on the abbreviation for the month of January found in cell B4

Excel provides other techniques for automatically filling in values and text. You can even create your own customized fill series. You can use Excel's online Help to explore other Auto Fill options.

Working with Date Functions

Entering the current date in a worksheet might not always address a date-related issue or need. If you want the current date to always appear in your workbook, versus the date you may have entered when you created the workbook, you can use a Date function rather than re-entering the current date each time you open the workbook. The **Date functions** provided by Excel store and calculate dates as numeric values, representing the number of days since January 1, 1900. For example, when you enter the date 1/1/2008 into a worksheet cell, you are actually entering the value 39448, because that date is 39,448 days after January 1, 1900. This method of storing dates allows you to work with dates using the same formulas you would use to work with any value. If you want to determine the number of days between two dates, you simply subtract one date from the other.

Excel automatically updates the values returned by the TODAY() and NOW() functions whenever you reopen the workbook. The **TODAY() function** displays the current date based on your computer's internal clock; the **NOW() function** displays both the date and time. If you want a permanent date (reflecting when the workbook was initially created, for example), enter the date directly into the cell without using either function.

If you have additional tasks to perform with a date or time, you can use one of the functions listed in Figure 2-22.

Figure 2-22 ▶ **Date and Time functions**

Function	Description
DATE(*year*, *month*, *day*)	Creates a date value for the date represented by the *year*, *month*, and *day* arguments
DAY(*date*)	Extracts the day of the month from the *date* value
MONTH(*date*)	Extracts the month number from the *date* value, where 1=January, 2=February, and so forth
YEAR(*date*)	Extracts the year number from the *date* value
WEEKDAY(*date*, [*return_type*])	Calculates the day of the week from the *date* value, where 1=Sunday, 2=Monday, and so forth. To choose a different numbering scheme, set the optional *return_type* value to "1" (1=Sunday, 2=Monday, ...), "2" (1=Monday, 2=Tuesday, ...), or "3" (0=Monday, 1=Tuesday, ...).
NOW()	Displays the current date and time
TODAY()	Displays the current date

You can use these functions to answer such questions as: On what day of the week does 1/1/2008 fall? You can calculate the day of the week with the **WEEKDAY function** as =*WEEKDAY(1/1/2008)*. This formula returns the value 7, which is Saturday—the seventh day of the week.

Because Amanda intends to use this worksheet as a model for future budgets, she wants the date on the Documentation sheet to always display the current date. You will replace the date you entered when you first opened the workbook with the TODAY() function.

To enter the TODAY() function on the Documentation sheet:

1. Switch to the Documentation sheet.

2. Click cell **B4**, type **=TODAY()**, and then click the **Enter** button ✓ on the Formula bar. Note that there are no arguments in the TODAY() function, but you still have to include the opening and closing parentheses, and there are no spaces between the parentheses. Excel displays the current date as shown in Figure 2-23.

Inserting the current date ◀ **Figure 2-23**

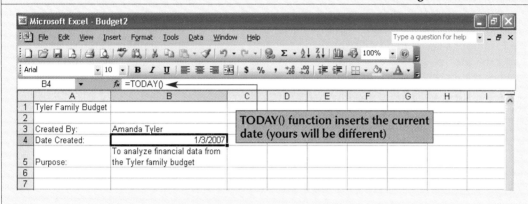

You have completed your work on the Budget2 workbook.

3. Save your changes to the workbook, and then close it.

Using Math and Statistical functions, you have been able to calculate the monthly and end-of-year values Amanda requested. With these values in place, Amanda has a better picture of the family's finances, and she is more confident about how she will manage the family budget in the year to come.

Session 2.1 Quick Check

Review

1. What is the function you enter to calculate the minimum value in the range B1:B50?
2. Cell A10 contains the formula =A1+B1. When you copy the content of cell A10 and paste it into cell B11, what formula is inserted into the destination cell?
3. Cell A10 contains the formula =$A$1+B1. When you copy the content of cell A10 and paste it into cell B11, what formula is inserted into the destination cell?
4. Express the reference to cell A1 as (a) a relative reference, (b) an absolute reference, and (c) a mixed reference (both possibilities).
5. List the steps you use in Excel to create a series of odd numbers from 1 to 99 in column A of your worksheet.
6. To display the current date in a workbook each time you reopen it, you enter the _____ function in the cell where you want the date to appear.

(**Note:** This session presents topics related to Financial functions and Logical functions. This session *is optional and may be skipped* without loss of continuity of the instruction.)

Working with Financial Functions

After reviewing the figures calculated in the Budget worksheet, Amanda thinks she has a better understanding of the family finances. Now she would like to determine whether the family could afford the monthly payments required to purchase a house if they were to take a loan from a bank. To do this, she wants to create a worksheet containing a "typical" month's income and expenses, and then she wants to use an Excel Financial function to calculate the monthly payments required for a loan of $175,000. Excel's **Financial functions** are the same as those widely used in the world of business and accounting to perform various financial calculations. For instance, these functions allow you to calculate the depreciation of an asset, determine the amount of interest paid on an investment, compute the present value of an investment, and so on. Although she is not a business or financial professional, Amanda's question is a financial one: Given the family budget, how great a loan payment can they afford if they want to buy a home? There are four principal factors involved in negotiating a loan:

- The size of the loan
- The length of time in which the loan must be repaid
- The interest rate charged by the lending institution
- The amount of money to be paid to the lending institution in periodic installments, called *payment periods*. (For most home loans, payments are due monthly, so the payment period is a month.)

To be sure, this is a simplified treatment of loans. Often other issues are involved, such as whether payments are due at the beginning of the payment period or at the end. For the purposes of this exercise, the above are the major factors on which Amanda will concentrate for now. Once you know any three of these factors, you can use Excel to calculate the value of the remaining fourth. Amanda is interested in a loan with the following conditions:

- The size of the loan is equal to $175,000.
- The length of time to repay the loan is equal to 30 years.
- The annual interest rate is equal to 5.5%.

She wants to calculate the fourth value—the monthly payment required by the lending institution to pay back the loan. To answer this question, you'll add a new worksheet to her workbook in which she can analyze various loan possibilities.

To create the Loan Analysis worksheet:

1. If you took a break after the last session, make sure that Excel is running and that the Budget2 workbook is open.

2. Insert a new worksheet at the end of the workbook named **Loan Analysis**, and then save the workbook as **Budget3** in the Tutorial.02\Tutorial folder included with your Data Files.

3. Click cell **A1**, type **LOAN ANALYSIS**, and then press the **Enter** key.

   Now you need to copy the labels and the average values from the Budget worksheet, which you completed in the previous session.

▶ **4.** Switch to the Budget worksheet, select the nonadjacent range **A29:A48;C29:C48**, and then click the **Copy** button 🖹 on the Standard toolbar.

▶ **5.** Switch to the Loan Analysis worksheet, and then click cell **A3** to make it the active cell.

Rather than pasting the formulas into this worksheet, you will simply paste the values.

▶ **6.** Click the **Paste** list arrow 🖹 ▾ on the Standard toolbar, and then click **Values** in the list of paste options. Excel pastes the labels from column A in the Budget worksheet into column A on the Loan Analysis worksheet and also pastes the average values from column C in the Budget worksheet into column B in the current worksheet. See Figure 2-24.

 **Pasting the income and expense categories and the average values** Figure 2-24

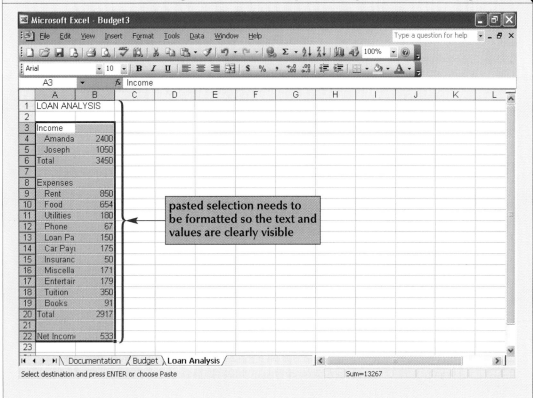

Excel pastes the cells as an adjacent range, not as a nonadjacent range. The result is that the values pasted from column C are shifted to the left into column B—right next to the labels in column A. These are the values you will need; their new location is not an issue. You will have to make some minor changes to the data, but first you need to increase the width of the columns so the values are easier to read. Then you will insert the formulas back into cells B6, B20, and B22 to calculate the total income, total expenses, and net income for a typical month.

To modify the layout of the worksheet and replace some of the values with formulas:

▶ **1.** Click cell **A1** to remove the selection highlight from the pasted range.

▶ **2.** Increase the width of column A to **18** characters (**131** pixels) and the width of column B to **10** characters (**75** pixels).

3. Click cell **B6**, click the **AutoSum** button Σ on the Standard toolbar, and then press the **Enter** key. Excel inserts the formula *=SUM(B4:B5)* into cell B6 to calculate the total average monthly income.

4. Click cell **B20**, click the **AutoSum** button Σ on the Standard toolbar, and then press the **Enter** key. Excel inserts the formula *=SUM(B9:B19)* into cell B20 to calculate the total average monthly expenses.

5. Click cell **B22**, type **=B6-B20** to calculate the average monthly net income, and then press the **Enter** key.

Now that you've entered the average monthly income and expense values for Amanda's budget and have widened the columns, you can enter the conditions for the loan. When you enter the amount of the loan, you will enter it as a negative value rather than as a positive value. The reason that you enter it as a negative value is because the loan is the amount owed to the lending institution; therefore, it is an expense. As you'll see later, Excel's Financial functions require loans to be entered as negative values because they represent negative cash flow. You will enter the labels and the conditions in columns D and E.

To enter the conditions of the loan in the worksheet:

1. Click cell **D3**, type **Loan Conditions**, and then press the **Enter** key to move to the next row where you will enter the Loan Amount label and the loan amount as a negative value.

2. Type **Loan Amount** in cell D4, press the **Tab** key, and then enter **-175,000** in cell E4.

   Next you will enter the length of the loan in years.

3. Type **Length of Loan** in cell D5, press the **Tab** key, and then enter **30** in cell E5.

   Now you will enter the annual interest rate, which is 5.5%.

4. Type **Annual Interest Rate** in cell D6, press the **Tab** key, and then enter **5.5%** in cell E6. Note that Excel may enter a zero, which doesn't change the value of the percentage.

   Next, you will enter the conditions under which the loan is to be repaid. In this case, you will assume that payments are due monthly.

5. Click cell **D8**, type **Payment Conditions**, and then press the **Enter** key.

   You will enter the number of payments to be made each year, which is 12.

6. Type **Payments per Year** in cell D9, press the **Tab** key, type **12** in cell E9, and then press the **Enter** key.

   Next you will enter the formula to calculate the total number of payments required to pay back the loan, which is the length of the loan (found in cell E5) multiplied by the payments per year (found in cell E9).

7. Type **Total Payments** in cell D10, press the **Tab** key, type **=E5*E9** in cell E10, and then press the **Enter** key.

8. Type **Payment Amount** in cell D11, and then press the **Tab** key.

   Before you continue, you will widen the columns so information is clearly visible.

9. Increase the width of column D to **18** characters (**131** pixels) and the width of column E to **10** characters (**75** pixels). Figure 2-25 shows the Loan Analysis worksheet with the values, loan conditions, and payment conditions entered.

Entering conditions for the loan and the monthly payments ◄ **Figure 2-25**

Paying off this loan will require 12 payments per year for 30 years, or 360 total payments. But how much will Amanda have to pay each month? To answer that question, you can use one of Excel's Financial functions.

Using the PMT Function

The monthly payment required to pay off a loan can be determined using the **PMT function**. The syntax of the PMT function is

=PMT(*rate, nper, pv,* [*fv*=0], [*type*=0])

where *rate* is the interest rate per payment period (determined by dividing the annual interest rate by the number of payment periods in a year), *nper* is the total number of payments, and *pv* is the present value of the future payments that will be made. In the case of a loan, the *pv* argument must be entered as a negative number. There are two optional parameters in this function: *fv* and *type*. The *fv* parameter indicates the future value of the loan and has a default value of 0. A future value of 0 means that the loan is paid off completely. The *type* parameter specifies whether payments are due at the beginning of the period (*type*=1) or at the end (*type*=0). The default value of the *type* parameter is 0.

Note that you can also use the PMT function for investments in which a specified amount of money is saved each month at a specified interest rate. In that case, the value of the *pv* argument would be positive since it represents an investment (a positive cash flow) rather than a loan (a negative cash flow).

Because the PMT function, like many Excel functions, has several required arguments, in addition to some optional arguments, you might not always remember all of the function's arguments and the order in which they should be entered. To make your task easier, you'll use the Insert Function dialog box to determine the payment amount for the loan Amanda is considering.

To select the PMT function using the Insert Function dialog box:

1. With E11 as the active cell, click the **Insert Function** button f_x on the Formula bar. The Insert Function dialog box opens.

   To locate the PMT function, you'll enter a text description of this function in the Search for a function text box.

2. Type **loan payment** in the Search for a function text box, and then click the **Go** button. Excel displays a list of functions related to loan payments. See Figure 2-26.

Figure 2-26	Searching for functions related to loan payments

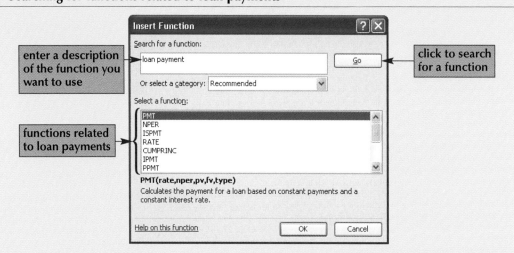

3. Verify that **PMT** is selected in the list of functions, read the description provided in the lower portion of the dialog box, and then click the **OK** button. The Function Arguments dialog box for the PMT function opens, as shown in Figure 2-27.

Figure 2-27	Function Arguments dialog box for the PMT function

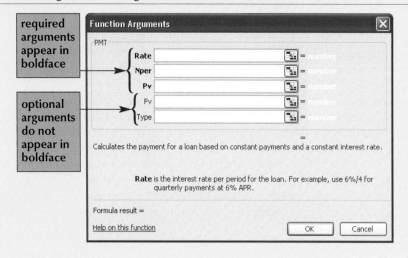

Note that, in the Function Arguments dialog box, required arguments are displayed in a boldfaced font, whereas optional arguments are not. Neither the Fv nor Type argument is displayed in a bold font. You will use this dialog box to enter values for the PMT function's arguments. The first argument that you will enter is for the rate, which is determined by dividing the annual interest rate by the number of payment periods in a year.

To enter values for the PMT function:

1. Click the **Collapse Dialog Box** button [icon] located to the right of the Rate box.

2. Click cell **E6** to enter the cell reference for the annual interest rate.

   To determine the rate, you will divide the value in cell E6 by the number of payment periods in a year (cell E9).

3. Type **/** (the division sign), and then click cell **E9** to enter the cell reference.

4. Click the **Expand Dialog Box** button [icon] to restore the Function Arguments dialog box. The expression E6/E9 should now appear in the Rate box.

   Next you will enter the value for the second argument, the *nper* argument, which is the total number of payments that need to be made for the 30-year loan. This number is displayed in cell E10.

5. Click in the **Nper** box, and then enter **E10** either by typing it directly into the reference box or by selecting the cell from the workbook.

   Finally, you will enter the *pv* (present value) argument. In the case of a loan, the present value is the amount of the loan Amanda's family is seeking. This value is stored in cell E4.

6. Click in the **Pv** box, and then enter **E4** using the method you prefer. Figure 2-28 shows the completed Function Arguments dialog box and illustrates how this dialog box relates to the function that will be inserted into cell E11.

Entering the PMT function ◀ **Figure 2-28**

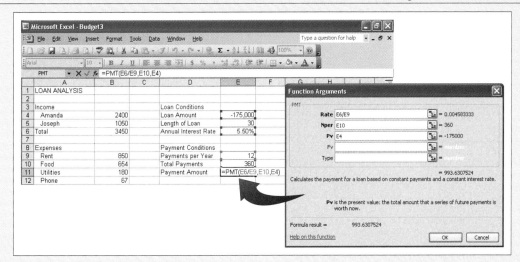

7. Click the **OK** button. Excel displays the value $993.63 in cell E11. Therefore, the required monthly payment is $993.63 for a loan of $175,000 at a 5.5% annual interest rate for 30 years.

   To see how this would affect Amanda's family budget, you will enter this information into the Expenses portion of the worksheet.

8. Click cell **A9**, type **House Payment** to replace the word "Rent," and then press the **Tab** key.

   Now you will enter a formula in cell B9 so the value House Payment is equal to the value Payment Amount.

9. Type **=E11** in cell B9, and then press the **Enter** key. The average total monthly expenses are recalculated.

If Amanda and Joseph were to buy a home with a $175,000 mortgage under the loan conditions specified in this workbook, their average monthly expenses would increase from $2,917 to $3,060.63 (cell B20), and the amount of money they could save each month would drop from $533 to about $389 (cell B22). By replacing the rent expense with the monthly home loan payment, Amanda can quickly gauge the effects of the loan on the family budget. Because the differences don't seem too unreasonable, Amanda now wants you to increase the size of the loan to $250,000, but keep all of the other factors constant.

To explore a what-if analysis for the mortgage:

1. Click cell **E4**, type **-250,000** as the new loan amount, being sure to enter this as a negative value, and then press the **Enter** key. Under this scenario, the monthly payment increases to about $1,419 and the family's monthly expenses increase to about $3,486, which is more than they make in a typical month. Obviously a loan of this size is more than they can afford.

2. Click the **Undo** button 🔄 on the Standard toolbar to restore the worksheet to its previous condition.

   This time Amanda wants to know what would happen if the interest rate changed. To determine the difference between the low interest rate of 5.5% and a higher one, you will change the interest rate to 6.5%.

3. Click cell **E6**, type **6.5%**, and then press the **Enter** key. Excel calculates the monthly payment to be about $1,106. Amanda can see that if the interest rate increases by 1%, then the monthly payment increases by about $113. She wants you to change the interest rate back to 5.5%.

4. Click the **Undo** button 🔄 on the Standard toolbar to change the interest rate back to its previous value.

The PMT function is just one of the many Financial functions supported by Excel. Figure 2-29 describes some of the other functions that can be used for mortgage analysis. For example, you can use the PV function to calculate the size of the loan that Amanda could afford given a specific interest rate, monthly payment, and total number of payments. If Amanda wanted to know the size of the loan she could afford by using the $850 rent payment as a loan payment, you would enter the formula =PV(5.5%/12,360,850), which would return the value –$149,703.50, or a total loan of almost $150,000.

Figure 2-29 ▷ **Financial functions**

Function	Description
PMT(*rate*, *nper*, *pv*, [*fv*=0], [*type*=0])	Calculates the payments required each period on a loan or investment, where *rate* is the interest rate per period, *nper* is the total number of periods, *pv* is the present value or principal of the loan, *fv* is the future value of the loan, and *type* indicates whether payments should be made at the end of the period (0) or the beginning (1)
PV(*rate*, *nper*, *pmt*, [*fv*=0], [*type*=0])	Calculates the present value of a loan or investment based on periodic, constant payments
NPER(*rate*, *pmt*, *pv*, [*fv*=0], [*type*=0])	Calculates the number of periods required to pay off a loan or investment
RATE(*nper*, *pmt*, *pv*, [, *fv*=0], [*type*=0])	Calculates the interest rate of a loan or investment based on periodic, constant payments

You can use the other functions described in Figure 2-29 to calculate the interest rate and the total number of payment periods. Once again, if you know three of the conditions for the loan, there is an Excel function that you can use to calculate the value of the fourth.

From the calculations you have performed, Amanda now knows that a monthly mortgage payment of $993 is required to pay off a $175,000 loan in 30 years at 5.5% interest. This leaves the family with a net income of about $390 per month. The question remains whether Amanda feels that the mortgage is affordable. Amanda knows that she and Joseph will have to purchase a second car soon, that there are other expenses on the horizon, and that a new house will, no doubt, bring with it additional expenses that she may not have considered yet, such as property taxes. To prepare for those new future expenses, Amanda wants the family's net income to exceed their expenses by about $5,000 per year.

Does her current budget, with a home loan payment of $993 per month, meet that requirement? To find out, you will enter the amount of money Amanda feels that the family needs to save each year and a formula to calculate if they can achieve this goal.

To calculate the family's yearly net income:

▶ 1. Click cell **D13**, type **Is the loan affordable?** and then press the **Enter** key.

   You will enter the amount Amanda wants the family to save each year.

▶ 2. Type **Required Savings** in cell D14, press the **Tab** key, type **5,000** in cell E14, and then press the **Enter** key.

   Next, you'll enter the formula to calculate how much the family saved in one year using the average monthly net income multiplied by 12 months.

▶ 3. Type **Calculated Savings** in cell D15, press the **Tab** key, type **=B22*12** in cell E15, and then press the **Enter** key. See Figure 2-30. Note that the value in cell E15 shows five places to the right of the decimal. You'll learn how to specify the number of decimal places in Tutorial 3.

Calculating the yearly savings   **Figure 2-30**

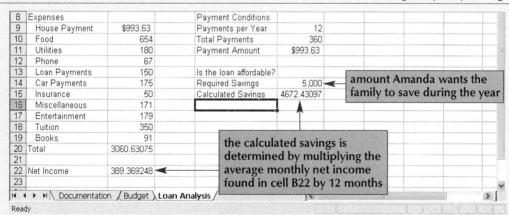

Under the proposed loan and assuming only the current expenses, the family could save about $4,672 per year, which is less than Amanda had hoped. So, Amanda would need to look at getting a smaller loan or hope that interest rates decrease in the future.

Amanda appreciates the type of information the worksheet provides, but she is concerned about getting lost in all of the numbers. She would like the worksheet to display a simple text message: "Yes" if the loan is affordable given the conditions she has set for the budget and "No" if otherwise. To add such a feature to the worksheet, you'll need to use a Logical function.

Working with Logical Functions

A **Logical function** is a function that tests, or evaluates, whether a condition in the workbook is true or false. The condition is usually entered as an expression. For example, the expression A1=10 would be true if cell A1 contains the value 10; otherwise, the expression is false.

Using the IF Function

The most commonly used Logical function is the **IF function**, which has the following syntax:

=IF(*logical_test*, *value_if_true*, [*value_if_false*])

where *logical_test* is an expression that is either true or false, *value_if_true* is the value displayed in the cell if the logical test is true, and *value_if_false* is the value displayed if the logical test is false. Note that the *value_if_false* argument is optional, though in most cases you will use it so that the function covers both possibilities.

For example, the formula =*IF(A1=10, 20, 30)* tests whether the value in cell A1 is equal to 10. If the expression A1=10 is true, the function displays the value 20 in the cell containing the function; otherwise, the cell displays the value 30. You can also construct logical tests that involve text values. The formula =*IF(A1="Retail", B1, B2)* tests whether cell A1 contains the text "Retail"; if it does, the function returns the value of cell B1; otherwise, it returns the value of cell B2.

Expressions in the logical test always include a comparison operator. A **comparison operator** indicates the relationship between two values. Figure 2-31 describes the comparison operators supported by Excel.

Figure 2-31 ▷ **Comparison operators**

Operator	Example	Description
=	A1 = B1	Tests whether the value in cell A1 *is equal to* the value in cell B1
>	A1 > B1	Tests whether the value in cell A1 *is greater than* the value in cell B1
<	A1 < B1	Tests whether the value in cell A1 *is less than* the value in cell B1
>=	A1 >= B1	Tests whether the value in cell A1 *is greater than or equal to* the value in cell B1
<=	A1 <= B1	Tests whether the value in cell A1 *is less than or equal to* the value in cell B1
<>	A1 <> B1	Tests whether the value in cell A1 *is not equal to* the value in cell B1

You'll use the IF function to display a text message in the worksheet indicating whether a $175,000 loan is affordable. In this case, the logical expression will test whether the value in cell E14 (the required savings) is less than the value in cell E15 (the calculated savings). The expression is E14 < E15. If this expression is true, then the loan is affordable for Amanda's family; otherwise, it is not. You will now enter the formula that includes the IF function =*IF(E14 < E15, "Yes", "No")*.

To insert the IF function to evaluate whether the loan is affordable:

▶ **1.** Click cell **D16**, type **Conclusion**, and then press the **Tab** key.

▶ **2.** In cell E16, type **=IF(E14<E15,"Yes","No")** and then press the **Enter** key. The text "No" appears in cell E16, indicating that the value in cell E14 is not less than the value in cell E15, and, therefore, the conditions of the mortgage are not acceptable to Amanda.

Amanda asks you to reduce the size of the loan to $165,000 to see whether this amount changes the conclusion about the mortgage's affordability.

▶ **3.** Click cell **E4**, type **-165,000** as the new loan amount, and then press the **Enter** key. As shown in Figure 2-32, the monthly payment drops to about $936 and the net yearly savings rise to about $5,354. Cell E16 displays the text string "Yes," indicating that this loan does satisfy Amanda's conditions for affordability.

Inserting a Logical function ◀ | **Figure 2-32**

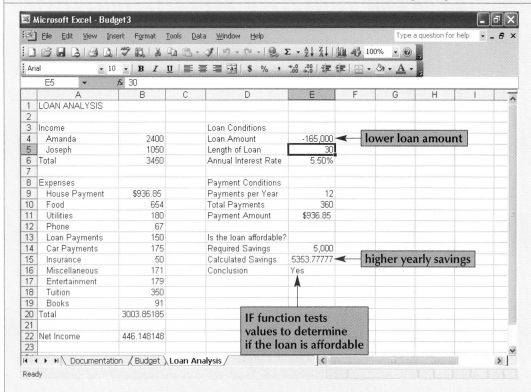

Now Amanda knows that buying a house is something that her family budget can support in the near future if she and Joseph manage their budget well. You will now save and close the Budget3 workbook.

▶ **4.** Save your changes to the workbook, and then close it.

Excel has several other Logical functions that you can use to create more complicated tests. Figure 2-33 describes the syntax of each of these functions.

Figure 2-33 > **Logical functions**

Function	Description
IF(logical_test, value_if_true, [value_if_false])	Returns the value value_if_true if the logical_test expression is true and value_if_false if otherwise
AND(logical1, [logical2, logical3, ...])	Returns the value TRUE if all logical expressions in the function are true and FALSE if otherwise
OR(logical1, [logical2, logical3, ...])	Returns the value TRUE if any logical expression in the function is true and FALSE if otherwise
FALSE()	Returns the value FALSE
TRUE()	Returns the value TRUE
NOT(logical)	Returns the value FALSE if the logical expression is true and the value TRUE if the logical expression is false

Amanda's budget workbook contains much of the information that she and Joseph can use to build a more stable financial picture for themselves in the future.

Review

Session 2.2 Quick Check

1. What are the four principal factors in a loan?
2. If you were to take a five-year loan for $10,000 at 7% annual interest rate, with monthly payments, what formula would you enter to calculate the monthly payment on the loan?
3. To calculate the present value of a loan based on a set, monthly payment, you could use the _____ function.
4. What formula would you use to display the text string "Yes" if the value in cell A1 is greater than the value in cell B1 and "No" if otherwise?
5. To change a logical expression from FALSE to TRUE or from TRUE to FALSE, use the _____ function.

Review

Tutorial Summary

In Session 2.1, you learned about the general syntax used by all Excel functions, and you learned about some of the Math and Statistical functions supported by Excel. You used the SUM function in a formula to calculate income and expenses for the month of January. You then learned how to copy and paste these formulas into other cells in the worksheet to calculate total figures for every month of the year. You learned the difference between the three types of cell references—relative, absolute, and mixed—and then you used an absolute reference to calculate a running total of the net income. You learned about the AVERAGE, MIN, and MAX functions, and then used them to summarize the entire year's budget figures. Once you entered the formulas that used these functions, you learned how to copy and paste the formulas using the Auto Fill feature. You also learned how to change the magnification of the workbook window so you can see more or less of the data in a worksheet. Finally, you used the TODAY() function to display the current date in the Documentation sheet.

In Session 2.2, you learned about the PMT function, which is a Financial function supported by Excel. You used the PMT function to calculate the monthly payment required to pay off a specified mortgage. You also learned about one of Excel's most commonly used Logical functions, the IF function. You used the IF function to display a text string indicating whether a loan was affordable.

Key Terms

Session 2.1	MAX function	TODAY() function
absolute reference	MIN function	WEEKDAY function
argument	mixed reference	***Session 2.2***
Auto Fill	NOW() function	comparison operator
AVERAGE function	optional argument	Financial function
Date function	relative reference	IF function
destination cell	source cell	Logical function
destination range	source range	PMT function
F4 key	SUM function	
fill handle	syntax	

Practice

Practice the skills you learned in Session 2.1 using the same case scenario.

Review Assignments

Data File needed for the Review Assignments: Family1.xls

Amanda appreciates the work you did on her family budget. Her friends Ken and Ava Giles have examined the workbook you created and have asked you to create a similar workbook for their budget.

Once you have completed a budget worksheet for the Giles family, they may want you to help them determine if they can afford to purchase their dream house in the country. The mortgage would be substantially higher than the family's current mortgage, but with Ava now working full time, the couple feels that they may be able to afford the higher mortgage. They would like you to create a workbook that will help them to determine if purchasing the house is possible.

To complete this task:

1. Open the **Family1** workbook located in the Tutorial.02\Review folder included with your Data Files, and then save the workbook as **Family2** in the same folder.
2. In the Documentation sheet, enter your name in cell B3, and then enter the current date in cell B4 using the TODAY() function.
3. Switch to the Budget worksheet, and then enter the formulas in the ranges C7:N7 and C14:N14 to calculate the total income and expenses, respectively, for each month. (*Hint*: Enter the formula in cells C7 and C14 first, and then copy and paste the formulas to the other cells in the ranges.)
4. In the range C16:N16, enter a formula to calculate the family's net income. (*Hint*: Enter the formula in cell C16 first, and then copy and paste the formula to the other cells in the range.)
5. In the range D17:N17, enter a formula using the SUM function to calculate the running total for net income from February through December. (*Hint*: Use an absolute reference for the appropriate cell reference.)
6. In the range C4:N4, use Auto Fill to fill in the month names January, February, March, and so forth.

7. In the range C21:F23, enter a formula to calculate the total, average, minimum, and maximum values of the two incomes.
8. In the range C25:F30, enter a formula to calculate the total, average, minimum, and maximum values of each expense category.
9. In the range C32:F32, enter a formula to calculate the total, average, minimum, and maximum values for net income.
10. Print the contents of the Budget worksheet, and save the changes you have made. If you are not continuing with the remaining steps, close the workbook.

Practice the skills you learned in Session 2.2 using the same case scenario.

   (**Note:** The following steps are *optional*. You should attempt them only if you have completed **Session 2.2** in the tutorial.)

11. Save the workbook as **Family3** to the Tutorial.02\Review folder.
12. Add a worksheet named "Loan Analysis" to the end of the workbook, and then enter the text "Loan Analysis" in cell A1 of the worksheet.
13. Switch to the Budget worksheet, copy the nonadjacent range A21:B32;D21:D32, switch to the Loan Analysis worksheet, and then paste the values, but not the formulas, into range A3:C14, using the Paste Special option. Increase the width of columns A and C to 12 characters (89 pixels) each, and column B to 15 characters (110 pixels). Edit the entries in cells C5, C12, and C14 so they contain formulas that calculate the total income, total expense, and net income.
14. Enter the following labels in the cells as indicated:
    - Cell E3: Loan Conditions
    - Cell E4: Loan Amount
    - Cell E5: Length of Loan
    - Cell E6: Annual Interest Rate
    - Cell E8: Payment Conditions
    - Cell E9: Payments per Year
    - Cell E10: Total Payments
    - Cell E11: Payment Amount
15. Widen column E to 21 characters (152 pixels).
16. In the range F4:F9, enter values for the following loan and payment conditions:
    - Loan Amount = –300,000
    - Years = 15
    - Annual Interest Rate = 6%
    - Payments per Year = 12
17. In cell F10, enter a formula to calculate the total number of payments. In cell F11, enter a formula using the PMT function to calculate the monthly loan payment.
18. In cell C8, enter the formula to make the mortgage expense equal to the result of the calculation in cell F11.
19. Enter the following labels in the cells as indicated:
    - Cell E13: Is the loan affordable?
    - Cell E14: Minimum Loan Payment
    - Cell E15: Conclusion
20. The family does not want a monthly loan payment greater than $2,500. Enter this value into cell F14, and then in cell F15 enter a formula using the IF function to display the text string "Yes" if the monthly payment is less than or equal to the value you entered in cell F14, and "No" if otherwise. Is the loan affordable under the loan conditions you have entered?
21. Print the contents of the Loan Analysis worksheet.

22. Change the loan from a 15-year loan to a 20-year loan. What effect does this have on the monthly loan payment and the conclusion about the affordability of the loan? Print the contents of the revised Loan Analysis worksheet.
23. Save your changes to the workbook, and then close it.

Case Problem 1

Apply

Apply the lessons you learned in Session 2.1 by creating a worksheet that analyzes the performance of a stock.

Data File needed for this Case Problem: Stock1.xls

Hardin Financial   Carol Gilson works at Hardin Financial compiling reports on different stocks for portfolios managed by the company. Carol would like to use Excel to create a summary report for a particular stock, Point Electronics (PEC). She has entered the stock's performance for the past 50 days of trading and needs to summarize these values over the last 5 days, 10 days, and 50 days. She has asked you to help her complete the workbook. To complete this task:

1. Open the **Stock1** workbook located in the Tutorial.02\Cases folder included with your Data Files, and then save the file as **Stock2** in the same folder.
2. In the Documentation sheet, enter your name and enter the current date using the TODAY() function.
3. Switch to the Stock History worksheet, and in the range E3:E52 enter the numbers 50 through 1 in descending order using Auto Fill.
4. Column F needs to contain the opening value of the PEC stock. The opening value of the stock is equal to the closing value of the stock on the previous day. For example, the value in cell F3 should equal the value in cell I4. Enter the formula for the opening value for Day 50, and then use Auto Fill to fill in the opening values of the stock in the range F4:F51. (*Note:* The closing value for Day 1 has already been entered in cell F52 for you.)
5. In cell C4, enter a formula that calculates the highest value of the stock in the last 5 days (Day 46 through 50) using the values in column H.
6. In cell C5, enter a formula to calculate the lowest value of the stock in the same time period using the values in column G.
7. In cell C6, enter a formula to calculate the range (the difference between the maximum and minimum) of the stock's value in that time period.
8. In cell C7, enter a formula to display the stock's average closing value in the 5-day period.
9. Repeat Steps 5 through 8 for the 10-day statistics, placing the maximum, minimum, range, and average closing values in the range C9:C12.
10. Repeat Steps 5 through 8 for the 50-day statistics, placing the maximum, minimum, range, and average closing values in the range C14:C17.

Explore

11. Select range A1:C20, and then print just the selection.
12. Save your changes to the workbook, and then close it.

Create

Using what you learned in Session 2.1, create a workbook that summarizes regional sales information.

Case Problem 2

There are no Data Files needed for this Case Problem.

Maxwell Scientific Lisa Dunn manages orders for Maxwell Scientific, a mail-order company that sells science kits and education products to schools and educators. Lisa has asked you to help her with some projects. To begin, Lisa wants you to enter sales information for three different Maxwell Scientific products by region in an Excel workbook. After you enter the sales data, you need to enter formulas to calculate total, average, minimum, and maximum sales for each product and each region, and then for all the models and regions. You will also need to calculate the percentage of sales for each product.

To complete this task:

1. Open a new blank workbook and save it as **Maxwell1** in the Tutorial.02\Cases folder included with your Data Files.
2. Rename the first sheet in the workbook "Documentation," and then enter your name, the current date, and the purpose of the project in this sheet.
3. Rename the second worksheet "Sales Summary," and then enter the sales data shown in Figure 2-34.

Figure 2-34

Region	Night Disks	Units Sold Planet Cards	Solar Mobiles
Region 1	2305	1483	824
Region 2	1281	1782	1005
Region 3	1885	2285	721
Region 4	2100	2108	1287

4. For each product, enter formulas to calculate the total sales for all regions, the average sales per region, and the maximum and minimum sales over all the regions.
5. For each product, enter a formula that uses absolute cell references to calculate the percentage of units sold per region.
6. Summarize the sales for all three of these Maxwell Scientific products by calculating the total, average, maximum, and minimum units sold for all products in all regions.
7. Calculate the percent of units sold for all products in each region.
8. Print the Sales Summary worksheet, and save your changes to the workbook. If you are not continuing with the remaining steps, close the workbook.

   (**Note:** The following steps are *optional*. You should attempt them only if you completed **Session 2.2** in the tutorial.)

Using what you learned in Session 2.2, create another worksheet that determines discount prices and shipping expenses.

9. Rename the third worksheet "Orders," and then save the workbook as **Maxwell2** in the Tutorial.02\Cases folder. Lisa has asked you to help her with another project. She wants you, using the Orders worksheet, to calculate the cost of each order and the total cost of all customer orders. Maxwell Scientific offers a 5% discount if customers order more than 50 units of a particular product. Also, customers can choose between two shipping options: standard shipping for a cost of $4.95, and express shipping for a cost of $9.95. You need to include both of these factors when calculating the cost of the order. Figure 2-35 shows a preview of the worksheet you'll create.

Figure 2-35

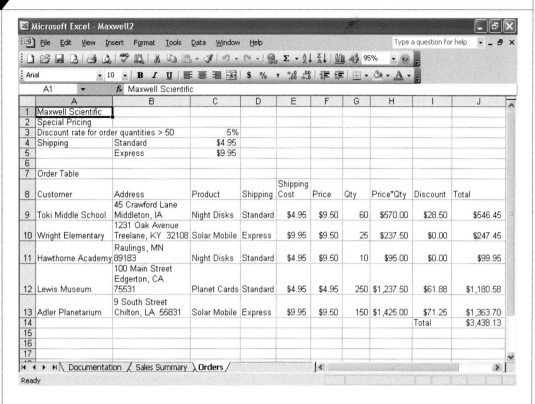

10. Enter formulas to calculate the total amount of each order and the total amount of all the customer orders. Use IF functions to calculate the shipping cost and discount for each order.

11. Preview the completed Orders worksheet, and then print it.

12. Save your changes to the Maxwell2 workbook.

13. Maxwell Scientific is considering changing its bulk discount rate from 5% to 8%. It is also looking at changing standard shipping charges to $5.50 and express shipping to $10.95. Lisa wants you to make these changes in the Orders worksheet. Change the discount rate and the shipping charges. What effect does the changes have on the current orders?

14. Print the revised Orders worksheet.

15. Save the workbook as **Maxwell3** in Tutorial.02\Cases folder, and then close the workbook.

Challenge

Go beyond what you learned in Session 2.2 to use the IF function as you create a payroll worksheet.

Case Problem 3

Data File needed for this Case Problem: Sonic1.xls

Sonic Sounds Jeff Gwydion manages the payroll at Sonic Sounds. He has asked you for help in setting up an Excel worksheet to store payroll information. The payroll contains three elements: each employee's salary, 401(k) contribution, and health insurance cost. The company's 401(k) contribution is 3% of an employee's salary for those who have worked for the company at least one year; otherwise, the company's contribution is zero. Sonic Sounds also supports two health insurance plans: Premier and Standard. The cost of the Premier plan is $6,500, and the cost of the Standard plan is $5,500. The workbook has already been set up for you. Your job is to enter the formulas to calculate the 401(k) contributions and health insurance costs for each employee. Figure 2-36 shows the worksheet as it will appear at the end of this exercise.

Figure 2-36

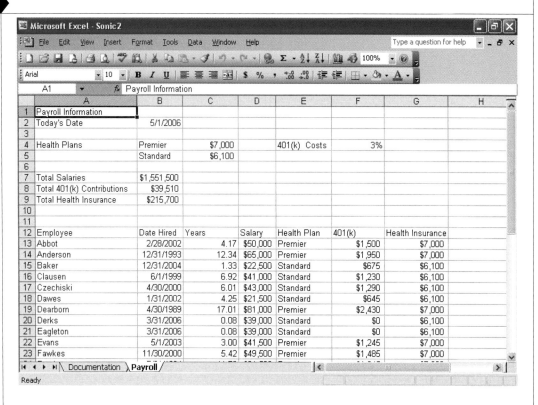

To complete this task:

1. Open the **Sonic1** workbook located in the Tutorial.02\Cases folder included with your Data Files, and then save the workbook as **Sonic2** in the same folder.
2. In the Documentation sheet, enter your name and then enter the date using the TODAY() function.
3. Switch to the Payroll worksheet. In cell C13, enter a formula to calculate the number of years the first employee has worked at Sonic Sounds. Use an absolute reference for cell B2. Divide the difference by 365. (*Hint*: You need to subtract the date the employee was hired from the current date, which is in cell B2, and then divide the difference by the number of days in a year. For the purposes of this exercise, do not try to account for leap years.)
4. Use Auto Fill to calculate the number of years the remaining employees in the table have worked for the company.

Explore

5. In the range F13:F45, insert a formula to calculate the 401(k) contributions for each employee. The formula should determine that if the number of years employed is greater than or equal to 1, then the contribution is equal to the contribution percentage in cell F4 multiplied by the employee's salary; otherwise, the contribution is zero.

Explore

6. In the range G13:G45, enter a formula to calculate the health insurance cost for each employee by testing whether the name of the employee's plan is equal to the name of the health plan in cell B4. If it is, then the cost of the health plan is equal to the value of cell C4; otherwise, the cost is equal to the value of cell C5.

7. In the range B7:B9, enter the formulas to calculate the total salaries, 401(k) contributions, and health insurance costs.
8. Print the contents of the Payroll worksheet.
9. Rework the analysis, assuming that the cost of the Premier plan has risen to $7,000 and the cost of the Standard plan has risen to $6,100.
10. Print the revised Payroll worksheet.
11. Save your changes to the workbook, and then close it.

Challenge

Go beyond what you learned in Session 2.2. Use the PMT, PPMT, and IPMT functions to create a payment schedule for a small business.

Case Problem 4

Data File needed for this Case Problem: Soup1.xls

The Soup Shop   Ken Novak is the owner of a diner in Upton, Ohio, named The Soup Shop. Business has been very good lately, so Ken is considering taking out a loan to cover the cost of upgrading and expanding the diner. Ken wants your help in creating an Excel workbook that provides detailed information about the loan. He would like the workbook to calculate the monthly payment needed for a five-year, $125,000 loan at 6.5% interest. Ken believes that the expansion will increase business, so he also wants to know how much he would save on interest payments by paying off the loan after one, two, three, or four years.

To do this type of calculation, you need to know what part of each monthly payment is used to reduce the size of the loan (also referred to as payments toward the principal) and what part is used for paying interest on the loan. Excel provides two functions to calculate these values, both of which are similar to the PMT function used to calculate the total monthly payment. To calculate how much of a monthly payment is used to pay off the principal, you use the PPMT function, which has the following syntax:

=PPMT(*rate, period, nper, pv* [,*fv*=0] [,*type*=0])

where *rate* is the interest rate period, *period* is the payment period you want to examine (such as the first period, the second period, and so forth), *nper* is the total number of payment periods, *pv* is the amount of the loan, *fv* is the future value of the loan (assumed to be zero), and *type* indicates whether the payment is due at the beginning (*type*=1) or at the end (*type*=0) of the month. The function to calculate how much of the monthly payment is used for paying the interest is the IPMT function, which has a similar syntax:

=IPMT(*rate, period, nper, pv* [,*fv*=0] [,*type*=0])

As with the PMT function, the value of the *pv* argument should be negative when you are working with loans—as you are in this case.

Ken wants you to use these two functions to create a payment schedule that indicates for each of the 60 months of the loan, how much of the monthly payment is being used to pay off the loan and how much is being used to pay interest on the loan. You can then use this schedule to discover how much Ken could save in interest charges by paying off the loan early. Figure 2-37 shows the worksheet as it will appear at the end of this exercise.

Figure 2-37

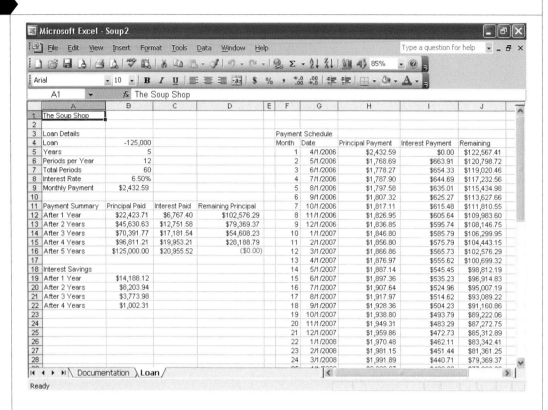

To complete this task:

1. Open the **Soup1** workbook located in the Tutorial.02\Cases folder included with your Data Files, and then save the workbook as **Soup2** in the same folder.
2. Enter your name and the current date in the Documentation sheet.
3. Switch to the Loan worksheet, and then in the range B4:B8, enter the following loan details:
   - Loan Amount = −125,000
   - Years = 5
   - Periods per Year = 12
   - Interest Rate = 6.5% (annually)

   In cell B7, enter a formula to calculate the total number of payment periods.
4. In cell B9, enter a formula using the PMT function to calculate the total monthly payment required to pay off the loan. Assume that payments are made at the beginning of each period, *not* at the end, which is the default. (*Hint*: Use the *fv* and *type* arguments.)
5. In the range F5:F64, enter the numbers 1 through 60 using Auto Fill. Each number indicates the payment period in the payment schedule.
6. Ken would like his payment schedule to include the dates on which the payments are due. In cell G5, enter the date 4/1/2006. This is the due date for the first payment. In cell G6, enter the date 5/1/2006. This is the due date for the second payment. Use the Auto Fill to enter the rest of the due dates into the range G7:G64.

Explore

7. In cell H5, enter a formula using the PPMT function to calculate the amount of the first month's payment devoted to reducing the principal of the loan. The details of the loan should reference the appropriate cells in the B4:B8 range of the worksheet using absolute references. The period number should reference the value in cell F5 using a relative reference. Be sure to indicate in the function that the payments are made at the beginning, not the end, of the month.

Explore

8. In cell I5, enter a formula using the IPMT function to calculate the amount of the first month's payment that is used for paying the interest on the loan.

Explore

9. In cell J5, enter a formula that calculates the amount of the principal remaining to be paid. Ken would like this expressed as a positive value. To calculate this value, construct a formula that is equal to the *negative* of the value in cell B4 (the amount of the loan) minus the running total of the principal payments. To calculate a running total of the principal payments, use the formula =SUM($H$5:H5). Note that this formula uses both an absolute reference and a relative reference, much like the running total example in the tutorial.

10. Using Auto Fill, copy the formulas in the range H5:J5 to the range H5:J64. (*Hint*: The value displayed in cell J64 should be $0.00, indicating that the loan is completely paid off. Also, the interest payment for the last month should be $13.11.)

11. In cell B12, enter a formula to calculate the total amount of payments made to the principal in the first 12 months of the schedule. In cell C12, enter a formula to calculate the total amount of the interest payments. In cell D12, enter a formula to calculate the amount of the remaining principal. Once again, Ken wants this expressed as a positive value, so the formula must subtract the value in cell B12 from the *negative* of the value in cell B4.

12. Repeat Step 11 for the range B13:D13, calculating the totals for the first 24 months. In the range B14:D14, calculate the totals for the first 36 months. In the range B15:D15, calculate the 48-month totals. In the range B16:D16, calculate the 60-month totals.

13. In the range B19:B22, enter a formula to calculate the amount of money Ken would save in interest payments if he paid off the loan after one year, two years, three years, and four years.

Explore

14. Preview the worksheet before printing it. Open the Page Setup dialog box, change the page orientation of the worksheet to landscape orientation, and then select the option so the worksheet will print on one page. Preview the worksheet again and then print it.

15. Save your changes to the workbook and then close it.

Research

Use the Internet to find and work with data related to the topics presented in this tutorial.

Internet Assignments

The purpose of the Internet Assignments is to challenge you to find information on the Internet that you can use to work effectively with this software. The actual assignments are updated and maintained on the Course Technology Web site. Log on to the Internet and use your Web browser to go to the Student Online Companion for New Perspectives Office 2003 at **www.course.com/np/office2003**. Click the Internet Assignments link, and then navigate to the assignments for this tutorial.

Assess

SAM Assessment and Training

If you have a SAM user profile, you may have access to hands-on instruction, practice, and assessment of the skills covered in this tutorial. Log in to your SAM account and go to your assignments page to see what your instructor has assigned.

Quick Check Answers

Session 2.1

1. =MIN(B1:B50)
2. =B2+C2
3. =$A$1+C2
4. (a) A1 (b) $A$1 (c) $A1 and A$1
5. Enter the values 1 and 3 in the first two rows of column A. Select the two cells and then drag the fill handle down over the range A1:A99, completing the series.
6. TODAY()

Session 2.2

1. the loan amount, the interest rate, the number of payment periods, and the payment due each period
2. =PMT(7%/12,5*12,10000)
3. PV
4. =IF(A1>B1, "Yes", "No")
5. NOT

Objectives

Session 3.1
- Format data using the Comma, Currency, and Percent styles
- Copy and paste formats using the Format Painter
- Modify and apply number formatting styles
- Change font type, style, size, and color
- Change alignment of cell contents
- Apply borders and background colors and patterns

Session 3.2
- Merge a range of cells into a single cell
- Hide rows, columns, and worksheets
- Add a background image to a worksheet
- Format worksheet tabs
- Clear and replace formats
- Create and apply styles
- Apply an AutoFormat
- Set up a worksheet for printing
- Add headers and footers to printouts

Developing a Professional-Looking Worksheet

Formatting a Sales Report

Case

NewGeneration Monitors

NewGeneration Monitors is a computer equipment company that specializes in computer monitors. Joan Sanchez, sales manager, has been entering sales data for three of the company's monitors into an Excel workbook. She plans on including the sales data in a report to be presented later in the week. Joan has made no attempt to change or enhance the presentation of this data. She has simply entered the numbers. She needs you to transform her raw figures into a presentable report.

To create a professional-looking document, you will learn how to work with Excel's formatting tools to modify the appearance of the data in each cell, the cell itself, and the entire worksheet. You will also learn how to format printouts, create headers and footers, and control which parts of the worksheet are printed on which pages.

Student Data Files

▼ Tutorial.03

▽ Tutorial folder	▽ Review folder	▽ Cases folder
Back.jpg	Region1.xls	Blades1.xls
Sales1.xls		Running1.xls
		WBus1.xls

Session 3.1

Formatting Worksheet Data

The data for Joan's sales report has already been stored in an Excel workbook. Before going further, you will open the workbook and save it with a new filename.

To open the Sales report workbook:

1. Start Excel and then open the **Sales1** workbook located in the Tutorial.03\Tutorial folder included with your Data Files.

2. On the Documentation worksheet, enter *your name* in cell B3, and enter the *current date* in cell B4.

3. Save the workbook as **Sales2** in the Tutorial.03\Tutorial folder.

4. Click the **Sales** tab to display the unformatted worksheet, shown in Figure 3-1.

Figure 3-1 ▶ **The unformatted Sales worksheet**

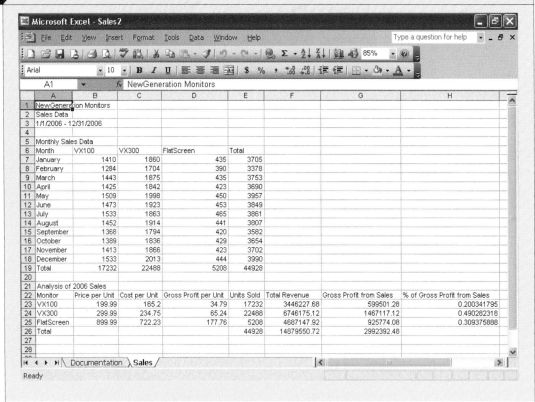

The Sales worksheet contains two tables. The table in the upper portion of the worksheet displays the monthly sales figures for three of NewGeneration's monitors: the VX100, the VX300, and the FlatScreen. The other table presents an analysis of these sales figures. Although the data in the worksheet is accurate and complete, the numbers are not as easy to read as they could be, which also makes interpreting the data more difficult. To help improve the readability of the data presented in a worksheet, you can change its appearance by formatting it.

Formatting is the process of changing the appearance of your workbook. A properly formatted workbook can be easier to read, appear more professional, and help draw attention to the important points you want to make. Formatting only changes the appearance of the data; it does not affect the data itself. For example, if a cell contains the value 0.124168, and you format the cell to display only up to the thousandths digit (so the value appears as 0.124), the cell still contains the precise value, even though you cannot see it displayed in the worksheet.

Unless you specify different formatting, Excel automatically displays numbers in the worksheet cells using the **General number format**, which, for the most part, formats numbers just the way you enter them. There are some exceptions to this approach. For example, if the cell is not wide enough to show the entire number, the General number format rounds numbers that contain decimals and uses scientific notation for large numbers.

If you don't want to use the General number format, you can choose from a wide variety of number formats. Formats can be applied using either the Formatting toolbar or the Format menu. Formats can also be copied from one cell to another, giving you the ability to apply a common format to different cells in your worksheet.

Using the Formatting Toolbar

The Formatting toolbar is one of the fastest ways to format a worksheet. By clicking a single button on the Formatting toolbar, you can increase or decrease the number of decimal places displayed in a selected range of cells, and display a value as currency with a dollar sign or a percentage with a percent sign. You also can use the Formatting toolbar to change the font type (for example, Times New Roman or Arial), style (such as bold), color, or size.

When Joan entered the monthly sales figures for the three monitors, she was concerned with entering the figures as accurately and as efficiently as possible and wasn't concerned with the appearance of the numbers in the worksheet. She entered the sales figures without including a comma to separate the thousands from the hundreds and so forth. Now, to make the numbers easier to read, Joan wants all the values to appear with commas, and for the figures that are whole numbers, she doesn't want any zeros after the decimal point (also referred to as "trailing zeros"). She believes that these changes will make the worksheet easier to read.

To insert commas in the figures in Joan's worksheet, you will apply the Comma style using its button on the Formatting toolbar. By default, Excel automatically adds two decimal places to the numbers that you have formatted with the Comma style. You will then need to use the Decrease Decimal button on the Formatting toolbar to change the number of decimal places displayed in a number.

To apply the Comma style and remove the trailing zeros:

1. Select the range **B7:E19** in the Sales worksheet.

2. Click the **Comma Style** button ⬛ on the Formatting toolbar. Excel adds the comma separator to each of the values in the table and displays the values with two digits to the right of the decimal point.

    Trouble? If you do not see the Comma Style button ⬛ on the Formatting toolbar, click the Toolbar Options button ⬛ on the Formatting toolbar, point to Add or Remove Buttons, point to Formatting, and then click ⬛ on the menu of available buttons.

    Because Joan wants whole numbers displayed without trailing zeros, you will remove any that are displayed.

3. Click the **Decrease Decimal** button ⬛ on the Formatting toolbar twice to remove the zeros. Figure 3-2 shows the worksheet with the formatting changes you have made so far.

Figure 3-2   Applying the Comma style

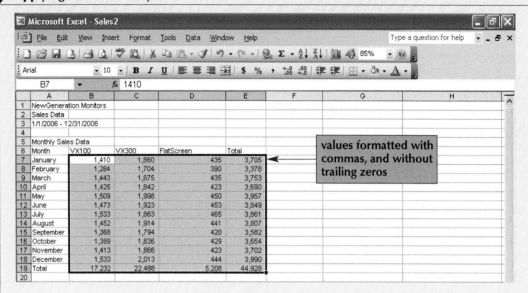

Joan wants the price and production cost of each monitor as well as last year's total sales and gross profit displayed using dollar signs, commas, and two decimal places. A quick and easy way to format the values with these attributes is to use the Currency style, which is available as a button on the Formatting toolbar. When you apply the Currency style, Excel adds a dollar sign and comma separator to the value and displays two decimal places. Try applying the Currency style to the total sales and profit values.

To apply the Currency style:

1. Select the nonadjacent range **B23:D25;F23:G26**.

   Trouble? To select a nonadjacent range, select the first range, press and hold the Ctrl key, and then select the next range.

2. Click the **Currency Style** button $ on the Formatting toolbar. As shown in Figure 3-3, Excel adds the dollar signs and commas, and keeps two decimal places to display the values as currency. Also note that the alignment of the dollar signs is along the left edge of the cell and the decimal points are aligned vertically.

Figure 3-3   Applying the Currency style

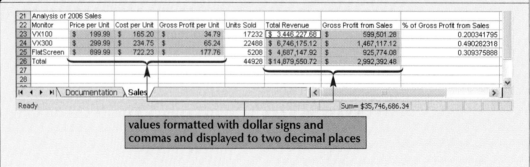

Finally, the range H23:H25 displays the percentage that each monitor contributes to the overall profit from sales. Joan wants these values displayed with a percent sign and two decimal places. To format a value as a percent, you can apply the Percent style. By default, Excel does not display any decimal places with the Percent style; therefore, you will need to increase the number of decimal places displayed.

To apply the Percent style and increase the number of decimal places:

▶ 1. Select the range **H23:H25**.

▶ 2. Click the **Percent Style** button % on the Formatting toolbar. The values appear with percent signs and without zeros.

▶ 3. Click the **Increase Decimal** button on the Formatting toolbar twice to display the percentages to two decimal places. Figure 3-4 shows the values in column H formatted with percent signs and to two decimal places.

Applying the Percent style ◀ **Figure 3-4**

21	Analysis of 2006 Sales							
22	Monitor	Price per Unit	Cost per Unit	Gross Profit per Unit	Units Sold	Total Revenue	Gross Profit from Sales	% of Gross Profit from Sales
23	VX100	$ 199.99	$ 165.20	$ 34.79	17232	$ 3,446,227.68	$ 599,501.28	20.03%
24	VX300	$ 299.99	$ 234.75	$ 65.24	22488	$ 6,746,175.12	$ 1,467,117.12	49.03%
25	FlatScreen	$ 899.99	$ 722.23	$ 177.76	5208	$ 4,687,147.92	$ 925,774.08	30.94%
26	Total				44928	$14,879,550.72	$ 2,992,392.48	
27								
28								

|◀ ◀ ▶ ▶|\ Documentation \ Sales /

Ready   Sum=100.00%

values formatted with percent signs and displayed to two decimal places

By displaying the percentages, you can quickly see that one monitor, the VX300, accounts for almost half of the profit from monitor sales.

Copying Formats

As you look over the sales figures, you see that one area of the worksheet still needs to be formatted. The Units Sold column in the range E23:E26 still does not display the comma separator you used with the sales figures. To fix a formatting problem like this one, you can use the Format Painter button located on the Standard toolbar. When you use the **Format Painter** option, you "paint" a format from one cell to another cell or to a range of cells. This is a fast and efficient way of copying a format from one cell to another.

Copying Formatting Using the Format Painter   Reference Window

- Select the cell or range whose formatting you want to apply to other cells.
- To apply the formatting to one cell or an adjacent range of cells, click the Format Painter button on the Standard toolbar, and then click the destination cell or drag the Format Painter pointer over the adjacent range.
- To apply the formatting to nonadjacent ranges, double-click the Format Painter button on the Standard toolbar, and then drag the Format Painter pointer over the first range and then over the other ranges you want to format.

You will use the Format Painter button to copy the format used in the sales figures and to paste that format into the range E23:E26.

To copy the formatting to the range E23:E26 using the Format Painter button:

▶ **1.** Select cell **B7**, which contains the formatting that you want to copy. You do not have to copy the entire range, because the range is formatted in the same way.

▶ **2.** Click the **Format Painter** button on the Standard toolbar. As you move the pointer over the worksheet area, the pointer changes to ⊕.

▶ **3.** Drag the pointer over the range **E23:E26** to apply the modified Comma style format to the sales figures.

Another approach is to use the fill handle discussed in Tutorial 2 to fill in the format (not the values) from one cell to another. To use this approach, you have click the Auto Fill Options button and select the Fill Formatting option. This technique only works when the cell or cells that you want to format are adjacent to the cell containing the format you want to copy. You can also use the Paste Special command from the Copy and Paste buttons to paste only the format of a selected group of cells into a new range of cells. This technique was also discussed in Tutorial 2. One of the advantages of the Format Painter button is that it does what these two methods do, but it does so in fewer steps. However, you should use the approach with which you feel most comfortable.

The Format Painter button and the buttons on the Formatting toolbar are fast and easy ways to copy and apply cell formats, but on occasion you will need more control over your formatting choices than is provided by these toolbar buttons. In those cases, you will need to use the Format Cells dialog box.

Using the Format Cells Dialog Box

Joan agrees that formatting the values has made the worksheet easier to read, but she has a few other suggestions. She does not like the way the currency values are displayed with the dollar signs placed at the left edge of the cell, leaving a large blank space between the dollar sign and the numbers, which is characteristic of values that use an accounting format. She would rather see the dollar sign placed directly to the left of the dollar amounts, which would eliminate the blank space.

The convenience of the Formatting toolbar's one-click access to many of the formatting tasks you will want to perform does have its limits. As you can see in the worksheet, when you use the Formatting toolbar, you cannot specify how the format is applied. To make the change that Joan suggests, you will open the Format Cells dialog box, which gives you more control over the formatting by providing categories of formats from which you can choose and modify to suit your needs.

To open the Format Cells dialog box:

1. Select the nonadjacent range **B23:D25;F23:G26**.

2. Click **Format** on the menu bar, and then click **Cells**. The Format Cells dialog box opens, as shown in Figure 3-5. In addition to the General format category, there are 11 number format categories from which to choose.

Format Cells dialog box 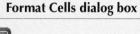 **Figure 3-5**

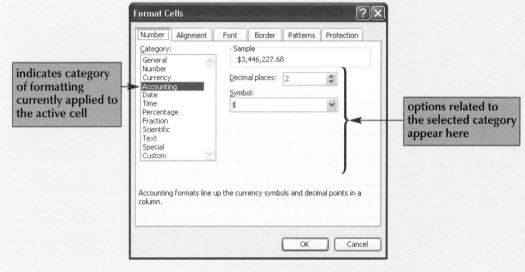

indicates category of formatting currently applied to the active cell

options related to the selected category appear here

The Format Cells dialog box contains the following six tabs, each dedicated to a different set of format properties. You can apply the options available in this dialog box to any cell or range of cells that you select. The six tabs are:

- **Number:** Provides options for formatting the appearance of numbers, including dates and numbers treated as text (for example, telephone numbers)
- **Alignment:** Provides options for controlling how data is aligned within a cell
- **Font:** Provides options for selecting font types, sizes, and styles and other formatting attributes, such as underlining and colors
- **Border:** Provides options for adding borders around cells
- **Patterns:** Provides options for creating and applying background colors and patterns to cells
- **Protection:** Provides options for locking or hiding cells to prevent other users from modifying their contents

Excel supports several categories of number formats, ranging from Accounting, which you applied using the Currency Style button, to Scientific, which might be used for recording engineering data. Figure 3-6 describes the number format categories.

Figure 3-6 — **Number format categories**

Category	Description
General	Default format that displays numbers as they are entered
Number	Used for a general display of numbers, with options for the formatting of negative numbers and the number of decimal places
Accounting	Used for displaying monetary values with dollar signs aligned at the left edge of the cell, the decimal points aligned vertically, and comma separators inserted
Currency	Used for displaying monetary values with dollar signs aligned next to leftmost digit and comma separators inserted (decimal points are not aligned)
Date, Time	Used for displaying date and time values
Percentage	Used for displaying decimal values as percentages
Fraction, Scientific	Used for displaying values as fractions or in scientific notation
Text	Used for displaying values as text strings
Special	Used for displaying ZIP codes, phone numbers, and social security numbers
Custom	Used for displaying numbers used in coding or specialized designs

As shown in the Format Cells dialog box in Figure 3-5, the Accounting format displays numbers with a dollar sign, a comma separator, and two decimal places. The Currency format is similar to the Accounting format. When you apply the Currency format to a number, the number appears with a dollar sign, a comma separator, and two decimal places. However, the difference between the two formats is how these attributes appear in the cell. The Accounting format lines up the decimal points and aligns the dollar signs at the left edge of the cell border (creating blank spaces between the dollar signs and the values, as you saw earlier). The Currency format aligns the dollar sign closer to the number, which removes the blank spaces. Joan prefers the Currency format, so you will apply this format to the nonadjacent range that you already selected.

To modify and apply the Currency format:

1. On the Number tab, click **Currency** in the Category list box. The Format Cells dialog box displays the options available for customizing the Currency category and provides a preview of the selected format. As shown in the Negative numbers list box, Excel displays negative currency values either with a minus sign (-) or with a combination of a red font and parentheses. Joan wants negative currency values to be displayed with a minus sign, which is one of the variations of the Currency format available to you.

2. Click the first entry in the Negative numbers list box, and then click the **OK** button. Excel changes the format of the currency values, removing the blank spaces between the dollar signs and the values and changing the alignment of the decimal points.

By using the Format Cells dialog box, you can control the formatting to ensure that text and values are displayed the way you want them to be.

Changing Font Type, Size, Style, and Color

A **font** is a set of characters that use the same typeface, style, and size. A **typeface** is the specific design of a set of printed characters, including letters, numbers, punctuation marks, and symbols. Some of the more commonly used fonts are Arial, Times Roman, and Courier. Each font can be displayed using one of the following **font styles**: regular, *italic*, **bold**, or ***bold italic***. Fonts can also be displayed with special effects, such as ~~strikeout~~, <u>underline</u>, and color.

Fonts can also be rendered in different sizes. **Font sizes** are measured using points. A **point** is a unit of measurement used in printing and is equal to approximately 1/72 of an inch. By default, Excel displays characters using a 10-point Arial font in a regular style. To change the font used in a selected cell, you either click the appropriate buttons on the Formatting toolbar or select options in the Format Cells dialog box.

In the logo that the company uses on all its correspondence and advertising materials, the name "NewGeneration Monitors" appears in a large Times New Roman font, which is a serif font. Characters that are designed as **serif fonts** have small lines stemming from and at an angle to the upper and lower ends of the character. **Sans serif fonts** do not include the small lines. A serif font is considered easier to read than a sans serif font. Joan wants the title in cell A1 to reflect this company-wide format, so you will format the title accordingly.

To change the font and font size of the title:

▶ **1.** Click cell **A1** to make it the active cell.

▶ **2.** Click the **Font** list arrow `Arial ▾` on the Formatting toolbar, scroll down the list of available fonts, and then click **Times New Roman**.

   Trouble? If you do not have the Times New Roman font installed on your computer, choose a different Times Roman font or choose MS Serif or another serif font in the list.

▶ **3.** Click the **Font Size** list arrow `10 ▾` on the Formatting toolbar, and then click **18**. Figure 3-7 shows the revised format for the title in cell A1.

Changing the font and font size | **Figure 3-7**

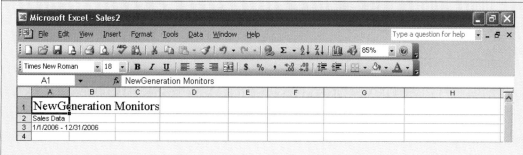

Joan wants the column titles of both tables displayed in bold font and the word "Total" in both tables displayed in italics. To make these modifications, you will again use the Formatting toolbar.

To apply the bold and italic styles:

▶ **1.** Select the nonadjacent range **A6:E6;A22:H22**.

▶ **2.** Click the **Bold** button **B** on the Formatting toolbar. The titles in the two tables now appear in a boldface font.

   Trouble? Some of the title text may appear truncated within their cells. You'll fix this problem shortly.

> **3.** Select the nonadjacent range **A19;A26**.
>
> **4.** Click the **Italic** button *I* on the Formatting toolbar. The word "Total" in cells A19 and A26 is now italicized.

Joan points out that NewGeneration's logo usually appears in a red font. Color is another one of Excel's formatting tools and can dramatically enhance the presentation of your data if you have a color printer. Excel provides a palette of 40 different colors. If the color you want is not listed, you can modify Excel's color configuration to create a different color palette. Excel's default color settings will work for most situations, so in this case you will not modify Excel's color settings. You will apply a red color to the name of the company and the two subtitles, which describe the contents of this worksheet.

To change the font color of the title to red:

> **1.** Select the range **A1:A3**.
>
> **2.** Click the **Font Color** list arrow **A ·** on the Formatting toolbar to display a color palette, and then position the pointer over the Red square (third row, first column from the left) on the palette, as shown in Figure 3-8.

Figure 3-8	Choosing a font color

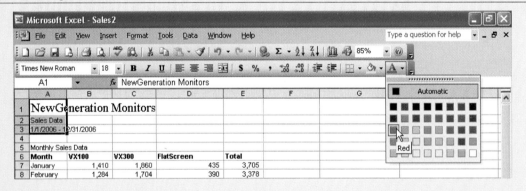

> **3.** Click the **Red** square to change the color of the font in the selected cells to red. See Figure 3-9.

Figure 3-9	Changing the font color of a cell

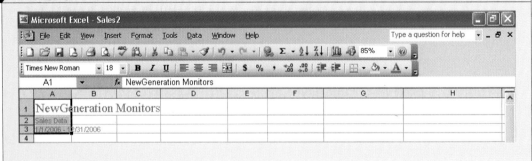

Aligning Cell Contents

When you enter numbers and formulas into a cell, Excel automatically aligns them with the cell's right edge and bottom border. Text entries are aligned with the left edge and bottom border. The default Excel alignment does not always create the most readable worksheets. As a general rule, you should center column titles, and format columns of numbers so that the decimal places are lined up within a column. You can change horizontal alignment using the alignment tools on the Formatting toolbar or the options on the Alignment tab in the Format Cells dialog box.

Next, you will center the column titles above the values in each column in the two tables.

To center the column titles:

▶ 1. Select the nonadjacent range **B6:E6;B22:H22**.

▶ 2. Click the **Center** button ≣ on the Formatting toolbar. Excel centers the text in the selected cells in each column.

The Formatting toolbar also provides the Align Left button and the Align Right button so that you can left-align and right-align cell contents. If you want to align cell contents vertically, you have to open the Format Cells dialog box and choose the vertical alignment options on the Alignment tab.

Another alignment option available in the Format Cells dialog box is to center text across a range of cells. Joan wants the text in the cell range A1:A3 to be centered at the top of the worksheet across the first eight columns of the worksheet. This time you will open the Format Cells dialog box to make this formatting change.

To center the titles and subtitles across the first eight columns of the worksheet:

▶ 1. Select the range **A1:H3**.

▶ 2. Click **Format** on the menu bar, and then click **Cells** to open the Format Cells dialog box.

▶ 3. Click the **Alignment** tab.

▶ 4. Click the **Horizontal** list arrow in the Text alignment pane, click **Center Across Selection**, and then click the **OK** button. See Figure 3-10.

Centering text within and across columns ◀ **Figure 3-10**

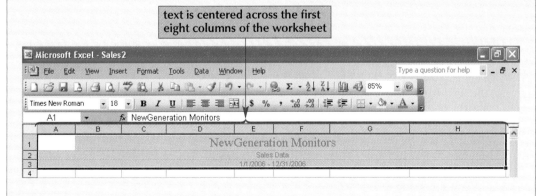

The text in these cells is centered horizontally across the selection. Note that centering the text does not affect the location. The title and subtitles are still placed in cells A1 through A3. In general, you should only use this approach for text that is in the leftmost column of the selection, and there should be no text in any other column. If you had text in column B in the previous set of steps, then that text would have been centered across columns B through H, and the text in column A would have remained where it was.

Indenting and Wrapping Text

Sometimes you will want a cell's contents offset, or indented, a few spaces from the cell's edge. This is particularly true for text entries that are aligned with the left edge of the cell. Indenting is often used for cell entries that are considered "subsections" of your worksheet. Joan wants you to indent the names of the months in the range A7:A18 and the monitor titles in the range A23:A25. You will indent the text using one of the indent buttons on the Formatting toolbar.

To indent the months and monitor titles:

1. Select the nonadjacent range **A7:A18;A23:A25**.
2. Click the **Increase Indent** button on the Formatting toolbar. Excel shifts the contents of the selected cells to the right. See Figure 3-11.

Figure 3-11 **Indenting text within cells**

4								
5	Monthly Sales Data							
6	**Month**	**VX100**	**VX300**	**FlatScreen**	**Total**			
7	January	1,410	1,860	435	3,705			
8	February	1,284	1,704	390	3,378			
9	March	1,443	1,875	435	3,753			
10	April	1,425	1,842	423	3,690			
11	May	1,509	1,998	450	3,957			
12	June	1,473	1,923	453	3,849			
13	July	1,533	1,863	465	3,861			
14	August	1,452	1,914	441	3,807			
15	Septembe	1,368	1,794	420	3,582			
16	October	1,389	1,836	429	3,654			
17	November	1,413	1,866	423	3,702			
18	December	1,533	2,013	444	3,990			
19	*Total*	17,232	22,488	5,208	44,928			
20								
21	Analysis of 2006 Sales							
22	**Monitor**	**Price per Unit**	**Cost per Unit**	**Gross Profit per Unit**	**Units Sold**	**Total Revenue**	**Gross Profit from Sales**	**% of Gross Profit from Sales**
23	VX100	$199.99	$165.20	$34.79	17,232	$3,446,227.68	$599,501.28	20.03%
24	VX300	$299.99	$234.75	$65.24	22,488	$6,746,175.12	$1,467,117.12	49.03%
25	FlatScreer	$899.99	$722.23	$177.76	5,208	$4,687,147.92	$925,774.08	30.94%
26	*Total*				44,928	$14,879,550.72	$2,992,392.48	
27								

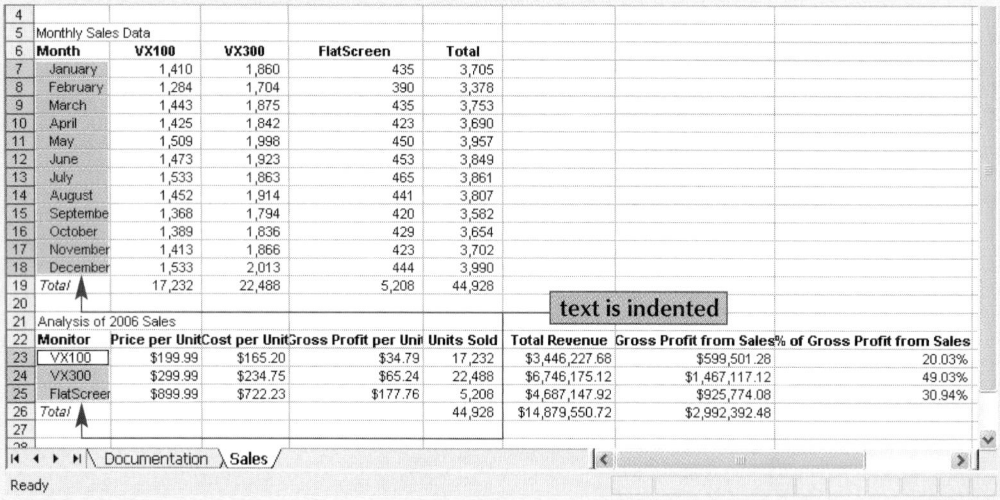

Clicking the Increase Indent button increases the amount of indentation by roughly one character. To decrease or remove an indentation, click the Decrease Indent button or modify the Indent value using the Format Cells dialog box.

If you enter text that is too wide for a cell, Excel either extends the text into the adjoining cells (if the cells are empty) or truncates the display of the text (if the adjoining cells contain text or values). To avoid cutting off the display of text in a cell, you can widen the columns, or place the text on several lines using the method you learned in Tutorial 1 (pressing the Alt key to move to a second line with a cell). You can also have Excel wrap the text within the cell for you. To wrap text within a cell, you click the Wrap text check box on the Alignment tab of the Format Cells dialog box.

Joan notes that some of the column titles in the second table are long. For example, the "Cost per Unit" label in cell C22 is much longer than the values below it. This formatting has caused some of the columns to be wider than they need to be. Another problem is that the text for some cells has been truncated because the columns are not wide enough. Joan suggests that you wrap the text within the column titles and then change the width of the columns where necessary. To make this change, you will use the Format Cells dialog box.

To have Excel automatically wrap text within a cell:

▶ **1.** Select the range **A22:H22**.

▶ **2.** Click **Format** on the menu bar, and then click **Cells** to open the Format Cells dialog box.

▶ **3.** Make sure that the Alignment tab is selected, select the **Wrap text** check box in the Text control pane, and then click the **OK** button. The text in many of the selected cells now appears on two rows within the cells.

▶ **4.** Change the width of columns **A** and **D** to about **12** characters (**89** pixels) each, columns **B** and **C** to about **10** characters (**75** pixels) each, columns **F** and **G** to about **13** characters (**96** pixels) each, and column **H** to about **17** characters (**124** pixels) each. See Figure 3-12.

Wrapping text and resizing the worksheet columns   **Figure 3-12**

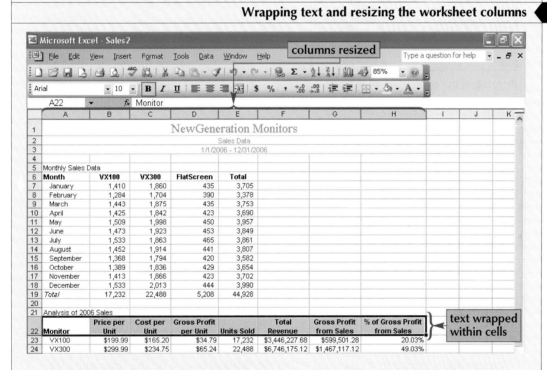

Trouble? If your screen does not match Figure 3-12, resize the columns so the values are easy to read. If some of the text is still hidden, you may need to resize the height of row 22 by dragging the bottom row border down (see Tutorial 1 for a description of resizing rows and columns).

Other Formatting Options

Excel supports even more formatting options than have been discussed so far. For example, instead of wrapping the text, you can have Excel shrink it to fit the size of the cell. If you reduce the cell later on, Excel will automatically resize the text to match. You can also rotate the contents of the cell, displaying the cell entry at almost any angle (see Figure 3-13). Joan does not need to use either of these options in her workbook, but they might be useful later for another project.

| Figure 3-13 | Rotating text within a cell |

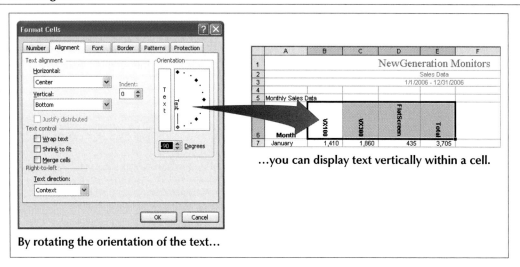

By rotating the orientation of the text…

…you can display text vertically within a cell.

Working with Cell Borders and Backgrounds

Up to now, all the formatting you have done has been applied to the contents of a cell. Excel also provides a range of tools to format the cells themselves. Specifically, you can add borders to cells and color a cell's background.

Adding a Cell Border

As you may have noticed from the printouts of other worksheets, the gridlines that appear in the worksheet window are not normally displayed on the pages that you print. **Gridlines** provide a visual cue for the layout of the cells in a worksheet. Although you can choose to print the gridlines using the Page Setup dialog box, you might want to display borders around individual cells in a worksheet. This would be particularly useful when you have different sections or tables in a worksheet, as in the Sales worksheet.

You can add a border to a cell using either the Borders button on the Formatting toolbar or the options on the Border tab in the Format Cells dialog box. The Borders button allows you to create borders quickly, whereas the Format Cells dialog box lets you further refine your choices. For example, you can specify the style, thickness, and color using the options available in the Format Cells dialog box.

Joan wants you to place a border around each cell in the two tables in the worksheet. You'll select the appropriate border style from the list of available options on the Borders palette.

To create a grid of cell borders in the two tables:

1. Select the nonadjacent range **A6:E19;A22:H26**.

2. Click the **Borders** list arrow 🔲 ▾ on the Formatting toolbar, then move the pointer over the gallery of borders to highlight the All Borders option as shown in Figure 3-14.

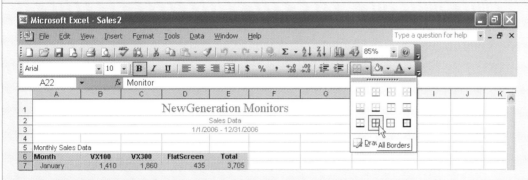

3. Click the **All Borders** option (third row, second column from the left) in the borders gallery. A thin border appears around each cell in the selected range.

4. Click any cell to deselect the range and to see the applied border.

You can also place a border around the entire range itself (and not the individual cells) by selecting a different border style. Try this by creating a thick border around the cell range.

To create a thick border around a selected range:

1. Select the nonadjacent range **A6:E19;A22:H26** again.

2. Click the **Borders** list arrow 🔲 ▾ on the Formatting toolbar, and then click the **Thick Box Border** option (third row, fourth column from the left) in the borders gallery.

3. Click any cell to deselect the range so you can see the thick border applied to the tables. The interior borders should be unchanged.

If you want a more interactive way of drawing borders on your worksheet, you can use the Draw Borders button, which is another option on the borders gallery. To see how this option works, you will add a thick black line under the column titles in both of the tables.

To draw borders using the Draw Borders button:

1. Click the **Borders** list arrow 🔲 ▾ on the Formatting toolbar, and then click the **Draw Borders** button 📝 at the bottom of the borders gallery. The pointer changes to ✐, and a floating Borders toolbar opens with four tools. The Draw Border button (currently selected) on the Borders toolbar draws a border line on the worksheet; the Erase Border button erases border lines; the Line Style button specifies the style of the border line; and the Line Color button specifies the line color.

2. Click the **Line Style** list arrow ⸺ ▾ to display a list of line style options, and then click the **thick line** option (the ninth from the top) in the list.

3. Click and drag the pointer over the lower border of the range **A6:E6**. The lower border thickens, matching the top border in thickness.

4. Click and drag the pointer over the lower border of the range **A22:H22**. The lower border thickens.

5. Click the **Close** button ✖ on the floating Borders toolbar to close it.

Finally, you will add a double line above the Total row in each table. You will add the line using the options in the Format Cells dialog box.

To create the double border lines:

1. Select the nonadjacent range **A18:E18;A25:H25**.

2. Click **Format** on the menu bar, and then click **Cells** to open the Format Cells dialog box.

3. Click the **Border** tab. The Border tab displays a diagram showing what borders, if any, are currently surrounding the selected cells.

    The bottom border is currently a single thin line. You want to change this to a double line.

4. Click the **double line** style in the Style list box located on the right side of the tab, and then click the **bottom border** in the border diagram to apply the double-line style. The bottom border changes to a double line. See Figure 3-15.

| Figure 3-15 | Border tab in the Format Cells dialog box |

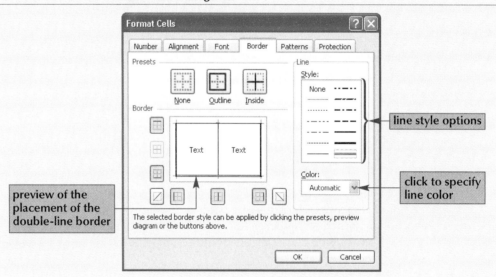

5. Click the **OK** button to close the dialog box, and then click cell **A1** to deselect the ranges. Figure 3-16 shows all of the border styles you've applied to the two tables.

Border styles applied to the worksheet | **Figure 3-16**

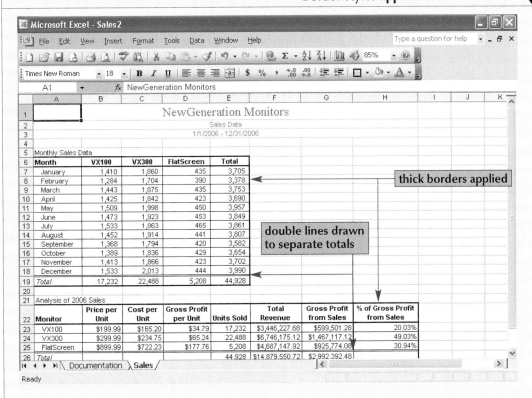

You can also specify a color for the cell borders by using the Color list box located on the Border tab (see Figure 3-15). Joan does not need to change the border colors, but she would like you to change the background color for the column title cells. When you copy the formatting of a cell, any border that you have applied is also copied.

Applying Background Colors and Patterns

Patterns and color can be used to turn a plain worksheet full of numbers and labels into a powerful presentation of information that captures your attention and adds visual emphasis to the different sections of the worksheet. If you have a color printer or a color projection device, you might want to take advantage of Excel's color tools. By default, worksheet cells are not filled with any color (the white you see in your worksheet is not a fill color for the cells). To change the background color in a worksheet, you can use the Fill Color button on the Formatting toolbar, or you can use the Format Cells dialog box, which also provides patterns that you can apply to the background. When choosing to apply color to a worksheet, you must always give consideration to the availability of a color printer. Also, if you plan to print a worksheet as an overhead, black print on a clear overhead transparency is easier to read than other colors.

Joan wants to change the background color of the worksheet. When she prints her report later in the week, she will be using the company's color laser printer. Therefore, she would like you to explore using background color in the column titles for the two sales tables. She suggests that you try formatting the column titles with a light-yellow background.

To apply a fill color to the column titles:

1. Select the nonadjacent range **A6:E6;A22:H22**.

2. Click the **Fill Color** button list arrow ![fill color icon] on the Formatting toolbar. The color palette appears.

3. Position the pointer over the **Light Yellow** square (fifth row, third column from the left) on the color palette, as shown in Figure 3-17.

Figure 3-17
Selecting a fill color

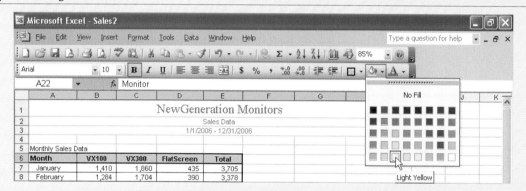

4. Click the **Light Yellow** square to apply the color to the selected range, and then click any cell to deselect the range and to see the applied color. The column titles now have light-yellow backgrounds.

Joan would also like to investigate whether you can apply a pattern to the fill background. Excel supports 18 different fill patterns. To create and apply a fill pattern, you have to open the Format Cells dialog box.

To apply a fill pattern to the column titles:

1. Select the nonadjacent range **A6:E6;A22:H22**.

2. Click **Format** on the menu bar, click **Cells** to open the Format Cells dialog box, and then click the **Patterns** tab to display the options provided.

3. Click the **Pattern** list arrow to display a gallery of patterns and a palette of colors that you can apply to the selected pattern. The default pattern color is black. First, you will choose a crosshatch pattern, which is a pattern using crossed diagonal lines.

4. Click the **50% Gray** pattern (first row, third column) in the pattern gallery, as shown in Figure 3-18.

Selecting a fill pattern   Figure 3-18

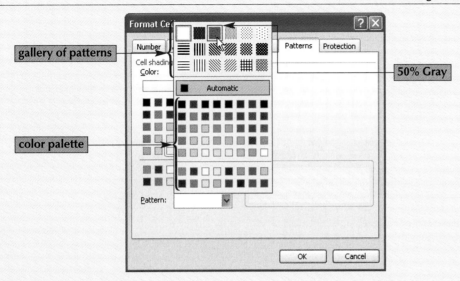

5. Click the **OK** button, and then click any cell to deselect the ranges and to see the pattern.

The background pattern you have chosen overwhelms the text in these column titles. You can improve the appearance by changing the color of the pattern itself from black to a light orange.

To change the pattern color:

1. Select the range **A6:E6;A22:H22**. The default (or automatic) color of a selected pattern is black, but you want to choose a brighter and lighter color for the pattern.

2. Click **Format** on the menu bar, and then click **Cells** to open the Format Cells dialog box again. The Patterns tab should be displayed automatically because it is the last set of options you used.

3. Click the **Pattern** list arrow to display the gallery of patterns and the color palette.

4. Click the **Light Orange** square (third row, second column) in the color palette, click the **OK** button to close the dialog box, and then click cell **A1** to deselect the range and to see the color applied to the pattern. See Figure 3-19. The column titles now appear in a light-orange patterned background. The pattern and the color do not overwhelm the column titles.

Figure 3-19

Cells with formatted backgrounds

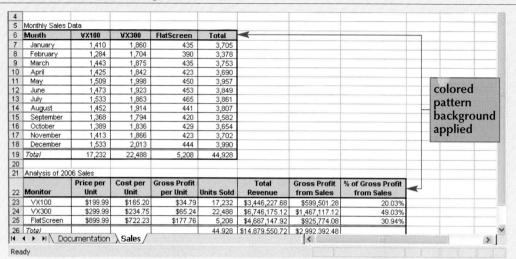

5. Save your changes to the workbook.

Joan is pleased with the progress you have made. In the next session, you will explore other formatting features.

Session 3.1 Quick Check

1. Describe two ways of applying the Currency style to cells in your worksheet.
2. If the number 0.05765 has been entered into a cell, what will Excel display if you:
   a. format the number using the Percent style with one decimal place?
   b. format the number using the Currency style with two decimal places and a dollar sign?
3. Which two buttons can you use to copy a format from one cell range to another?
4. A long text string in one of your worksheet cells has been truncated. List three ways to correct this problem.
5. How do you center the contents of a single cell across a range of cells?
6. Describe three ways of creating a cell border.
7. How would you apply a colored background pattern to a selected cell range?

Session 3.2

Formatting the Worksheet

In the previous session, you formatted individual cells within the worksheet. Excel also provides tools for formatting the columns and rows in a worksheet. You will explore some of these tools as you continue to work on Joan's sales report.

Merging Cells into One Cell

Joan has several other formatting changes that she would like you to make to the Sales worksheet. She wants you to format the titles for the two tables in her report so that they are centered in a bold font above the tables. You could do this by centering the cell title across a cell range, as you did for the title in the last session. Another way is to merge several cells into one cell and then center the contents of that single cell. Merging a range of cells into a single cell removes all of the selected cells from the worksheet, except the cell in the upper-left corner of the range. Any content in the other cells of the range is deleted. To merge a range of cells into a single cell, you can use the Merge cells check box on the Alignment tab in the Format Cells dialog box or click the Merge and Center button on the Formatting toolbar.

To merge and center the cell ranges containing the table titles:

▶ 1. If you took a break after the previous session, make sure that Excel is running and that the Sales2 workbook is open.

▶ 2. In the Sales worksheet, select the range **A5:E5**.

▶ 3. Click the **Merge and Center** button on the Formatting toolbar. The cells in the range A5:E5 are merged into a single cell whose cell reference is A5. The text in the merged cell is centered as well.

▶ 4. Click the **Bold** button **B** on the Formatting toolbar.

▶ 5. Select the range **A21:H21**, click the **Merge and Center** button on the Formatting toolbar, and then click the **Bold** button **B** on the Formatting toolbar.

▶ 6. Click cell **A1** to deselect the range. Figure 3-20 shows the merged and centered table titles.

Merging and centering cells ◀ **Figure 3-20**

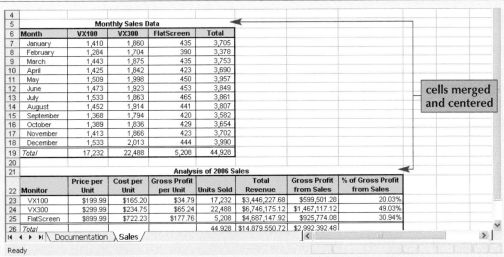

To split a merged cell back into individual cells, regardless of the method you used to merge the cells, you select the merged cell and then click the Merge and Center button again. You can also merge and unmerge cells using the Alignment tab in the Format Cells dialog box.

Hiding Rows, Columns and Worksheets

Sometimes Joan does not need to view the monthly sales for the three monitors. She does not want to remove this information from the worksheet, but she would like the option of temporarily hiding that information. Excel provides this capability. Hiding a row or column does not affect the data stored there, nor does it affect any other cell that might have a formula referencing a cell in the hidden row or column. Hiding part of your worksheet is a good way of temporarily concealing nonessential information, allowing you to concentrate on the more important data contained in your worksheet. To hide a row or column, first you must select the row(s) or column(s) you want to hide. You can then use the Row or Column option on the Format menu or right-click the selection to open its shortcut menu.

You will hide the monthly sales figures in the first table in the worksheet.

To hide the monthly sales figures:

1. Select the headings for rows **7** through **18**.
2. Right-click the selection, and then click **Hide** on the shortcut menu. Excel hides rows 7 through 18. Note that the total sales figures in the range B19:E19 are not affected by hiding the monthly sales figures. See Figure 3-21.

Figure 3-21 | **Hiding worksheet rows**

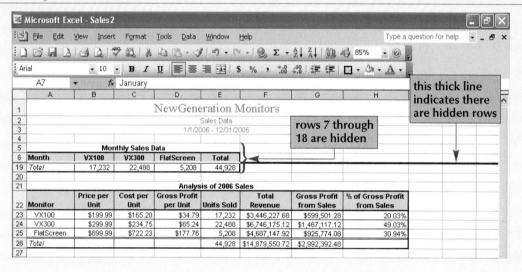

To unhide a hidden row or column, you must select the headings of the rows or columns that border the hidden area; then you can use the right-click method or the Row or Column command on the Format menu to choose the Unhide option. You will let Joan know that it is easy to hide any row or column that she does not want to view. But for now you will redisplay the hidden sales figures.

To unhide the monthly sales figures:

1. Select the row headings for rows **6** and **19**.
2. Right-click the selection, and then click **Unhide** on the shortcut menu. Excel redisplays rows 7 through 18.
3. Click cell **A1** to deselect the rows.

Hiding and unhiding a column follows the same process, except that you select the worksheet column headings rather than the row headings. For example, to hide column B, you select the column heading B. To unhide the column, you must select columns A and C.

On other occasions Joan would like to hide an entire worksheet. This could occur in situations where a worksheet contains detailed information and she only wants to display the summary figures from another sheet. To show how to hide an entire worksheet, you should suggest that she hide the documentation sheet located at the front of the workbook.

To hide the Documentation sheet:

1. Click the **Documentation** sheet tab to make it the active sheet.
2. Click **Format** on the menu bar, point to **Sheet**, and then click **Hide**.

The Documentation sheet disappears from the workbook. It is still present in the workbook, it is just hidden at this point. Excel maintains a list of the hidden worksheets in the current workbook, so you can always select one of those sheets to be redisplayed. Do this now to unhide the Documentation sheet.

To unhide the Documentation sheet:

1. Click **Format** on the menu bar, point to **Sheet**, and then click **Unhide**. Excel displays the Unhide dialog box, listing all hidden worksheets in the workbook.
2. Verify that **Documentation** is selected in the list of hidden worksheets, and click the **OK** button.

   The Documentation sheet should be redisplayed in the workbook and made the active sheet.
3. Click the **Sales** sheet tab to return to the Sales worksheet.

Adding a Background Image

In the previous session you learned how to create a background color for individual cells within the worksheet. Excel also allows you to use an image file as a background for a worksheet. The image from the file is tiled repeatedly until the images fill up the entire worksheet. Images can be used to give the background a textured appearance, like that of granite, wood, or fibered paper. The background image does not affect the format or content of any cell in the worksheet, and if you have already defined a background color for a cell, Excel displays the color on top, hiding that portion of the image.

Adding a Background Image to the Worksheet

Reference Window

- Click Format on the menu bar, point to Sheet, and then click Background.
- Locate the image file that you want tiled over the worksheet background.
- Click the Insert button.

If you add a background and then decide against it, you can remove the background image by clicking Format on the menu bar, pointing to Sheet, and then clicking Delete Background. The image will automatically be removed.

Joan wants you to experiment with using a background image for the Sales worksheet. You will add the image file that she has selected.

To add a background image to the worksheet:

1. Click **Format** on the menu bar, point to **Sheet**, and then click **Background**. The Sheet Background dialog box opens.

2. Navigate to the Tutorial.03\Tutorial folder, click the **Back** image file, and then click the **Insert** button. The Back image file is applied repeatedly to, or is "tiled over," the worksheet, creating a textured background for the Sales sheet. Notice that the tiling is hidden in the cells that already contain a background color. To make the sales figures easier to read, you'll change the background color of those cells to white.

3. Select the nonadjacent range **A7:E19;A23:H26**.

4. Click the **Fill Color** list arrow ⬛ ▾ on the Formatting toolbar, click the **White** square (lower-right corner) in the color palette, and then click cell **A1** to deselect the range, making the background image easier to see. Figure 3-22 shows the Sales worksheet with the formatted background.

| Figure 3-22 | Inserting a background image |

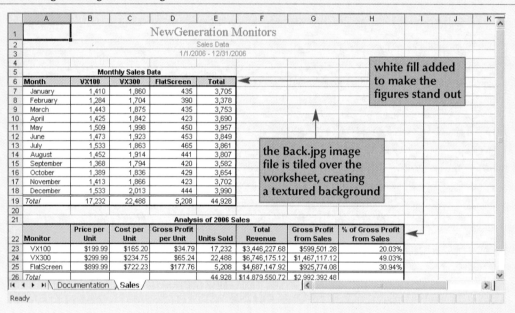

Note that you cannot apply a background image to all of the sheets in a workbook at the same time. If you want to apply the same background to several sheets, you must format each sheet separately.

Formatting Sheet Tabs

In addition to the sheet background, you can also format the background color of worksheet tabs. This color is only visible when the worksheet is not the active sheet in the workbook. By default, the tab of the active sheet in a workbook is white. If you change the color of a tab, the tab changes to white with a narrow colored stripe at the bottom of the tab when the sheet is active. You can use tab colors to better organize the various sheets in your workbook. For example, worksheets that contain sales information could be formatted with blue tabs, whereas sheets that describe the company's cash flow or budget could be formatted with green tabs. To explore how to color worksheet tabs, you will change the tab color of the Sales worksheet to light orange.

To change the tab color:

▶ 1. Right-click the **Sales** tab, and then click **Tab Color** on the shortcut menu. The Format Tab Color dialog box opens.

▶ 2. Click the **Light Orange** square (third row, second column from the left) in the color palette, and then click the **OK** button. Because the Sales sheet is the active worksheet, the tab is white with a light-orange horizontal stripe at the bottom of the tab.

▶ 3. Switch to the Documentation sheet so you can see the light-orange color of the Sales sheet tab, and then switch to the Sales sheet again.

Clearing and Replacing Formats

Sometimes you might want to change or remove some of the formatting from your workbooks. As you experiment with different formats, you can use the Undo button on the Standard toolbar to remove formatting choices that did not work out as well as you expected. Another choice is to clear the formatting from the selected cells, returning the cells to their previous format. To see how this option works, you will remove the formatting from the company name in cell A1 on the Sales worksheet.

To clear the formatting from cell A1:

▶ 1. Make sure cell **A1** is selected.

▶ 2. Click **Edit** on the menu bar, point to **Clear**, and then click **Formats**. Excel removes the formatting that was applied to the text and removes the formatting that merged the cells and then centered the text across the range.

▶ 3. Click the **Undo** button ↺ on the Standard toolbar to undo your action, restoring the formats you cleared.

Sometimes you will want to make a formatting change that applies to several different cells. If those cells are scattered throughout the workbook, you may find it time consuming to search for and replace the formats for each individual cell. If the cells share a common format that you want to change, you can use the Find and Replace command to locate the formats and modify them.

Finding and Replacing a Format

- Click Edit on the menu bar, and then click Replace.
- Click the Options >> button, if necessary, to display the format choices.
- Click the top Format list arrow, and then click Format.
- Specify the format you want to find in the Find Format dialog box, and then click the OK button.
- Click the bottom Format list arrow, and then click Format.
- Enter the new format, which will replace the old format, and then click the OK button.
- Click the Replace All button to replace all occurrences of the old format; click the Replace button to replace the currently selected cell containing the old format; or click the Find Next button to find the next occurrence of the old format before replacing it.
- Click the Close button.

In the Sales worksheet, the table titles and column titles are displayed in a bold font. After seeing how the use of color has made the worksheet come alive, Joan wants you to change the titles to a boldface blue. Rather than selecting the cells that contain the table and column titles and formatting them, you will replace all occurrences of the boldface text with blue boldface text.

To find and replace formats:

1. Click **Edit** on the menu bar, and then click **Replace**. The Find and Replace dialog box opens. You can use this dialog box to find and replace the contents of cells. In this case, you will use it only for finding and replacing formats, leaving the contents of the cells unchanged.

2. Click the **Options >>** button to display additional find and replace options. See Figure 3-23. The dialog box expands to display options that allow you to find and replace cell formats. It also includes options to determine whether to search within the active sheet or the entire workbook. Currently no format options have been set.

Figure 3-23 ▶ **Find and Replace dialog box**

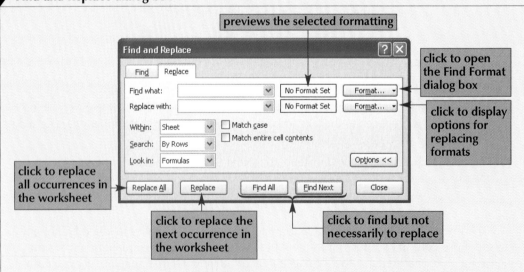

Trouble? If the button on your workbook appears as Options <<, the additional options are already displayed, and you do not need to click any buttons.

3. Click the top **Format** button to open the Find Format dialog box. Here is where you specify the format you want to search for. In this case, you are searching for cells that contain boldface text.

▶ **4.** Click the **Font** tab, and then click **Bold** in the Font style list box. See Figure 3-24.

Find Format dialog box ◀ **Figure 3-24**

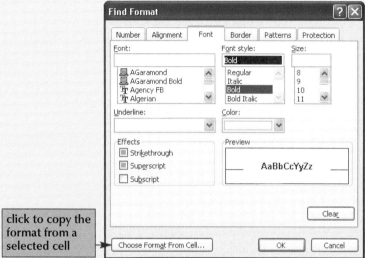

click to copy the format from a selected cell

▶ **5.** Click the **OK** button.

Next, you will specify the new format that you want to use to replace the boldface text. In this case, you will specify blue boldface text.

▶ **6.** Click the bottom **Format** button to open the Replace Format dialog box again, and then click **Bold** in the Font style list box.

▶ **7.** Click the **Color** list box, click the **Blue** square (second row, sixth column from the left) in the color palette, and then click the **OK** button.

▶ **8.** Click the **Replace All** button to replace all boldface text in the worksheet with blue bold-face text. Excel indicates that it has completed its search and made 15 replacements.

▶ **9.** Click the **OK** button, and then click the **Close** button to close the Find and Replace dialog box. See Figure 3-25. The boldface text has been replaced with blue boldface text.

Sales worksheet with blue boldface text ◀ **Figure 3-25**

bold formatting found and replaced with bold blue formatting

4					
5		Monthly Sales Data			
6	Month	VX100	VX300	FlatScreen	Total
7	January	1,410	1,860	435	3,705
8	February	1,284	1,704	390	3,378
9	March	1,443	1,875	435	3,753
10	April	1,425	1,842	423	3,690
11	May	1,509	1,998	450	3,957
12	June	1,473	1,923	453	3,849
13	July	1,533	1,863	465	3,861
14	August	1,452	1,914	441	3,807
15	September	1,368	1,794	420	3,582
16	October	1,389	1,836	429	3,654
17	November	1,413	1,866	423	3,702
18	December	1,533	2,013	444	3,990
19	Total	17,232	22,488	5,208	44,928
20					
21			Analysis of 2006 Sales		

	Monitor	Price per Unit	Cost per Unit	Gross Profit per Unit	Units Sold	Total Revenue	Gross Profit from Sales	% of Gross Profit from Sales
22	Monitor	Price per Unit	Cost per Unit	Gross Profit per Unit	Units Sold	Total Revenue	Gross Profit from Sales	% of Gross Profit from Sales
23	VX100	$199.99	$165.20	$34.79	17,232	$3,446,227.68	$599,501.28	20.03%
24	VX300	$299.99	$234.75	$65.24	22,488	$6,746,175.12	$1,467,117.12	49.03%
25	FlatScreen	$899.99	$722.23	$177.76	5,208	$4,687,147.92	$925,774.08	30.94%
26	Total				44,928	$14,879,550.72	$2,992,392.48	

Documentation \ Sales /

Ready

Using Styles

If you have several cells that employ the same format, you can create a style for those cells. This can be a faster and more efficient way of updating formats than copying and replacing formats. A **style** is a saved collection of formatting options—number formats, text alignment, font sizes and colors, borders, and background fills—that can be applied to cells in a worksheet. When you apply a style, Excel remembers which styles are associated with which cells in the workbook. If you want to change the appearance of a particular type of cell, you need only modify the specifications for the style, and the appearance of any cell associated with that style will be automatically changed to reflect the new style.

You can create a style in one of two ways: by selecting a cell from the worksheet and basing the style definition on the formatting choices already defined for that cell or by manually entering the style definitions into a dialog box. Once you create and name a style, you can apply it to cells in the workbook.

Excel has eight built-in styles: Comma, Comma [0], Currency, Currency [0], Followed Hyperlink, Hyperlink, Normal, and Percent. You have been using styles all of this time without knowing it. Most cells are formatted with the Normal style, but when you use the Percent Style button, Excel formats the selected text using the definitions contained in the Percent style. Similarly, the Currency Style button applies the format as defined in the Currency style. As you'll see, you can modify these style definitions or create some of your own.

Creating a Style

Joan wants you to further modify the appearance of the worksheet by changing the background color of the months in the first table and the monitor names in the second table to yellow. Rather than applying new formatting to the cells, you will create a new style called "Category" and then apply the new style to the category columns of the tables in the worksheet. You will create the style using the format already applied to cell A7 as a basis.

To create a style using a formatted cell:

1. Click cell **A7** to select it. The format applied to this cell becomes the basis of the new style that you want to create.

2. Click **Format** on the menu bar, and then click **Style**. The Style dialog box opens. All of the formatting options associated with the style of the active cell are listed. For example, the font is 10-point Arial. The check boxes indicate whether these various formatting categories are part of the style definition. If you deselect one of the formatting categories, such as Border, then that category will not be part of the style definition.

   To create a new style for this cell, you simply type a different name into the list box.

3. Type **Category** in the Style name list box, as shown in Figure 3-26. At this point, cell A7 is no longer formatted using the Normal style; rather it is formatted using the Category style you just created.

Style dialog box **Figure 3-26**

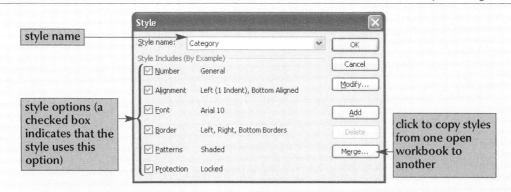

Now you will modify the properties of this style.

4. Click the **Border** check box to deselect it. Category style will not include any border format options.

Next, you will modify the pattern of the style.

5. Click the **Modify** button to open the Format Cells dialog box, and then click the **Patterns** tab.

6. Click the **Yellow** square (fourth row, third column from the left) in the color palette, and then click the **OK** button to close the Format Cells dialog box and redisplay the Style dialog box.

If you click the OK button in the Style dialog box, the style definition changes and is applied to the active cell and the Style dialog box closes. If you click the Add button in the dialog box, the style change is saved and applied, but the Style dialog box remains open for further style changes.

7. Click the **OK** button to save the new style and apply it to the background color of cell A7.

Now you need to apply this style to other cells in the workbook.

Applying a Style

To apply a style to cells in a worksheet, you first select the cells you want associated with the style and then open the Style dialog box.

To apply the Category style:

1. Select the nonadjacent range **A8:A18;A23:A25**.

2. Click **Format** on the menu bar, and then click **Style**. The Style dialog box opens.

3. Click the **Style name** list arrow, and then click **Category**. The formatting options change to reflect the associated options for the selected style.

4. Click the **OK** button to close the dialog box and apply the Category style to the selected range, and then click cell **A1** to deselect the cells. A yellow background color is applied to all of the month and monitor cells in the two tables.

The yellow background appears a bit too strong. You decide to change it to a light-yellow background. Since all the month and monitor cells are now associated with the Category style, you need only modify the definition of the Category style to make this change.

To modify the Category style:

1. Click **Format** on the menu bar, and then click **Style**.

2. Click the **Style name** list arrow, and then click **Category**. The options in the Style dialog box change to reflect the selected Category style.

3. Click the **Modify** button to open the Format Cells dialog box, and then click the **Patterns** tab, if necessary.

4. Click the **Light Yellow** square (fifth row, third column from the left) in the color palette, and then click the **OK** button.

5. Click the **Add** button in the Style dialog box. Excel changes the background color of all the cells associated with the Category style.

   Trouble? If you clicked the OK button instead of the Add button, the Category style would have been applied to the active cell as well as the ranges formatted with the Category style. Click the Undo on the Standard toolbar to undo the application of the Category style to cell A2, and then skip Step 6.

6. Click the **Close** button. See Figure 3-27. The updated Category style is applied to the ranges using that format.

| Figure 3-27 | Category style in the Sales worksheet |

The Category style becomes part of the Sales2 workbook, but it is not available to other workbooks. However, you can copy styles from one workbook to another. Copying styles allows you to create a collection of workbooks that share a common look and feel.

To copy styles from one workbook to another, open the workbook containing your customized styles, and then open the workbook into which you want to copy the styles. Open the Styles dialog box, click the Merge button, and select the first workbook. All of the styles in that workbook will be copied into the second workbook for use on that workbook's contents. Note that if you make changes to the style definitions later on, you will have to copy them again. Excel will not automatically update styles across workbooks.

Using AutoFormat

Excel's **AutoFormat** feature provides a gallery of 17 predefined formats that you can select and apply to your worksheet cells. Rather than spending time testing different combinations of fonts, colors, and borders, you can apply an existing format to your worksheet.

You have done a lot of work already formatting the data in the Sales worksheet to give it a more professional and polished look, but you decide to see how the formatting you have done compares to one of Excel's AutoFormat designs.

You'll apply an AutoFormat design to the sales figures table so that you can compare a predefined format to the format you have worked on.

To apply an AutoFormat design to the table:

▶ 1. Select the range **A5:E19**.

▶ 2. Click **Format** on the menu bar, and then click **AutoFormat**. The AutoFormat dialog box opens. See Figure 3-28. The dialog box displays a preview of how each format will appear when applied to cells in a worksheet.

AutoFormat gallery ◀ Figure 3-28

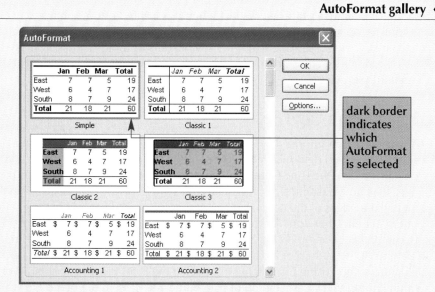

dark border indicates which AutoFormat is selected

▶ 3. Click **Classic 3** in the list of available designs, click the **OK** button, and then click cell **A1** to remove the highlighting from the table. Figure 3-29 shows the appearance of the Classic 3 design to the cells containing the monthly sales data.

Applying an AutoFormat ◀ Figure 3-29

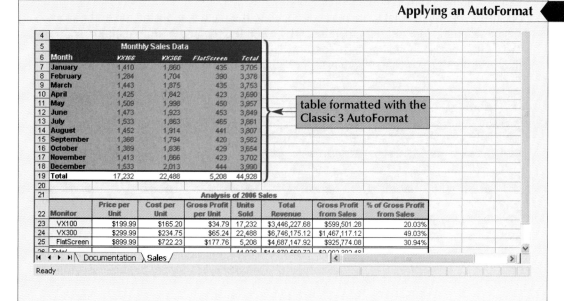

table formatted with the Classic 3 AutoFormat

The colors and contrast of the AutoFormat design do not complement the background, so you will revert to the format you created.

▶ **4.** Click the **Undo** button ↺ on the Standard toolbar to remove the AutoFormat design.

Although you will not use AutoFormat in this case, you can see how an AutoFormat design can be a starting point. You could start with an AutoFormat design and then make modifications to the worksheet to fit your own needs.

Formatting the Printed Worksheet

You have settled on an appearance for the Sales worksheet—at least the appearance that is displayed on your screen. But that is only half of your job. Joan also wants you to format the appearance of this worksheet when it is printed out. You have to decide on the position of the report on the page, the size of the page margins, the orientation of the page, and whether the page will have any headers or footers. You can make many of these choices using the Page Setup dialog box, which you can open from the File menu or from within Print Preview.

Defining the Page Setup

As you learned in Tutorial 1, you can use the Page Setup dialog box to change the page orientation, which determines if the page is wider than it is tall or taller than it is wide. You can also use the Page Setup dialog box to control how a worksheet is placed on a page. You can adjust the size of the **margins**, which are the spaces between the page content and the edges of the page. You can center the worksheet text between the top and bottom margins (horizontally) or between the right and left margins (vertically). You can also use the Page Setup dialog box to display text that will appear in the area at the top of a page or at the bottom of a page for each page of a worksheet. You can open the Page Setup dialog box using the File menu or using the Print Preview toolbar. Working from within Print Preview can be helpful. Each time you close a dialog box in which you have made a change or selected an option, you will see how that action impacts the worksheet before printing it.

By default, Excel places a one-inch margin above and below the report and a ¾-inch margin to the left and right. Excel also aligns column A in a worksheet at the left margin and row 1 at the top margin. Depending on how many columns and rows there are in the worksheet, you might want to increase or decrease the page margins or center the worksheet between the left and right margins or between the top and bottom margins.

You will increase the margin size for the Sales worksheet to one inch all around. You will also center the worksheet between the right and left margins.

To change the margins and positioning of the worksheet:

▶ **1.** Click the **Print Preview** button 🔍 on the Standard toolbar. The Print Preview window opens, displaying the worksheet as it will appear on the printed page.

▶ **2.** Click the **Setup** button on the Print Preview toolbar, and then click the **Margins** tab. The Margins tab, as shown in Figure 3-30, provides a diagram that shows you the placement of the worksheet on the page. In addition to adjusting the sizes of the margins, you can also adjust the positioning of the worksheet on the printout.

Margins tab in the Page Setup dialog box ◀ **Figure 3-30**

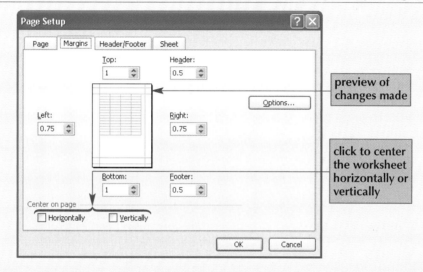

▶ **3.** Click the **Left** up arrow to set the size of the left margin to **1** inch, and then click the **Right** up arrow to increase the size of the right margin to **1** inch.

▶ **4.** Click the **Horizontally** check box, and then click the **OK** button to close the Page Setup dialog box and return to Print Preview.

Note that this printout does not fit on a single page. As indicated in the status line located in the lower-left corner of the Print Preview window, the worksheet covers two pages instead of one; two columns of the bottom table have been moved to the second page. You could try to reduce the left and right margins, so the worksheet fits on a single page, but as you learned in Tutorial 1, you also can change the page orientation to landscape, making the worksheet page wider than it is tall. This will accommodate all the columns of the bottom table so all the data will fit on the same page.

To change the page orientation:

▶ **1.** Click the **Setup** button on the Print Preview toolbar to open the Page Setup dialog box again.

▶ **2.** Click the **Page** tab and then click the **Landscape** option button, as shown in Figure 3-31.

Figure 3-31 **Changing the page orientation**

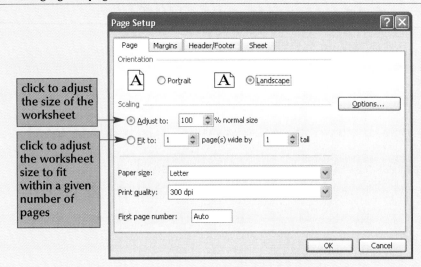

click to adjust the size of the worksheet

click to adjust the worksheet size to fit within a given number of pages

3. Click the **OK** button to close the dialog box and return to the Print Preview window. The preview of the printed worksheet in landscape orientation shows that the report will fit on a single page.

The Page tab in the Page Setup dialog box contains other useful formatting features. You can reduce or increase the size of the worksheet on the printed page. The default size is 100 percent. You can also have Excel automatically reduce the size of the report to fit within a specified number of pages.

Working with Headers and Footers

Joan wants you to add a header and footer to the report. A **header** is text printed in the top margin of every worksheet page. A **footer** is text printed at the bottom of every page. Headers and footers can add important information to your printouts. For example, you can create a header that displays your name and the date the report was created. If the report covers multiple pages, you can use a footer to display the page number and the total number of pages. You use the Page Setup dialog box to add headers and footers to a worksheet.

Excel tries to anticipate headers and footers that you might want to include in your worksheet. Clicking the Header or Footer list arrow displays a list of possible headers or footers (the list is the same for both). For example, the "Page 1" entry inserts the page number of the worksheet prefaced by the word "Page" in the header; the "Page 1 of ?" displays the page number and the total number of pages. Other entries in the list include the name of the worksheet or workbook.

If you want to use a header or footer not available in the lists, you click the Custom Header or Custom Footer button and create your own header and footer. The Header dialog box and the Footer dialog box are similar. Each dialog box is divided into three sections: left, center, and right. If you want to enter information such as the filename or the date into the header or footer, you can either type the text or click one of the format buttons located above the three section boxes. Figure 3-32 describes the format buttons and the corresponding format codes.

Header/Footer formatting buttons ◄ **Figure 3-32**

Button	Name	Formatting Code	Action
A	Font	None	Sets font, text style, and font size
	Page Number	&[Page]	Inserts page number
	Total Pages	&[Pages]	Inserts total number of pages
	Date	&[Date]	Inserts current date
	Time	&[Time]	Inserts current time
	File Path	&[Path]&[File]	Inserts path and filename
	Filename	&[File]	Inserts filename
	Tab Name	&[Tab]	Inserts name of active worksheet
	Insert Picture	&[Picture]	Inserts an image file
	Format Picture	None	Opens the Format Picture dialog box

Joan wants a header that displays the filename at the left margin and today's date at the right margin. She wants a footer that displays the name of the workbook author, with the text aligned at the right margin of the footer. You'll create the header and footer now.

To add a custom header and footer to the workbook:

▶ **1.** Click the **Setup** button on the Print Preview toolbar, and then click the **Header/Footer** tab. The Header/Footer dialog box opens.

▶ **2.** Click the **Custom Header** button. The Header dialog box opens. See Figure 3-33.

Header dialog box ◄ **Figure 3-33**

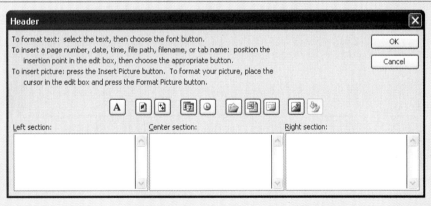

▶ **3.** In the Left section box, type **Filename:** and then press the **spacebar**.

▶ **4.** Click the **Filename** button 🖳 to insert the format code. The formatting code for the name of the file "&[File]" appears after the text that you entered.

▶ **5.** Click the **Right section** box, and then click the **Date** button 🗓. Excel inserts the &[Date] format code into the section box.

▶ **6.** Click the **OK** button to close the Header dialog box, and then click the **Custom Footer** button to open the Footer dialog box, which duplicates the layout of the Header dialog box. Now you will create a footer that centers the page number and the total number of pages at the bottom of the printout.

7. Click the **Center section** box, type **Page**, press the **spacebar**, click the **Page Number** button 🔳, press the **spacebar**, type **of**, press the **spacebar**, and then click the **Total Pages** button 🔳. The text and codes in the Center section should appear as "Page &[Page] of &[Pages]"—which, if the worksheet was divided into five pages, would appear as "Page 1 of 5."

Next, you will enter the workbook author in the right section of the footer.

8. Click the **Right section** box, type **Prepared by:**, press the **spacebar**, and then type your name.

9. Click the **OK** button to return to the Page Setup dialog box, which provides a preview of the custom header and footer that you created, and then click the **OK** button to return to Print Preview. As shown in Figure 3-34, the worksheet now is displayed with the new header and footer.

Figure 3-34	Preview of the custom header and footer

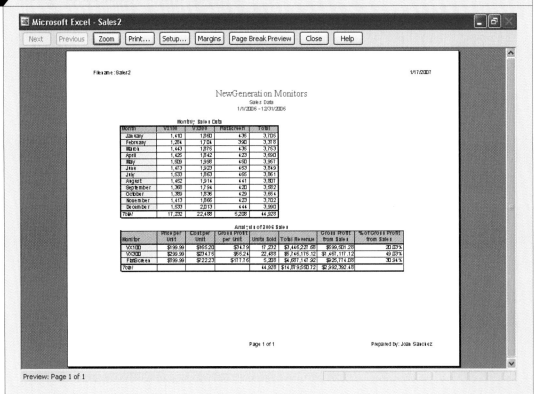

10. Click the **Close** button on the Print Preview toolbar.

Note that a header or footer is added only for the printed worksheet—not the entire workbook. You can define different headers and footers for each sheet in your workbook.

Working with the Print Area and Page Breaks

When you displayed the worksheet in the Print Preview window, how did Excel know which parts of the active worksheet you were going to print? The default action is to print all parts of the active worksheet that contain text, formulas, or values, which will not always be what you want. If you want to print only a part of the worksheet, you can define a **print area** that contains the content you want to print. To define a print area, you must first select the cells you want to print, and then select the Print Area command on the File menu.

A print area can include an adjacent range or nonadjacent ranges. You can also hide rows or columns in the worksheet in order to print nonadjacent ranges. For her report, Joan might decide against printing the sales analysis information. To remove those cells from the printout, you will define a print area that excludes the cells for the second table.

To define the print area:

▶ **1.** Select the range **A1:H19**.

▶ **2.** Click **File** on the menu bar, point to **Print Area**, and then click **Set Print Area**. Excel places a dotted black line around the selected cells of the print area. This is a visual indicator of what parts of the worksheet will be printed.

▶ **3.** Click the **Print Preview** button 🔍 on the Standard toolbar. The Print Preview window displays only the first table. The second table has been removed from the printout because it is not in the defined print area.

▶ **4.** Click the **Close** button on the Print Preview toolbar.

Another way to preview the print areas in your worksheet is through **page break preview**, which displays a view of the worksheet as it is divided up into pages. Anything outside of the print area is grayed out. Try previewing the contents of the Sales worksheet using page break preview.

To switch to page break preview:

▶ **1.** Click cell **A1** to remove the selection.

▶ **2.** Click **View** on the menu bar, and then click **Page Break Preview**. The workbook window adjusts to display the worksheet with any page break inserted in it and the Welcome to Page Break Preview dialog box, as shown in Figure 3-35. The dialog box serves to remind you that you can adjust the page breaks. A page number appears as a watermark on each page to be printed out. Notice that the second table is grayed out because it is not part of the printed area of the worksheet.

Figure 3-35 **Using Page Break Preview**

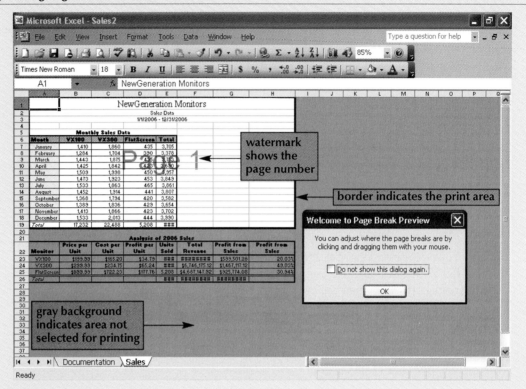

3. Click the **OK** button to close the dialog box before you change the dimensions of the printed area to include the other table.

4. Position the pointer at the bottom border of the print area (located at row 19) until the pointer changes to $\updownarrow$, and then click the border and drag it down to row **26**. The print area has now been expanded to the cell range A1:H26.

   Trouble? If you are unsure of the location of the bottom border, click row 19 to make the border easier to see, and then repeat Step 3.

5. Click **View** on the menu bar, and then click **Normal** to switch back to Normal view.

Another approach that Joan might take is to place the two tables on separate pages. You can do this for her by inserting a **page break**, which forces Excel to place a portion of a worksheet on a new page. Before you insert a page break, you need to indicate where in the worksheet you want the break to occur. If you select a cell in the worksheet, the page break will be placed directly above and to the left of the cell. Selecting a row or a column places the page break directly above the row or directly to the left of the column. You will place a page break directly above row 20, which will separate the first sales table from the second.

To insert a page break:

1. Click row **20**, click **Insert** on the menu bar, and then click **Page Break**. Another black dotted line appears—this time above row 20, indicating there is a page break at this point in the print area.

▶ **2.** Click cell **A1** to remove the selection, click **View** on the menu bar, click **Page Break Preview**, and then click the **OK** button to close the Welcome to Page Break Preview dialog box. As shown in Figure 3-36, the second table will now appear on page 2 of the printout.

Inserting a page break ◀ Figure 3-36

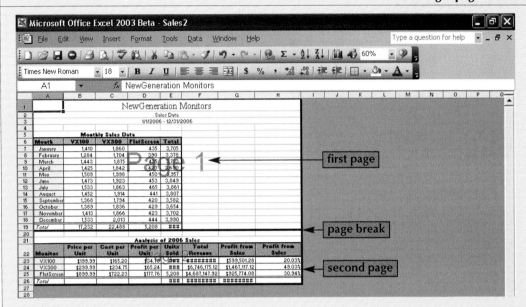

▶ **3.** Click **View** on the menu bar, and then click **Normal** to return to Normal view.

As Joan reviews the preview of the worksheet, she notices that the name of the company, "NewGeneration Monitors," and the two subtitles appear on the first page, but not on the second. That is not surprising because the range that includes the titles and subtitles is limited to the first page of the printout. However, Joan would like to have this information repeated on the second page.

You can repeat information, such as the company name, by specifying which cells in the print area should be repeated on each page. This is particularly useful in long tables that extend over many pages. In such cases, you can have the column titles repeated for each page of the printout.

To set rows or columns to repeat on each page, you will open the Page Setup dialog box from the worksheet window.

To repeat the first three rows on each page:

▶ **1.** Click **File** on the menu bar, click **Page Setup**, and then click the **Sheet** tab. The Sheet tab displays options you can use to control how the worksheet is printed. Note that the print area you have defined is already entered into the Print area box. Because Joan wants the first three rows of the worksheet to be repeated on each printed page, you will have to select them.

▶ **2.** Click the **Rows to repeat at top** box, move your pointer over to the worksheet, and then click and drag over the range **A1:A3**. A flashing border appears around the first three rows in the worksheet. This is a visual indicator that the contents of the first three rows will be repeated on all pages of the printout. In the Rows to repeat at top box, the cell reference $1:$3 appears. See Figure 3-37.

Figure 3-37	Sheet tab of the Page Setup dialog box

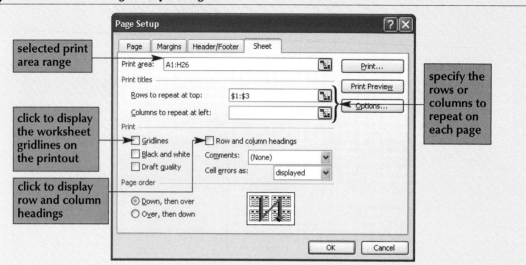

Trouble? If the Page Setup dialog box is in the way, you can move it to another location in the workbook window, or you can select the range using the Collapse Dialog Box button.

▶ **3.** Click the **Print Preview** button, and then click the **Next** button on the Print Preview toolbar to display the second page of the printout. Now the title and two subtitles appear on this page as well. See Figure 3-38.

Figure 3-38	Second page of the printout

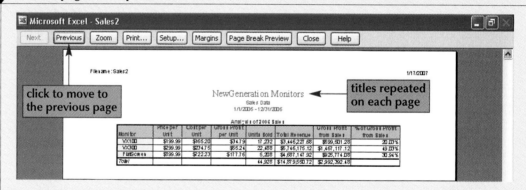

▶ **4.** Click the **Print** button on the Print Preview toolbar, make sure the settings in the Print dialog box are correct, and then click the **OK** button.

For now, your work is done. When you save the workbook, your printing options are saved along with the file, so you will not have to re-create the print format in the future.

▶ **5.** Save your changes to the workbook, and then close it.

Note that the Sheet tab also provides other options, such as the ability to print the worksheet's gridlines or row and column headings. You can also have Excel print the worksheet in black and white or draft quality. If there are multiple pages in the printout, you can indicate whether the pages should be ordered going down the worksheet first and then across, or across first and then down.

You show the final version of the workbook and the printout to Joan. She is very happy with the way in which you have formatted her report. She will spend some time going over the printout and will get back to you with any further changes she wants you to make.

Review

Session 3.2 Quick Check

1. Describe two ways of merging a range of cells into one.
2. How do you clear a format from a cell without affecting the underlying data?
3. How do you add a background image to the active worksheet?
4. To control the amount of space between the content on a page and its edges, you can adjust the page's _____.
5. By default, Excel prints what part of the active worksheet?
6. How do you define a print area? How do you remove a print area?
7. How do you insert a page break into your worksheet?

Review

Tutorial Summary

In this tutorial, you learned how to use Excel's formatting tools to design your worksheet. You saw how to quickly format cells using the buttons on the Formatting toolbar, and you learned how the Format Cells dialog box can give you even more control over the appearance of your worksheet. You saw how to create and edit cell borders using the Borders button and the Draw Borders button. You also learned how to change cell backgrounds using colors and patterns and external graphic files. The tutorial also demonstrated how to apply the formats in one cell range to another through the use of the Format and Replace dialog box and through styles. Finally, you learned how to format the appearance of your printed worksheet through the use of customized headers, footers, and print areas.

Key Terms

AutoFormat	General number format	point
font	gridline	print area
font size	header	sans serif font
font style	margin	serif font
footer	page break	style
Format Painter	page break preview	typeface
formatting		

Practice

Practice the skills you learned in the tutorial using the same case scenario.

Review Assignments

Data File needed for the Review Assignments: Region1.xls

Joan Sanchez has another report that she wants to format. The report displays regional sales for the three monitor brands you worked on earlier. As before, Joan wants to work on the overall appearance of the worksheet so the printout of the report is polished and professional looking. Figure 3-39 shows a preview of the worksheet you'll create for Joan.

Figure 3-39

	A	B	C	D	E	F	G
1			*NewGeneration Monitors*				
2			Regional Sales Report				
3			1/1/2006 - 12/31/2006				
4							
5	**Sales by Region**						
6	**Region**	**VX100**	**VX300**	**Flatscreen**	**Total**		
7	Northeast	1,723	2,248	520	4,491		
8	East	3,446	4,497	1,041	8,984		
9	Southeast	2,067	2,698	624	5,389		
10	Midwest	1,723	2,248	520	4,491		
11	Southwest	1,378	1,799	416	3,593		
12	West	4,308	5,622	1,302	11,232		
13	Canada	1,378	1,799	416	3,593		
14	Europe	861	1,124	260	2,245		
15	Asia	348	453	109	910		
16	**Total**	17,232	22,488	5,208	44,928		
17							
18	**Regional Analysis**						
19		**Region**	**Units Sold**	**Total Sales**	**Profit from Sales**	**% of Profit**	
20	VX100	Domestic	14,645	$ 2,928,853	$ 509,499	17.03%	
21		Foreign	2,587	$ 517,374	$ 90,001	3.01%	
22		Total	17,232	$ 3,446,227	$ 599,500	20.03%	
23	VX300	Domestic	19,112	$ 5,733,408	$ 1,246,866	41.67%	
24		Foreign	3,376	$ 1,012,766	$ 220,250	7.36%	
25		Total	22,488	$ 6,746,174	$ 1,467,116	49.03%	
26	Flatscreen	Domestic	4,423	$ 3,980,655	$ 786,232	26.27%	
27		Foreign	785	$ 706,492	$ 139,541	4.66%	
28		Total	5,208	$ 4,687,147	$ 925,773	30.94%	
29	Total	Domestic	38,180	$12,642,918	$ 2,542,598	84.97%	
30		Foreign	6,748	$ 2,236,632	$ 449,793	15.03%	
31		Total	44,928	$14,879,550	$ 2,992,391	100.00%	
32							

To format the report:

1. Open the **Region1** workbook located in the Tutorial.03\Review folder included with your Data Files.
2. Enter your name and the current date in the Documentation sheet, and then save the workbook as **Region2** in the Tutorial.03\Review folder.
3. Switch to the Regional Sales worksheet.
4. Format the text in cell A1 with a 20-point, italicized, red, Times New Roman font. Format the text in cells A2 and A3 with a red font. Select the range A1:F3, and center the text across the selection. Do not merge the cells.
5. Select the range A5:E16, and then apply the List 2 format from the AutoFormat gallery.
6. Change the format of all values in the Sales by Region table to display a comma separator, but no decimal places. Resize column E to about 14 characters.
7. Change the format of the Units Sold values in the second table to display a comma separator, but no decimal places.
8. Indent the region names in the range A7:A15 by one character.
9. Display the text in cell A18 in bold.
10. Change the format of the values in the Total Sales and Profit from Sales columns to display a dollar sign on the left edge of the cell and no decimal places.
11. Change the format of the values in the % of Profit column to display a percent sign and two decimal places.
12. Allow the text in the range B19:F19 to wrap to a second line of text. Bold and center the text within each cell.

13. Merge and center the cells in the range A20:A22, and change the vertical text alignment to center. (*Hint*: Use the correct Text alignment option in the Format Cells dialog box to vertically align the text; see Figure 3-13.) Apply this format to the cells in the following ranges: A23:A25, A26:A28, and A29:A31.

14. Change the background color of the cells in the range A19:F19;A20:A31 to Sea Green (third row, fourth column of the color palette). Change the font color to white.

15. Change the background color of the cells in the range B20:F31 to white. Change the background color of the cells in the range B22:F22;B25:F25;B28:F28;B31:F31 to Light Green (fifth row, fourth column of the color palette).

16. Apply a thin black border to each of the cells in the range A19:F31.

17. Place a double line on the bottom border of the cells in the range B22:F22;B25:F25;B28:F28.

18. Set the print area as the range A1:F31. Insert a page break above row 18. Repeat the first three rows of the worksheet on every page of any printouts you produce from this worksheet.

19. Set up the page to print in portrait orientation with one-inch margins on all sides. Center the contents of the worksheet horizontally on the page.

20. Add a footer with the following text in the Left section box of the footer (with the date on a separate line): "Filename: *the name of the file*" and "Date: *current date*," and then the following text in the Right section box of the footer: "Prepared by: *your name*." In the Center section, place the text "Page *page_number* of *total_pages*" where *page_number* is the number of the page and *total_pages* is the total number of pages in the printout.

21. Add a header with the text "Regional Sales Report" displayed in the Center section using a 14-point Times New Roman font with a double underline. (*Hint*: Select the text in the Center section, and then click the Font button in the Footer dialog box to open the Format Cells dialog box.)

22. Preview the two-page worksheet, and then print it.

23. Save your changes to the workbook and then close it.

Case Problem 1

Apply

Use the skills you learned in this tutorial to format a worksheet that presents an annual sales report.

Data File needed for this Case Problem: Running1.xls

Jenson Sportswear Quarterly Sales Carol Roberts is the national sales manager for Jenson Sportswear, Inc., a company that sells sportswear to major department stores. She has been using an Excel worksheet to track the results of her staff's sales incentive program. She has asked you to format the worksheet so that it looks professional. She also wants a printout before she presents the worksheet at the next sales meeting. To complete this task:

1. Open the **Running1** workbook located in the Tutorial.03\Cases folder included with your Data Files, and then save the file as **Running2** in the same folder.

Explore

2. In the Documentation sheet, enter your name and the current date. Format the date so that it appears as *Weekday, Month Day, Year* where *Weekday* is the day of the week, *Month Day* is the name of the month and the day, and *Year* is a four-digit year.

3. Switch to the Sales worksheet, and then enter the formulas to calculate the following results:
   a. the totals for each product
   b. the quarterly subtotals for the Shoes and Shirts departments
   c. the totals for each quarter and the grand total

4. Using Figure 3-40 as a guide, format the worksheet with the following attributes:

Figure 3-40

	A	B	C	D	E	F
1	**Jenson Sportswear, Inc.**					
2	Sales Report					
3	1/1/2006 - 12/31/2006					
4						
5		**Quarterly Sales by Product**				
6	**Shoes**	**Qtr1**	**Qtr2**	**Qtr3**	**Qtr4**	**Total**
7	Running	2,250	2,550	2,650	2,800	10,250
8	Tennis	2,800	1,500	2,300	2,450	9,050
9	Basketball	1,250	1,400	1,550	1,550	5,750
10	**Subtotal**	**6,300**	**5,450**	**6,500**	**6,800**	**25,050**
11						
12	**Shirts**	**Qtr1**	**Qtr2**	**Qtr3**	**Qtr4**	**Total**
13	Tee	1,000	1,150	1,250	1,150	4,550
14	Polo	2,100	2,200	2,300	2,400	9,000
15	Sweat	250	250	275	300	1,075
16	**Subtotal**	**3,350**	**3,600**	**3,825**	**3,850**	**14,625**
17						
18	**Grand Total**	**9,650**	**9,050**	**10,325**	**10,650**	**39,675**

5. Create a style named "Subtotal" that is based on the font, border, and pattern formats found in the cell ranges B10:F10 and B16:F16.
6. Use the Page Setup dialog box to center the table both horizontally and vertically on the printed page and to change the page orientation to landscape.
7. Add the filename, your name, and the date on separate lines in the Right section box of the footer.
8. Preview the sales report and then print it.
9. Save your changes to the workbook and then close it.

Apply

Use the skills you have learned in this tutorial to format a revenue report for women-owned businesses.

Case Problem 2

Data File needed for this Case Problem: WBus1.xls

Wisconsin Department of Revenue   Ted Crawford works for the Wisconsin Department of Revenue. Recently he compiled a list of the top 50 women-owned businesses in the state. He would like your help in formatting the report, in regard to both how it appears in the worksheet window and how it appears on the printed page. A preview of the worksheet you'll create is shown in Figure 3-41.

Figure 3-41

	A	B	C	D	E	F	G
1		**Wisconsin's top 50 women-owned businesses**					
2	**Rank**	**Name**	**Sales**	**Employees**	**Year Founded**	**Line**	
3	1	Jockey International	$ 450,000,000	500	1930	Manufacturing Clothing	
4	2	Astronautics	$ 425,000,000	1,400	1959	Manufacturing Flight & Electronic Equip.	
5	3	Pleasant Company	$ 74,000,000	280	1986	Mail Order Books, Dolls & Accessories	
6	4	Dawes Transport	$ 52,000,000	163	1981	Trucking	
7	5	East Capitol Drive Foods Inc.	$ 45,800,000	285	1984	Grocery Stores	
8	6	TSR Inc.	$ 40,000,000	140	1986	Manufacturing Toys & Games	
9	7	Ricom Electronics	$ 34,000,000	52	1982	Mail Order Consumer Electronics	
10	8	Rollette Oil Co.	$ 32,300,000	46	1960	Gasoline Service Stations	
11	9	Mainline Industrial Distributors	$ 31,000,000	125	1964	Industrial Equipment	
12	10	Mueller Graphics	$ 27,100,000	48	1982	Printing Equip. & Supplies	
13	11	Nor-Lake Inc.	$ 26,000,000	208	1947	Refrigeration & Heating Equip.	
14	12	V & J Foods	$ 25,000,000	1,200	1984	Restaurant	
15	13	Fuchs Holding Corporation	$ 24,000,000	103	1955	Trucking Firm	
16	14	O'Connor Oil Corporation	$ 18,600,000	110	1961	Petroleum Bulk Stations	
17	15	A. D. Schinner Co.	$ 17,000,000	34	1910	Distributor Packaging Products	
18	16	Pro-Track Corporation	$ 15,000,000	51	1982	Distributor Footwear	
19	17	Racine Travel Service Inc.	$ 15,000,000	36	1979	Travel Agencies	
20	18	Runzheimer International, Ltd.	$ 14,000,000	165	1933	Info-Management Consultant	
21	19	Triangle Wholesale	$ 14,000,000	55	1981	Distributor Liquor & Beer	

To complete this task:

1. Open the **WBus1** workbook located in the Tutorial.03\Cases folder included with your Data Files, and then save the file as **WBus2** in the same folder.
2. Enter your name and the current date in the Documentation sheet, and then switch to the Business Data worksheet.
3. Change the font in cell A1 to a boldface font that is 14 points in size. Merge and center the title across the range A1:F1.
4. Display the text in the range A2:F2 in bold, and then center the text in the range C2:F2. Place a double line on the bottom border of the range A2:F2.
5. Display the sales information in the Accounting format with no decimal places. Increase the width of the column, if necessary.
6. Display the employees' data using a comma separator with no decimal places.
7. Change the background color of the cells in the range A3:F3 to light green, and then change the background color of the cells in A4:F4 to white.
8. Use the Format Painter to apply the format found in the cell range A3:F4 to the cell range A5:F52.
9. Set up the worksheet page so it prints in landscape orientation with a bottom margin of 1.5 inches. Also, center the contents of the worksheet horizontally on the page.
10. Set the print area as the cell range A1:F52, and then repeat the first two rows of the worksheet in the printouts.

Explore ▶ 11. Remove the existing header and footer from the printed page. (*Hint*: Choose (none) from the list of available header and footer text to remove the previous header and footer text.) Insert a customized footer that displays the following text on three separate lines in the Right section box of the footer:
   Compiled by: *your name*
   current date
   Page *page number* of *total number of pages*

Explore ▶ 12. Fit the worksheet on a printout that is one page wide and two pages tall.
13. Preview the worksheet, and then print it.
14. Save your changes to the workbook, and then close it.

Challenge

Using Figure 3-42 as your guide, challenge yourself by experimenting with more formatting techniques to enhance a worksheet presenting regional sales figures.

Case Problem 3

Data File needed for this Case Problem: Blades1.xls

Sales Report at Davis Blades Andrew Malki is a financial officer at Davis Blades, a leading manufacturer of roller blades. He has recently finished entering data for the yearly sales report. Andrew has asked you to help him with the design of the main table in the report. A preview of the format you will apply is shown in Figure 3-42.

Figure 3-42

Davis Blades
Sales Report
1/1/2006 - 12/31/2006

Units Sold		Northeast	East	Southeast	Midwest	Southwest	West	All Regions
Black Hawk	Qtr 1	641	748	733	676	691	783	4,272
	Qtr 2	708	826	811	748	763	866	4,722
	Qtr 3	681	795	780	719	734	833	4,542
	Qtr 4	668	779	764	705	720	816	4,452
	Total	2,698	3,148	3,088	2,848	2,908	3,298	17,988
Blademaster	Qtr 1	513	598	587	541	552	627	3,418
	Qtr 2	567	661	648	598	611	693	3,778
	Qtr 3	545	636	624	575	587	666	3,633
	Qtr 4	534	623	611	564	576	653	3,561
	Total	2,159	2,518	2,470	2,278	2,326	2,639	14,390
The Professional	Qtr 1	342	399	391	361	368	418	2,279
	Qtr 2	378	441	432	399	407	462	2,519
	Qtr 3	363	424	416	383	391	444	2,421
	Qtr 4	356	415	407	376	384	435	2,373
	Total	1,439	1,679	1,646	1,519	1,550	1,759	9,592
All Models	Qtr 1	1,496	1,745	1,711	1,578	1,611	1,828	9,969
	Qtr 2	1,653	1,928	1,891	1,745	1,781	2,021	11,019
	Qtr 3	1,589	1,855	1,820	1,677	1,712	1,943	10,596
	Qtr 4	1,558	1,817	1,782	1,645	1,680	1,904	10,386
	Total	6,296	7,345	7,204	6,645	6,784	7,696	41,970

To complete this task:

1. Open the **Blades1** workbook located in the Tutorial.03\Cases folder included with your Data Files, and then save the file as **Blades2** in the same folder.
2. Enter your name and the current date in the Documentation sheet, and then switch to the Sales worksheet.
3. Change the font of the title in cell A1 to a 16–point, dark blue, boldface, Times New Roman font. Change the subtitles in cells A2 and A3 to an 8-point, blue font. Reduce the height of row 2 and row 3 to 12 characters.
4. Add a solid black bottom border to the range A1:K1.
5. Format the text in cell A5 in a 12-point, blue, Arial font. Vertically align the text in this cell with the bottom of the cell.

Explore
6. Merge the cells in the range A6:A10, and align the contents of the cell vertically at the top of the cell. Repeat this for the following ranges: A11:A15, A16:A20, and A21:A25.
7. Change the background color of the cell range A6:I10 to light yellow. Change the background color of the range A11:I15 to light green. Change the background color of the range A16:I20 to light turquoise. Change the background color of the range A21:I25 to pale blue.
8. Reverse the color scheme for the subtotal values in the range B10:I10, so that instead of black on light yellow, the font color is light yellow on a black background. Reverse the subtotal values for the other products in the table.
9. Apply the borders, as shown in Figure 3-42, to the cells in the range A6:I25.

Explore
10. Rotate the column titles in the range C5:I5 by 45 degrees. Align the contents of each cell along the bottom-right corner of the cell. Change the background color of these cells to white, and then add a border to each cell.

Explore
11. Open the Options dialog box from the Tools menu. Deselect the Row & column headings and Gridlines options to remove the row and column headings and gridlines from the Sales worksheet window.

12. Set the print area as the range A1:K25.
13. Leave the page orientation as portrait, but center the worksheet horizontally on the page.
14. Create a custom footer with the text "Filename: *the name of the file*" left-aligned and with the text "Prepared by: *your name*" and "*the current date*" right-aligned, with your name and date on separate lines.
15. Preview the worksheet and then print it.
16. Save your changes to the workbook and then close it.

Create

Using Figure 3-43 as a guide, test your knowledge of formatting by creating your own design for a payroll worksheet.

Case Problem 4

There are no Data Files needed for this Case Problem.

Oritz Marine Services Vince DiOrio is an information systems major at a local college. He works three days a week at a nearby marina, Oritz Marine Services, to help pay for his tuition. Vince works in the business office, and his responsibilities range from making coffee to keeping the company's books.

Recently, Jim Oritz, the owner of the marina, asked Vince if he could help computerize the payroll for the employees. He explained that the employees work a different number of hours each week at different rates of pay. Jim now does the payroll manually, and finds it time consuming. Moreover, whenever he makes an error, he is annoyed at having to take the additional time to correct it. Jim is hoping that Vince can help him.

Vince immediately agrees to help. He tells Jim that he knows how to use Excel and that he can build a worksheet that will save him time and reduce errors. Jim and Vince meet to review the present payroll process and discuss the desired outcome of the payroll spreadsheet. Figure 3-43 displays the type of information that Jim records in the spreadsheet.

Figure 3-43

Employee	Hours	Pay Rate	Gross Pay	Federal Withholding	State Withholding	Total Deductions	Net Pay
Bramble	16	9.50					
Cortez	30	10.50					
DiOrio	25	12.50					
Fulton	20	9.50					
Juarez	25	12.00					
Smiken	10	9.00					
Smith	30	13.50					
Total							

To complete this task:

1. Create a new workbook named **Payroll1**, and save it in the Tutorial.03\Cases folder included with your Data Files.
2. Name two worksheets "Documentation" and "Payroll," and then delete the third sheet.
3. On the Documentation sheet, include the name of the company, your name as the author of the workbook, the date the workbook is being created, and a brief description of the purpose of the workbook.
4. On the Payroll worksheet, enter the payroll table shown in Figure 3-43.

5. Enter the formulas to calculate total hours, gross pay, federal withholding tax, state withholding tax, total deductions, and net pay, using the following information:
   a. Gross pay is equal to the number of hours multiplied by the pay rate.
   b. Federal withholding tax is equal to 15% of the gross pay.
   c. State withholding tax is equal to 4% of the gross pay.
   d. Total deductions are the sum of federal and state withholdings.
   e. Net pay is equal to the difference between the gross pay and the total amount of deductions.
6. Format the appearance of the payroll table using the techniques you learned in this tutorial. The appearance of the payroll table is up to you; however, do not use an AutoFormat design to format the table.
7. Format the printed page, setting the print area and inserting an appropriate header and footer. Only a few employees are entered into the table at present. However, after Jim Oritz approves your layout, many additional employees will be added, which will cause the report to cover multiple pages. Format your printout so that the worksheet title and column titles appear on every page.
8. Preview your worksheet, and then print it. Save your changes.
9. Add the following new employees to the worksheet. The employee list should be in alphabetical order, so these new employees should be inserted at the appropriate places in the sheet:

Name	Hours	Pay Rate
Carls	20	10.50
Lopez	35	11.50
Nelson	20	9.50

10. Preview the revised worksheet, and then print it.
11. Save this revised workbook as **Payroll2** in the Tutorial.03\Cases folder, and then close the workbook.

Internet Assignments

Research

Use the Internet to find and work with data related to the topics presented in this tutorial.

The purpose of the Internet Assignments is to challenge you to find information on the Internet that you can use to work effectively with this software. The actual assignments are updated and maintained on the Course Technology Web site. Log on to the Internet and use your Web browser to go to the Student Online Companion for New Perspectives Office 2003 at **www.course.com/np/office2003**. Click the Internet Assignments link, and then navigate to the assignments for this tutorial.

SAM Assessment and Training

Assess

If you have a SAM user profile, you may have access to hands-on instruction, practice, and assessment of the skills covered in this tutorial. Log in to your SAM account and go to your assignments page to see what your instructor has assigned.

Review

Quick Check Answers

Session 3.1

1. Click the Currency Style button on the Formatting toolbar; or click Format on the menu bar, click Cells, click the Number tab, and then select Currency from the Category list box.
2. a. 5.8%
   b. $0.06
3. Format Painter button and Copy button
4. Increase the width of the column; decrease the font size of the text; or select the Shrink to fit check box or the Wrap text check box on the Alignment tab in the Format Cells dialog box.
5. Select the range, click Cells on the Format menu, click the Alignment tab, and then select Center Across Selection in the Horizontal list box.
6. Use the Borders button on the Formatting toolbar; use the Draw Borders button in the Border gallery; or click Cells on the Format menu, click the Border tab, and then choose the border options in the dialog box.
7. Click Cells on the Format menu, click the Patterns tab, click the Pattern list arrow, and then select the pattern type and color.

Session 3.2

1. Select the cells and either click the Merge and Center button on the Formatting toolbar; or click Cells on the Format menu, click the Alignment tab, and then click the Merge cells check box.
2. Select the cell, click Edit on the menu bar, point to Clear, and then click Formats.
3. Click Format on the menu bar, point to Sheet, and then click Background. Locate and select an image file to use for the background, and then click the Insert button.
4. margins
5. Excel prints all parts of the active worksheet that contain text, formulas, or values.
6. To define a print area, select a range in the worksheet, click File on the menu bar, point to Print Area, and then click Set Print Area. To remove a print area, point to Print Area on the File menu, and then click Clear Print Area.
7. Select the first cell below the row at which you want to insert the page break, and then select Page Break on the Insert menu.

Objectives

Session 4.1
- Create column and pie charts using the Chart Wizard
- Move and resize a chart
- Embed a chart in a worksheet
- Place a chart on a chart sheet
- Separate a slice from a pie chart

Session 4.2
- Edit the data source
- Change the location of a chart
- Modify chart objects
- Insert and format chart text
- Create 3-D charts
- Add and modify drawing objects using the Drawing toolbar
- Print a chart

Working with Charts and Graphics

Charting Sales Data

Case

Vega Telescopes

Alicia Kendall is a sales manager at Vega Telescopes, one of the leading manufacturers of telescopes and optics. She has been asked to present information on last year's sales for four of Vega's most popular telescopes: the 6- and 8-inch BrightStar and the 12- and 16-inch NightVision. Her presentation will be part of a sales conference that will be held next week in Charlotte, North Carolina.

As part of her presentation, Alicia would like to include a report that shows the sales figures for each model in the United States, Europe, and Asia. She knows that this kind of information is often best understood when presented visually, that is, in a graphical or pictorial form. She would like to use a column chart to show the sales data and a pie chart to show how each model contributes to Vega's overall sales of these four popular telescope models. Alicia is especially interested in making the charts visually appealing, and she wants to draw attention to the top-selling telescope model. She also will need printouts of the charts.

Alicia has asked you to help her create charts that will clearly and effectively present the sales data. Your task is to format the charts and individual chart components to enhance the presentation of the data, which will help Alicia explain and highlight the data at the sales conference. You will also add a drawing object that points out the top-selling telescope, and you will print the completed charts.

Student Data Files

▼ **Tutorial.04**

▽ Tutorial folder	▽ Review folder	▽ Cases folder
Space.jpg	VegaUSA1.xls	CIC1.xls
Vega1.xls		Powder1.xls
		Pixal1.xls

Session 4.1

Excel Charts

Alicia's sales data has already been entered into a workbook for you. You will begin by opening the workbook so you can examine the sales data.

To open Alicia's workbook:

▶ **1.** Start Excel and then open the **Vega1** workbook located in the Tutorial.04\Tutorial folder included with your Data Files.

▶ **2.** Enter *your name* and the *current date* in the Documentation sheet.

▶ **3.** Save the workbook as **Vega2** to the Tutorial folder, and then switch to the Sales worksheet to view the sales data as shown in Figure 4-1.

Figure 4-1 | **Sales worksheet for Vega Telescopes**

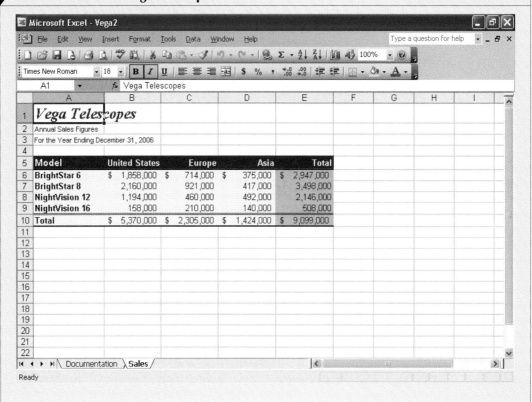

The Sales worksheet shows the annual sales, in U.S. dollars, for each of the four Vega telescope models. The sales data is broken down by world regions. As Alicia has explained, she wants two charts. The first chart should show the sales for each telescope in each region represented by columns, in which the height of the column represents the sales volume for each model. The second should be a pie chart that interprets how the total sales of each telescope model relate to overall sales. Sketches of the charts Alicia wants to create are shown in Figure 4-2.

Sketch of column and pie charts ◄ **Figure 4-2**

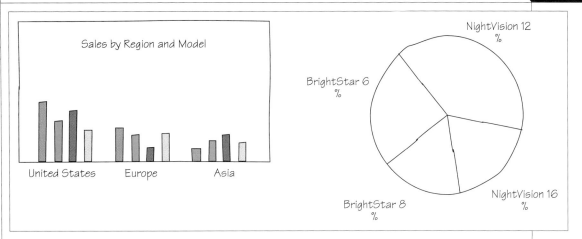

Charts, also known as graphs, provide a visual representation of the workbook data. Using charts, one can often see trends in the data that are more difficult to detect by viewing the raw numbers in a table. A chart can also be used to highlight items of interest, such as a region with low sales or an unexpectedly good sales month. Excel makes it easy to create charts through the use of the **Chart Wizard**, a series of dialog boxes that prompt you for information about the chart you want to create. This includes information such as the chart type, the cell range that the chart is based on, and features that the chart will contain. You will use the Chart Wizard to create the first chart that Alicia sketched for you—the column chart of the sales figures broken down by region and telescope model.

Creating a Chart Using the Chart Wizard

The Chart Wizard is a series of four dialog boxes, and each one is a step in the process of creating your chart. At each point in the process, you provide more detailed information about the chart you want Excel to create. Figure 4-3 describes the four steps in the Chart Wizard.

Tasks performed in each step of the Chart Wizard ◄ **Figure 4-3**

Dialog Box	Task Options
Chart Type	Select from list of available chart types and corresponding sub-types, or choose to customize a chart type
Chart Source Data	Specify the cells that contain the data on which the chart will be based and the cells that contain the labels that will appear in the chart
Chart Options	Change the appearance of the chart by selecting the options that affect titles, axes, gridlines, legends, data labels, and data tables
Chart Location	Specify where the chart will be placed: embedded as an object in the worksheet containing the data or on a separate worksheet, also called a chart sheet

You can stop the Chart Wizard at any time, and Excel will complete the remaining dialog boxes for you using the default specifications for the chart you have chosen.

Reference Window

Creating a Chart Using the Chart Wizard

- Select the data you want to chart.
- Click the Chart Wizard button on the Standard toolbar.
- In the first step of the Chart Wizard, select the chart type and sub-type, and then click the Next button.
- In the second step, make any modifications or additions to the chart's data source, and then click the Next button.
- In the third step, make any modifications to the chart's appearance, and then click the Next button.
- In the fourth step, specify the location for the chart, and then click the Finish button.

Before starting the Chart Wizard, you can select the cell range that contains the data that will be used in the chart. If you don't select a cell range, the Chart Wizard will "guess" at the cell range. If the selected range isn't correct, you can select the correct cell range as you work with the Chart Wizard. To create the first chart that Alicia wants, you'll select the data in the cell range A5:D9. The range needs to include both the labels and the sales figures for each telescope model. You will not include the total sales within each region.

To start the Chart Wizard:

1. Select the range **A5:D9**.

2. Click the **Chart Wizard** button 📊 on the Standard toolbar. The first step of the Chart Wizard is shown in Figure 4-4.

Figure 4-4 | **Step 1 of the Chart Wizard**

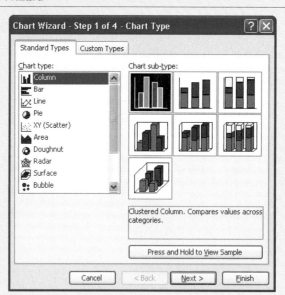

Choosing a Chart Type

The first step of the Chart Wizard provides the chart types, from which you choose the one that you feel will best display the data you want to plot. Excel supports 14 types of charts, ranging from the column chart, similar to the one shown in Alicia's first sketch, to stock market charts that can be used to record the daily behavior of stocks. Figure 4-5 provides information about some of the chart types. The charts are useful in different situations. When you want to compare the values from different categories (such as the sales of different telescope models), you will want to use a column, bar, or line chart. If you want to compare the values of individual categories to a whole collection of categories, you will want to use either a pie chart or a doughnut chart. If your data doesn't contain categories and you want to compare one set of numeric values with another, you will probably want to create an XY Scatter (scatter) chart or a bubble chart. Finally, for stock market data, you can use an Excel stock chart.

Excel chart types   **Figure 4-5**

Icon	Chart Type	Description
	Column	Compares values from different categories. Values are indicated by the height of the columns.
	Bar	Compares values from different categories. Values are indicated by the length of the bars.
	Line	Compares values from different categories. Values are indicated by the height of the line. Often used to show trends and changes over time.
	Pie	Compares relative values of different categories to the whole. Values are indicated by the size of the pie slices.
	XY (scatter)	Shows the patterns or relationship between two or more sets of numeric values. Often used in scientific studies and statistical analyses.
	Area	Similar to the line chart, except that areas under the lines are filled with colors indicating the different categories.
	Doughnut	Similar to the pie chart, except that it can display multiple sets of data.
	Radar	Compares a collection of values from several different data sets.
	Surface	Compares three sets of values in a three-dimensional chart.
	Bubble	Similar to the XY (scatter) chart, except the size of the data marker is determined by a third numeric value.
	Cylinder, Cone, Pyramid	Similar to the column chart, except that cylinders, cones, and pyramids are used in place of columns.

Each chart type has its own collection of sub-types that provide an alternative format for the chart's appearance. For example, the column chart type has seven different sub-types, including the clustered column and the stacked column. There are also 3-D, or three-dimensional, sub-types.

Finally, Excel also supports 20 additional "custom" chart types with additional formatting options. Some of the custom charts actually combine the properties of two or more of the main chart types. You can also create your own customized chart designs and add them to the custom chart list.

Alicia wants you to create a column chart for the sales data, in which values are arranged into separate columns. To see whether the chart you are creating is the right one, you will click the button in the first dialog box that lets you preview the chart before continuing with the Chart Wizard.

To select the chart type and preview it:

1. Verify that the **Column** chart type is selected in the Chart type list box and that the first sub-type, **Clustered Column**, is also selected.

2. Press the **Press and Hold to View Sample** button, but do not release the mouse button. A preview of the selected chart is displayed, as shown in Figure 4-6.

Figure 4-6 ▶ **Preview of the clustered column chart**

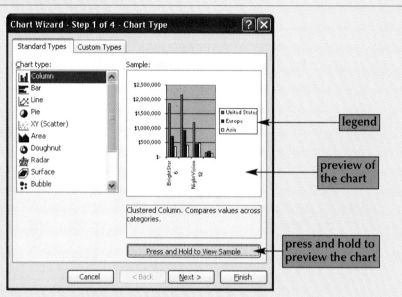

The Chart Wizard has assigned a different colored column to represent the sales values within each region. The legend on the right identifies the regions. The blue columns represent the United States, the maroon columns represent Europe, and the yellow columns represent Asia. Though the size of the Sample pane prevents you from viewing much of the chart's detail, you can see that the columns are clustered into groups; each group represents a different model. The first cluster represents sales for the BrightStar 6 telescope. The second cluster represents sales for the BrightStar 8 and so forth. Because this is the chart type that Alicia wants you to create, you can continue to the next step of the Chart Wizard.

3. Release the mouse button, and then click the **Next** button to go to step 2 of the Chart Wizard.

Choosing a Data Source

In the second step of the Chart Wizard, shown in Figure 4-7, you specify the **data source** for the chart, indicating the cell range that contains the chart's data. Excel organizes the data source into a collection of **data series**, where each data series is a range of data values that is plotted as a unit on the chart. In the case of this column chart, each data series contains the sales values of each sales region. A data series consists of **data values**, which are plotted on the chart's vertical axis, or **y-axis**. On the horizontal axis, or **x-axis**, are the data series' **category values**, or **x values**. In this chart, the data values are the sales values and the category values are the names of the different telescope models.

Specifying the data source ◄ **Figure 4-7**

data values are plotted on the vertical axis

category values are plotted on the horizontal axis

each column represents a different data series

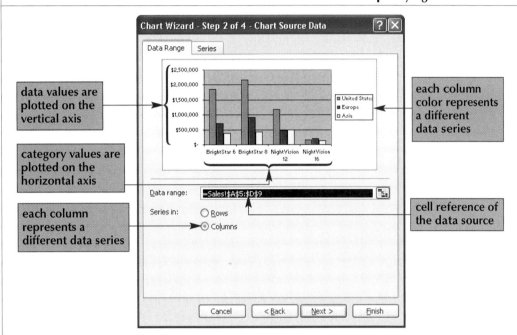

each column color represents a different data series

cell reference of the data source

In this case, the Chart Wizard has organized the data source by columns, so that the leftmost column contains the category values and the subsequent columns each contain a different data series. The first row of the data contains the labels that identify each data series. In general, if the data spans more rows than columns, then the Chart Wizard interprets the data series by columns; otherwise, the Chart Wizard interprets the data series by rows.

In Alicia's sketch, she has indicated that she wants the name of the region to be the category value, which means that each telescope model represents a different data series. Therefore, you need to ensure that the Chart Wizard organizes the data source by rows and not columns. The first row will contain the category values, and each subsequent row will contain a data series. The first column will then contain the labels of each series.

To organize the data source by rows:

1. Click the **Rows** option button. Excel changes the orientation of the data source. The category values now represent the three regions rather than the four telescope models. See Figure 4-8.

Figure 4-8 Changing the orientation of the data source

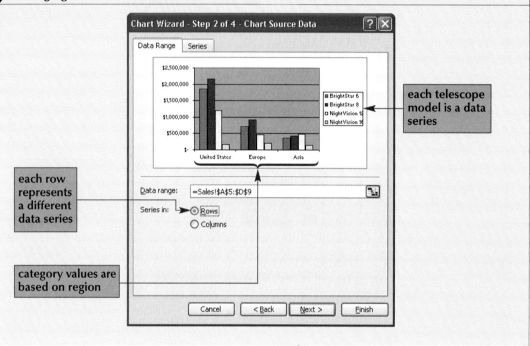

each row represents a different data series

category values are based on region

each telescope model is a data series

You can further define the data range using the Series tab. From this tab, you can add or remove individual data series from the chart or change the category values. Although it is recommended that you select the data series before starting the Chart Wizard, it is not necessary because you can define all of the data series and chart values using the Series tab. However, selecting the data series first does save time. You will switch to the Series tab so you can view its options.

To view the Series tab:

▶ **1.** Click the **Series** tab. The Series tab lists all of the data series used in the chart and the corresponding cell references for the cell that contains the name of the data series, the cells that contain the values for the data series, and the cells the contain the category labels. Note that the cell references include the name of the sheet from which the values are selected. See Figure 4-9.

Series tab ◀ **Figure 4-9**

You do not have to make any changes in the data series at this point, so you will continue in the Chart Wizard.

▶ **2.** Click the **Next** button to go to step 3 of the Chart Wizard.

Choosing Chart Options

The third step of the Chart Wizard provides the options that you can use to control the appearance of the chart. To better understand the options available to you, first you'll explore the terminology that Excel uses with respect to charts. Figure 4-10 shows the elements of a typical Excel chart.

Figure 4-10 **Excel chart elements**

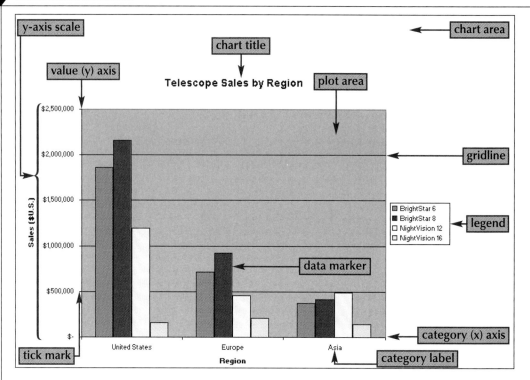

The basic element of the chart is the **plot area**, a rectangular area containing a graphical representation of the values in the data series. Each graphical representation is called a **data marker**. Each column in a column chart is an example of a data marker. Other types of data markers include the pie slices used in pie charts and the points used in XY (scatter) charts.

Most charts have two axes that border the plot area: an x-axis (or horizontal axis) and a y-axis (or vertical axis). As mentioned earlier, values from the data series are plotted along the y-axis, whereas the category labels are plotted along the x-axis. Each axis can have a title that describes the values or labels displayed on the axis. In Figure 4-10, the x-axis title is "Region" and the y-axis title is "Sales ($U.S.)."

The range of values that spans along an axis is called a **scale**. Excel automatically chooses a scale to match the range of values in the data series. In the chart shown in Figure 4-10, the scale of the y-axis ranges from $0 to $2,500,000. Next to the values on the scales are **tick marks**, which act like the division lines on a ruler, making it easier to read the scale. Your charts might also contain **gridlines**, which extend the tick marks across the plot area. Excel divides gridlines into two types. **Major gridlines** are the lines that extend the tick marks across the plot area; **minor gridlines** are the lines that divide the space between the major gridlines.

If your chart contains more than one data series, the chart will usually have a **legend** identifying the format of the data marker used for each series. Above the plot area, you can add a **chart title** to describe the contents of the plot area and the data series. The entire chart and all of the elements discussed so far are contained in the **chart area**.

You can format these various chart elements in the third step of the Chart Wizard. You can also format these features later on, after the chart has been created. As shown in Figure 4-11, step 3 of the Chart Wizard contains six tabs: Titles, Axes, Gridlines, Legend, Data Labels, and Data Table. Each tab provides tools for formatting different elements of your chart.

Step 3 of the Chart Wizard ◄ **Figure 4-11**

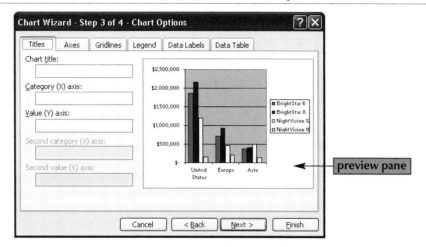

preview pane

Alicia wants you to add descriptive titles to the chart and to each of the axes. She also wants you to remove the gridlines because they are not necessary in such a simple, straight-forward chart. Using the Titles and Gridlines tabs, you will make these changes now.

To insert titles into the chart:

▶ **1.** Make sure that the **Titles** tab is active.

▶ **2.** Click the **Chart title** text box, type **Telescope Sales by Region**, and then press the **Tab** key. The preview pane updates the chart image to reflect the addition of the chart title to the chart area.

▶ **3.** Type **Region** in the Category (X) axis text box, and then press the **Tab** key.

▶ **4.** Type **Sales ($U.S.)** in the Value (Y) axis text box, and then press the **Tab** key. The preview pane shows all of the new titles you entered into the chart.

▶ **5.** Click the **Gridlines** tab.

▶ **6.** Click the **Major gridlines** check box for the Value (Y) axis to remove the major gridlines from the chart.

▶ **7.** Click the **Next** button to move to the last Chart Wizard dialog box, shown in Figure 4-12.

Step 4 of the Chart Wizard ◄ **Figure 4-12**

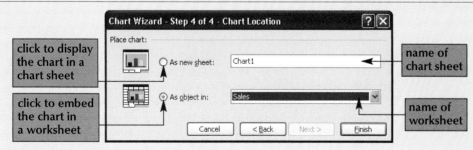

click to display the chart in a chart sheet

name of chart sheet

click to embed the chart in a worksheet

name of worksheet

Choosing the Chart Location

In the final step of the Chart Wizard, you choose a location for the chart. You can either create an embedded chart or a chart sheet. An **embedded chart** is a chart that is displayed within a worksheet. The advantage of creating an embedded chart is that you can place the chart alongside the data source, giving context to the chart. A **chart sheet** is a new sheet that is automatically inserted into the workbook, occupying the entire workbook window and thus providing more space and details for the chart. Figure 4-13 provides examples of each type of chart.

Figure 4-13	Example of an embedded chart and a chart sheet

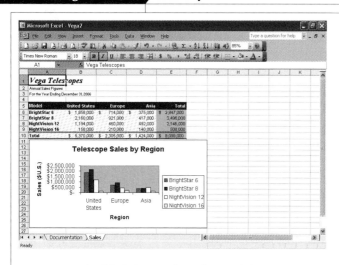

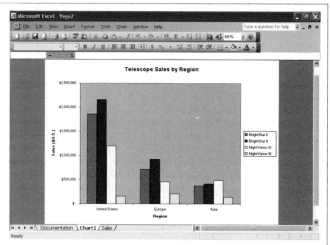

embedded chart in the Sales worksheet   chart sheet named "Chart1"

For this first chart, you'll embed the chart in the Sales worksheet.

To embed the clustered column chart in the Sales worksheet:

▶ **1.** Make sure that the **As object in** option button is selected and that **Sales** is selected in the adjacent list box.

▶ **2.** Click the **Finish** button. Excel creates the column chart with the specifications you selected and embeds the chart in the Sales worksheet, as shown in Figure 4-14.

Embedded column chart ◄ **Figure 4-14**

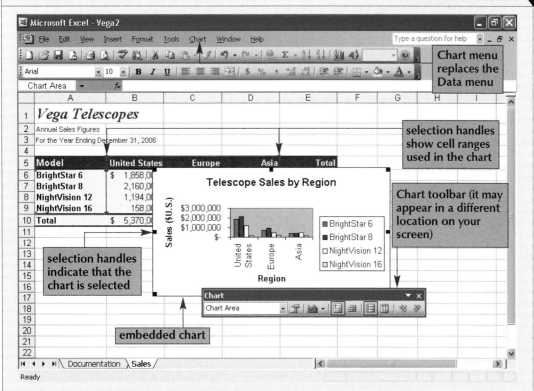

Trouble? If the Chart toolbar is not visible, it may have been closed during a previous Excel session. Click View on the menu bar, point to Toolbars, and then click Chart to redisplay the toolbar.

When the Chart Wizard creates the embedded chart, the chart appears with selection handles around it. The selection handles indicate that the chart is an **active chart** and is ready for additional formatting. The Chart toolbar also appears when the chart is selected. (Note that the Chart toolbar doesn't always appear when a chart is selected if the toolbar was closed in an earlier Excel session.) Another change that occurs is the Chart menu replaces the Data menu on Excel's menu bar. You will also find that certain Excel commands are not available to you when a chart is the active object in the workbook window. When a chart is not active, the default Excel menus return and the Chart toolbar disappears.

Try switching between the chart and the worksheet.

To switch between the embedded chart and the worksheet:

► **1.** Click anywhere in the worksheet outside of the chart to deselect it. The Chart toolbar disappears and the Data menu replaces the Chart menu on the menu bar. There are no selection handles around the chart.

► **2.** Move the pointer over a blank area of the chart so that the pointer changes to ⊿ and the ScreenTip "Chart Area" displays in the chart, and then click in the empty chart area. The Chart toolbar and the Chart menu reappear, and the selection handles appear around the chart.

Trouble? If you clicked one of the chart's elements, you made that element active rather than the entire chart. Click a blank area in the chart to select the entire embedded chart.

Moving and Resizing an Embedded Chart

The Chart Wizard has a default size and location for embedded charts, which might not match what you want in your worksheet. In this case, the new chart is covering some of the data in the Sales worksheet and the chart titles seem to overwhelm the plot area. You will move the chart so you can see all of the sales data, and then you will make the chart a little larger to make it easier to read.

To move and resize the embedded chart:

1. Verify that the embedded chart is still selected, and then move the pointer over a blank area of the chart so that the pointer changes to ⬚ and the ScreenTip "Chart Area" displays.

2. Drag the embedded chart so that the upper-left corner of the chart aligns with the upper-left corner of cell A11. Note that as you drag the chart with the pointer, an outline of the chart area appears, which you can use as a guideline.

3. Release the mouse button when the chart is positioned correctly. The chart moves to a new location in the worksheet.

   To resize the chart, you drag a selection handle in the direction that you want the chart resized. To keep the proportions of the chart the same, press and hold the Shift key as you drag one of the corner selection handles.

4. Move your pointer over the lower-right selection handle until the pointer changes to ⬉.

5. Drag the lower-right corner of the embedded chart until that corner is aligned with the lower-right corner of cell F26.

6. Release the mouse button when the chart is resized, and then, if necessary, scroll the worksheet so the chart is visible. Figure 4-15 shows the chart, repositioned and resized.

Figure 4-15	Embedded chart moved and resized

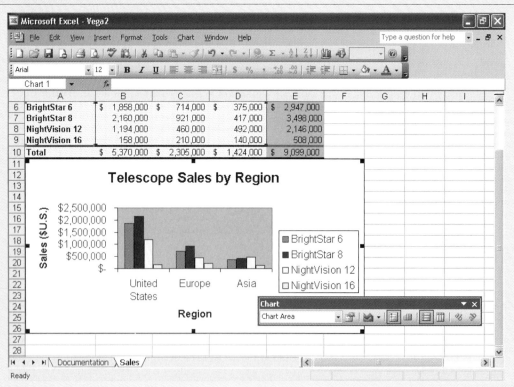

Updating a Chart

Every chart you create is connected to its data source. As a result, if you change values in the data source, Excel automatically updates the chart to reflect the change. This is true for category labels as well as for data values.

Alicia sees two changes that she would like you to make to the Sales worksheet. First, the European sales amount for the BrightStar 6 model should be $914,000, not $714,000. She also wants to change the label "United States" to "USA." You'll make these changes and observe how the embedded chart is automatically updated.

To update the column chart:

▶ **1.** Scroll the worksheet so both the chart and the sales data are visible.

▶ **2.** Click cell **C6**, type **914000**, and then press the **Enter** key. The data marker corresponding to European sales for the BrightStar 6 changes to reflect the new sales value.

▶ **3.** Click cell **B5**, type **USA**, and then press the **Enter** key. The x-axis reflects the change to the category name.

Creating a Pie Chart

The second chart that Alicia sketched (shown in Figure 4-2) is a pie chart that shows the relative contribution of each telescope model to the total sales. In a pie chart, the size of each slice is determined by the relative value of a single data point to the sum of all values in the data series. Unlike the column chart you just created, a pie chart has only one data series, which is the total sales for each model from all regions.

To create the pie chart:

▶ **1.** Select the nonadjacent range **A6:A9;E6:E9**, and then click the **Chart Wizard** button 📊 on the Standard toolbar. The first step of the Chart Wizard opens.

▶ **2.** Click **Pie** in the Chart type list box, make sure that the first chart sub-type **Pie** is selected, and then click the **Next** button.

Because you already selected the data series for the chart, which appears in columns, you do not have to make any changes, so you can bypass the second step of the Chart Wizard.

▶ **3.** Click the **Next** button to move to the third step of the Chart Wizard. You will enter the chart title that Alicia wants in this dialog box.

▶ **4.** Make sure that the **Titles** tab is active, click the **Chart title** text box, and then type **Total Telescope Sales**.

Next you will add data labels to the chart that display the percentage of sales for each model.

▶ **5.** Click the **Data Labels** tab, and then click the **Percentage** check box. The preview of the charts reflects the options you have chosen. See Figure 4-16.

Figure 4-16 ▶ Displaying percentage labels in a pie chart

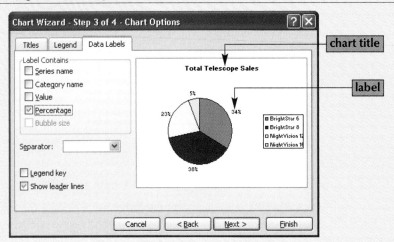

6. Click the **Next** button to display the final step of the Chart Wizard. You will place the pie chart in its own chart sheet and name the sheet "Pie Chart of Sales."

7. Click the **As new sheet** option button, and then type **Pie Chart of Sales** in the adjacent list box. The text you type in the text box will appear on the tab of the chart sheet.

8. Click the **Finish** button. Figure 4-17 shows the completed pie chart displayed on a chart sheet, which has been inserted before the Sales sheet. Note that the zoom magnification of the chart sheet on your screen might differ, depending on the settings and resolution of your monitor.

Figure 4-17 ▶ Pie chart of total telescope sales

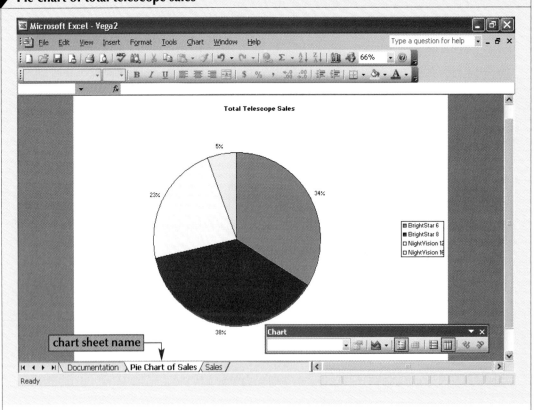

After reviewing the pie chart, Alicia has a few questions about the chart's appearance. She wonders why the slices are organized the way they are and whether the arrangement of the pie slices can be changed. The slices are arranged in a counterclockwise direction following the order that they appeared in the table. The first entry is for the BrightStar 6 telescope, the next is for the BrightStar 8, and so forth. Alicia asks whether it would be possible to move the placement of the BrightStar 6 telescope.

Rotating the Pie Chart

You cannot change the order in which the slices are arranged in the pie chart without changing their order in the data series, but you can rotate the chart. This is done by breaking the chart into 360-degree increments, starting from the top of the pie. Using this approach, the first slice starts at 0 degrees—a value that you can change. Based on Alicia's suggestion, you will change the starting point to 180 degrees, so that the first slice appears at the bottom of the pie chart.

To rotate the pie chart:

▶ 1. Double-click the pie chart to open the Format Data Series dialog box, and then click the **Options** tab.

▶ 2. Double-click the value in the Angle of first slice text box, and then click the **Degrees** up arrow to increase the angle of first slice value to **180**. As you click the up arrow, the pie chart in the preview pane rotates accordingly, as shown in Figure 4-18.

Rotating the pie chart 180 degrees ◀ **Figure 4-18**

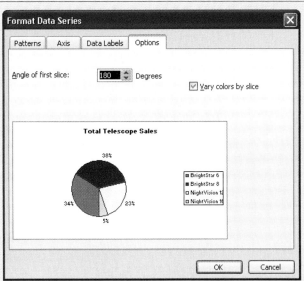

▶ 3. Click the **OK** button to close the dialog box.

Alicia tells you that the company is particularly interested in the sales performance of the BrightStar 6 telescope, because the company is considering replacing this scope with a six-inch version of the NightVision. Alicia has seen pie charts in which a single slice is removed from the others to give it greater emphasis. She wants the slice for the BrightStar 6 removed from the other slices to draw attention to this telescope.

Exploding a Slice of a Pie Chart

This method of emphasizing a particular pie slice over others is called separating or "exploding" the slice. An exploded slice is more distinctive because it is not connected to the other slices in the pie and it appears to be bigger. Excel allows you to explode any or all of the slices in the pie. A pie chart with one or more pie slices separated from the whole is referred to as an exploded pie chart.

Reference Window	**Creating an Exploded Pie Chart**

To explode one pie slice from a pie chart:
- Click the pie chart to select it, and then click the pie slice you want to explode.
- Drag the selected pie slice away from the rest of the pie, and then release the mouse button.

To explode all the pie slices in a pie chart:
- Click the pie chart to select it.
- Drag any pie slice to explode all the slices an equal distance apart, and then release the mouse button.

Next, you'll separate the BrightStar 6 telescope pie slice from the rest of the pie.

To explode the slice for the BrightStar 6 telescope:

▶ 1. Make sure that the pie chart is still selected, and then click the pie slice representing the total sales for the BrightStar 6. When you position the pointer over the pie slice, a ScreenTip appears with the corresponding worksheet cell information.

▶ 2. Drag the pie slice down and to the left. As you drag the pie slice, an outline marks your progress.

▶ 3. Release the mouse button, moving the slice into its new position. See Figure 4-19 for the location of the exploded pie slice.

Exploding a pie slice ◀ **Figure 4-19**

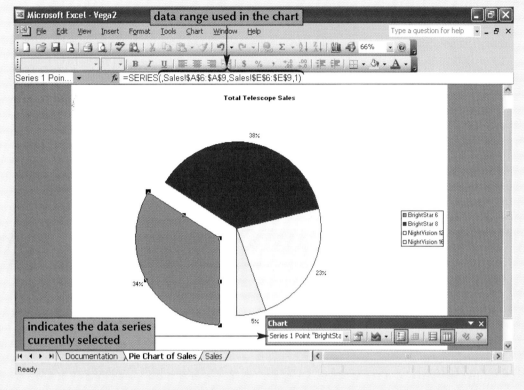

You have created the two charts that Alicia wanted, so you can save your work and then close the workbook and Excel.

▶ **4.** Save your changes to the workbook, and then close it.

Rotating the pie and exploding a pie slice are both examples of formatting the appearance of an Excel chart after it has been created with the Chart Wizard. In the next session, you will learn about the other tools available that you can use to format the charts that you create.

Session 4.1 Quick Check

Review

1. What is the difference between a chart type and a chart sub-type?
2. Which chart would you most likely use to track the daily values of a stock?
3. What is a data series?
4. What is the difference between the plot area and the chart area?
5. What are gridlines?
6. Describe the two types of chart locations.
7. A chart that shows the relative contribution of each data value to the whole is called a(n) _____ chart.
8. A pie chart in which all slices are separated from one another is called a(n) _____ chart.

Session 4.2

Modifying a Chart

In the last session, you used the Chart Wizard to create two charts. Although the Chart Wizard presents you with a variety of choices concerning your chart's appearance, the wizard does not provide every possibility. To make further modifications to your charts, you can use the formatting tools and commands available on the Chart toolbar and the Chart menu.

Editing the Data Source

After you create a chart, you can change the data that is used in the chart. You might need to change the data if you selected the wrong data or if you decide to display a different data series.

Reference Window	**Editing the Data Source of a Chart**

- Select the chart whose data source you want to edit.
- Click Chart on the menu bar, click Source Data, and then click the Series tab.
- To remove a data series, select the data series in the Series list box, and click the Remove button.
- To add a data series, click the Add button, and then select the cell references for the new data series.
- To revise a data series, select the data series in the Series list box, click the reference box for the data series, and then select a new cell reference.
- Click the OK button.

Alicia can see from the charts that 16-inch telescopes comprise a small portion of Vega's sales. For this reason, she wants you to remove the NightVision 16 from the two charts you created. You will begin by removing the NightVision 16 data series from the column chart.

To remove the NightVision 16 data series from the column chart:

1. If you took a break after the previous session, make sure that Excel is running and the Vega2 workbook is open.

2. Switch to the Sales worksheet, and then click the embedded column chart to select it.

3. Click **Chart** on the menu bar, and then click **Source Data**. The Source Data dialog box opens. Note that this dialog box is identical to the second dialog box in the Chart Wizard.

4. Click the **Series** tab, click **NightVision 16** in the Series list box, and then click the **Remove** button. The preview of the chart reflects the change you have made. See Figure 4-20.

Removing the NightVision 16 from the column chart | Figure 4-20

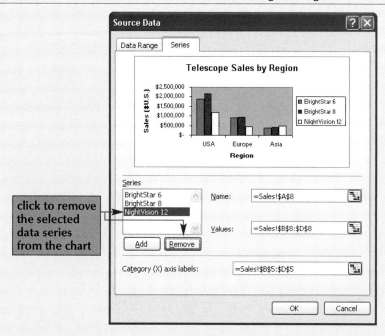

5. Click the **OK** button. The NightVision 16 sales data is no longer represented in the column chart.

Removing the NightVision 16 pie slice from the pie chart presents a slightly different challenge. Unlike the column chart (which has multiple data series), the pie chart has only one data series. To remove the NightVision 16 from the pie chart, you will have to change the cell reference of the chart's data source to exclude the NightVision 16 row.

To remove the NightVision 16 from the pie chart:

1. Switch to the Pie Chart of Sales worksheet.

2. Click **Chart** on the menu bar, click **Source Data** to open the Source Data dialog box, and then verify that the Series tab is selected. From this dialog box, you can see that the values for the data series are found in the cell range E6:E9 on the Sales worksheet and the category labels come from the range A6:A9 on the same sheet. You have to change these cell references to remove the NightVision 16 telescope from the chart.

3. Click the **Collapse Dialog Box** button for the Values reference box, select the range **E6:E8**, and then click the **Expand Dialog Box** button to redisplay the Source Data dialog box with the new value range.

4. Click the **Collapse Dialog Box** button for the Category Labels reference box, select the range **A6:A8**, and then click the **Expand Dialog Box** button to redisplay the Source Data dialog box. As shown in Figure 4-21, the preview pane displays the new pie chart with the NightVision 16 telescope excluded.

Figure 4-21 ▶ **Removing the NightVision 16 from the pie chart**

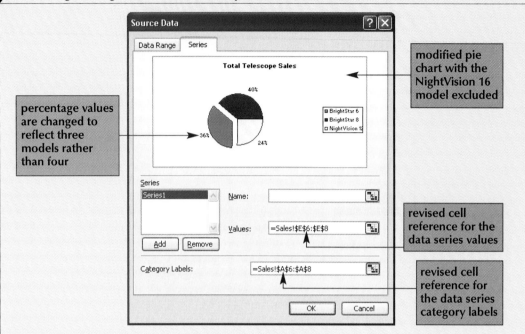

5. Click the **OK** button to save your changes to the chart.

Note that when you removed the NightVision 16 from the data series, the percentages in the pie chart changed as well to reflect a total sales figure based on only three models rather than four.

Changing the Chart Location

Alicia has decided that she prefers the chart sheet to the embedded chart. She wants you to move the embedded column chart on the Sales worksheet to a chart sheet. Rather than re-creating the chart using the Chart Wizard, you will use the Location command on the Chart menu. You will move the embedded chart to a chart sheet, which you will name "Column Chart of Sales."

To change the location of the embedded column chart:

▶ **1.** Switch to the Sales worksheet, and then, if necessary, click the embedded column chart to select it.

▶ **2.** Click **Chart** on the menu bar, and then click **Location**. The Chart Location dialog box opens. The dialog box is identical to the fourth dialog box in the Chart Wizard.

▶ **3.** Click the **As new sheet** option button, type **Column Chart of Sales** as the name of the chart sheet, and then click the **OK** button. The column chart moves into its own chart sheet.

Changing Chart Options

As mentioned, the dialog boxes to change the chart's data source and location look identical to the dialog boxes for steps 2 and 4 of the Chart Wizard. Dialog boxes for the remaining two Chart Wizard steps are also available through commands on the Chart menu. Recall that the third step of the Chart Wizard allowed you to format the chart's appearance by adding or removing chart titles, gridlines, legends, and labels.

Alicia wants to revisit some of the chart options selected earlier. After seeing that the percent labels in the pie chart provided useful information, she wants you to add labels to the column chart displaying the actual sales values for each column. You will use the Chart Options dialog box to make this change.

To revise the chart options for the column chart:

1. Click **Chart** on the menu bar, and then click **Chart Options**. The Chart Options dialog box opens. Note that the dialog box is identical to step 3 of the Chart Wizard.

2. Click the **Data Labels** tab.

3. Click the **Value** check box, and then click the **OK** button. The sales figures for each model now appear above the corresponding column. See Figure 4-22. The values appear to be a little crowded, and you will change this next.

Adding labels to the columns ◀ **Figure 4-22**

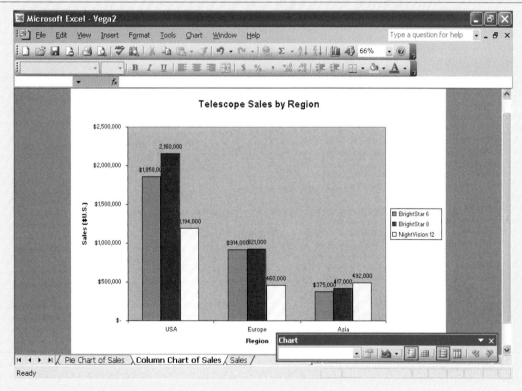

Alicia has a few changes that she wants you to make to the chart labels. You cannot make these changes by modifying the chart options. Instead, you have to format the individual elements within the chart.

Formatting Chart Elements

So far, all of the formatting that you have done has applied to the chart as a whole. You can also select and format individual chart elements, such as the chart title, legend, and axes. To select an individual chart element, you either click on the element or select the element's name from a drop-down list on the Chart toolbar. You can then use buttons on the Formatting toolbar or open a dialog box to modify the element's appearance. You can also double-click a chart element to both select it and open a dialog box or right-click the chart element and select a format from a shortcut dialog box.

In some cases, a chart element will be composed of several elements. For example, a data series will have several data markers. If you click on one data marker, you select all of the markers in the series. If you click that marker again, the selection is confined to that specific marker, removing the selection from other markers in the series. In this way, you can format all of the elements at once or confine your formatting to a specific element.

You'll have a chance to try these selection and formatting techniques in the steps that follow.

Formatting Chart Text

Alicia wants you to change the alignment of the data labels that appear above the columns. She feels that the labels would look better if you changed their alignment from horizontal to vertical. She would also like the labels to appear within and at the bottom of the columns themselves, so she suggests that you change the color of the data labels as well. You will make these changes by double-clicking the data label to open the Format Data Labels dialog box.

To format the data labels:

1. Double-click the data label **$1,858,000**, located above the first column in the chart. The Format Data Labels dialog box opens. The Format Data Labels dialog box has four tabs. You use the Font and Number tabs to change font-related options for text and values and to apply number formats to values as you did in the previous tutorial. You use the Patterns tab to change the fill color, patterns, and borders around labels. You use the Alignment tab to change the alignment of the text in the label.

   The $1,858,000 label is part of the set of labels for the BrightStar 6 data series. By double-clicking the first data label, you've selected all of the labels for this particular series. Any changes you make in this dialog box will apply to all of the labels for the BrightStar 6 sales data (but not for the labels in the other data series).

2. Click the **Font** tab, click the **Color** list box, and then click the **Yellow** square (fourth row, third column from the left) in the color palette.

   Trouble? If you are working with a black-and-white printer, select the White font color, located in the bottom-right corner of the color palette.

3. Click the **Alignment** tab.

4. In the Orientation section, change the value in the Degrees box to **90**. The text changes to a vertical orientation with an angle of 90 degrees.

5. Click the **Label Position** list arrow, and then select **Inside Base** to display the values label inside and at the base of each column in the chart. See Figure 4-23.

Changing the orientation of the data labels ◄ **Figure 4-23**

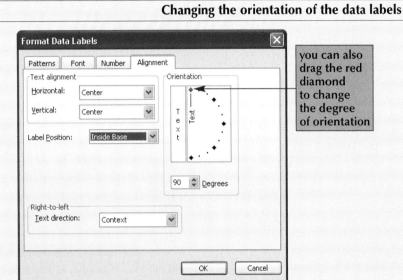

you can also drag the red diamond to change the degree of orientation

6. Click the **OK** button. The labels for the BrightStar 6 data series have been rotated 90 degrees and now appear in a yellow font at the base of the columns.

Next you'll make a similar change to the labels for the BrightStar 8 data series. Rather than double-clicking the label, you'll use the shortcut menu.

7. Right-click the **$2,160,000** label above the second column in the chart, click **Format Data Labels** from the shortcut menu, and then repeat Steps 2 through 6 to change the label to a white font rotated 90 degrees and displayed at the inside base of each column.

Finally, you'll select the data labels for the NightVision 12 data series using the Chart toolbar.

8. Click the **Chart Objects** list arrow [ ] on the Chart toolbar, scroll down the list of options, click **"NightVision 12" Data Labels** to select this chart element, and then click the **Format Data Labels** button [ ] on the Chart toolbar.

9. Repeat Steps 3 through 6 to rotate the label to **90** degrees and display it at the inside base of each column. You don't have to change the color of the font.

10. Click the **OK** button to save your changes. Figure 4-24 shows the revised labels for all of the data series in the chart.

Figure 4-24   **Revised data labels**

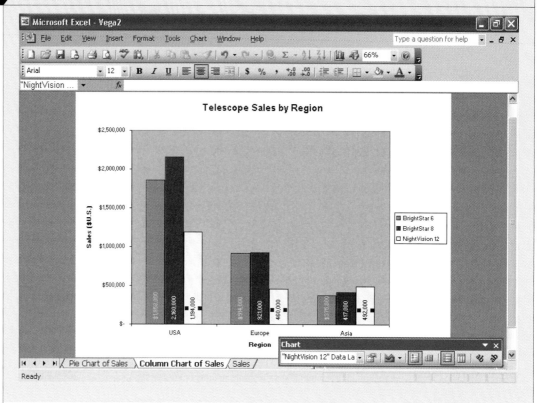

Next, Alicia wants you to add some additional text to the chart.

Inserting Unattached Text

Excel classifies chart text in three categories: label text, attached text, and unattached text. Label text includes the category names, the tick mark labels (which you've just worked with), and the legend text. Label text often is linked to cells in the worksheet. Attached text includes the chart title and the axes titles. Although the text appears in a predefined position, you can edit and move it. Unlike label text, attached text is not linked to any cells in the worksheet. Finally, unattached text is any additional text that you want to include in the chart. Unattached text can be positioned anywhere within the chart area and formatted with the same tools you use to format label and attached text.

To add unattached text to a chart, you type the text in the Formula bar. Excel automatically creates a text box for the text entry and places the text box in the chart area. You can then resize the text box and move it to another location in the chart area. You can format the text using the Format Text Box dialog box.

Inserting Unattached Text into a Chart

- Select the chart.
- In the Formula bar, type the text that you want to include in the chart.
- To resize the new unattached text box, click and drag one of the text box's selection handles.
- To move the unattached text box, click the border of the text box, and drag the text box to a new location in the chart area.
- To format the unattached text, select the text box and click the appropriate formatting buttons on the Formatting toolbar; or double-click the border of the text box to open the Format Text Box dialog box, use the options provided on the dialog box tabs, and then click the OK button.

Alicia wants you to add the text "Vega Sales from the Last Fiscal Year" to the upper-right corner of the plot area, and she wants the text to be ivory in color.

To add unattached text to the chart:

1. Click the column chart to select it, click in the Formula bar above the chart, type **Vega Sales from the Last Fiscal Year**, and then press the **Enter** key. Excel places a text box containing the new unattached text in the middle of the chart area. The text box is selected so you can modify its appearance.

2. Click the **Font Color** list arrow **A ·** on the Formatting toolbar, and then click the **Ivory** square (sixth row, third column from the left) in the color palette.

3. Move the pointer over the edge of the unattached text box until the pointer changes to ⬚, drag the text box to the upper-right corner of the plot area, and then release the mouse button. The text should now be placed in the upper-right corner of the plot.

You can double-click an unattached text box at any time to open the Format Text Box dialog box, in which you can change the font format, alignment, and color. You can also create a border around the text. Try this now by creating a yellow border.

To create a border for the text box:

1. Verify that the text box is still selected, and then double-click the border of the selected text box to open the Format Text Box dialog box.

   Trouble? If you double-clicked the text in the text box, the Format Text Box dialog box did not open. Try double-clicking the border of the text box again.

2. Click the **Colors and Lines** tab.

3. Click the **Color** list box in the Line section, click the **Ivory** square (sixth row, third column) in the color palette, and then click the **OK** button.

4. Click outside the chart to deselect it. Figure 4-25 shows the text box with the ivory border.

Figure 4-25 — **Adding unattached text to a chart**

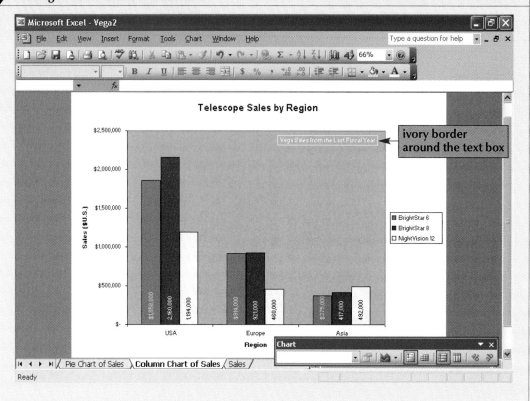

Now that you have formatted the chart labels and added unattached text, you can turn to some of the other features of Excel charts that need modifying.

Working with Colors and Fills

The formatted data labels and the unattached text help to clarify the sales data, but Alicia feels that the column chart lacks visual appeal. Alicia has seen objects filled with a variety of colors that gradually blend from one color to another. She wonders if you can do the same thing for the columns in the column chart. One idea she has is to make the columns appear more like tubes, such as telescope tubes.

When you want to fill a column (or area) in a chart with a pattern or color, you are actually modifying the appearance of the data marker in the chart. You will concentrate only on the fill color used in the data marker. Other data markers have other patterns that you can modify. For example, in an XY (scatter) chart, the data markers are points that appear in the plot. You can specify the color of those data points, their size, whether a line will connect the data points and, if so, the color, thickness, and style of that line.

You will format the data markers in the column chart beginning with the column that represents the BrightStar 6 telescope.

To format the fill color of the chart columns:

▶ **1.** Double-click the first column on the left in the chart to open the Format Data Series dialog box for that data series. You can use the options available on the different dialog box tabs to control one or more aspects of the selected data marker. For example, you use the options provided on the Patterns tab to control the border style that appears around the column as well as the interior appearance of the column. Currently, the column is format-ted with a black border and filled with a pale-blue color.

2. Click the **Fill Effects** button to open the Fill Effects dialog box. The tabs in this dialog box provide a full range of options that you can use to create sophisticated and lush colors and patterns.

3. Make sure the **Gradient** tab is displayed in the dialog box.

You use the options on the Gradient tab to create fill effects that blend together different and varying amounts of color. Three color options are:

- **One color:** To create a blend that uses different shades of one color
- **Two colors:** To create a blend from one color into another
- **Preset:** To apply a predefined blend style, including Early Sunset, Nightfall, Ocean, Rainbow, and Chrome

You can also specify the direction of the blending effect, choosing from horizontal, vertical, diagonal up, diagonal down, from corner, and from center. For the selected column in the current chart, you will create a blend fill effect using a single color starting from a dark shade of the pale-blue color. You will use a horizontal shading style to give the color dimension.

To create the fill effect:

1. Click the **One color** option button on the Gradient tab, and then drag the scroll box to the **Dark** end of the shading scale. Note that as you change the shading scale, the images in the Variants section reflect the degree of shading.

2. Click the **Vertical** option button in the Shading styles section. Now the images in the Variants section show the varying degrees of shading vertically.

3. Click the bottom-right Variants box, which shows the darker edges of the shading on the left and right edges of the object, as shown in Figure 4-26.

Specifying a fill effect   **Figure 4-26**

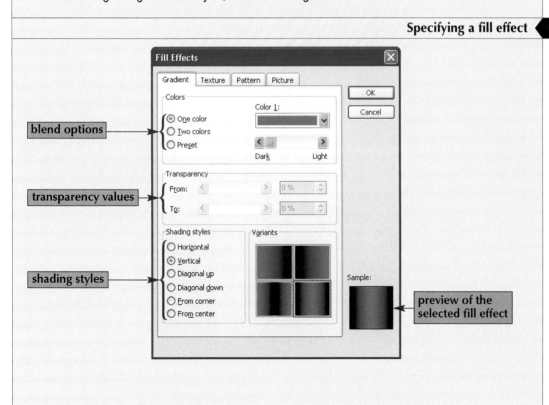

▶ **4.** Click the **OK** button twice to close the dialog boxes and redisplay the chart. Excel displays the first column series with a dark-blue color on the left and right side of the column, giving it the illusion of appearing as a tube.

Next you will create a similar blend for the other columns.

▶ **5.** Double-click the second column from the left in the chart to open the Format Data Series dialog box.

▶ **6.** Click the **Fill Effects** button to open the Fill Effects dialog box.

▶ **7.** Click the **One color** option button, drag the scroll box to the **Dark** end of the shading scale, make sure the **Vertical** option button is selected, select the bottom-right Variants option, and then click the **OK** button twice.

▶ **8.** Double-click the third column, and then repeat Steps 6 and 7 to create a one-color fill effect that goes from the dark end of the ivory scale to the light end.

▶ **9.** Click outside the chart area. Figure 4-27 shows the revised column chart with blends for each of the three data series.

| Figure 4-27 | Columns with the applied fill effects |

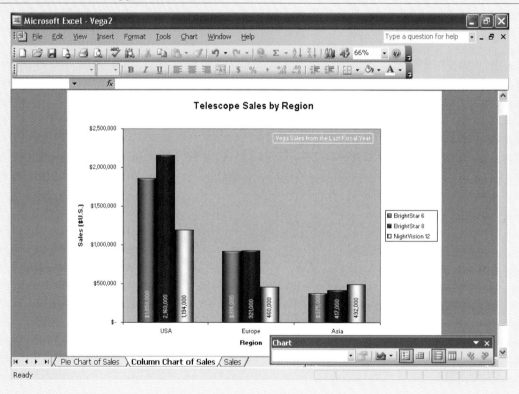

Using a Graphic Image as a Background

Next Alicia wants to replace the solid gray background with a graphic image. She has a graphic file that shows an image from the Hubble telescope, which she thinks would work well with the theme of telescope sales.

To insert this image into the chart, you will open the Format Plot Area dialog box.

To fill the plot area with an image:

▶ **1.** Click the **Chart Objects** list arrow [   ] on the Chart toolbar, click **Plot Area**, and then click the **Format Plot Area** button 🖼 on the Chart toolbar. The Format Plot Area dialog box opens.

▶ **2.** Click the **Fill Effects** button on the Patterns tab to open the Fill Effects dialog box.

▶ **3.** Click the **Picture** tab, and then click the **Select Picture** button. The Select Picture dialog box opens.

▶ **4.** Navigate to the Tutorial.04\Tutorial folder, select the **Space** file, and then click the **Insert** button. The image appears in the Fill Effects dialog box.

▶ **5.** Click the **OK** button twice to close the dialog boxes, and then click outside the chart area. Figure 4-28 shows the revised column chart with the new background image.

Chart with space background image ◀ **Figure 4-28**

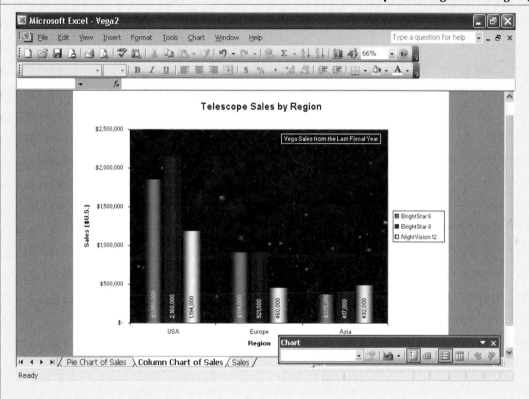

Graphic images can be applied to other elements in the chart. For example, you can replace the data markers in the chart with graphic images. To do this, select the data markers and open the Fill Effects dialog box that you used to create a background image for the chart. Select the image file that you want to use in place of the data marker. If you are working with a column chart, you can also choose to either stack or stretch the chosen image to the height of the column. Figure 4-29 shows the effect of these two options on the appearance of the column chart.

Figure 4-29 **Replacing columns with graphics**

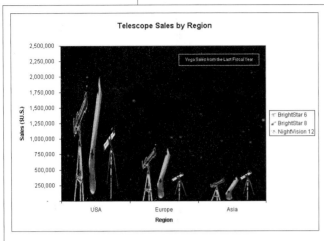

the Stretch option stretches the graphic over the height of the column

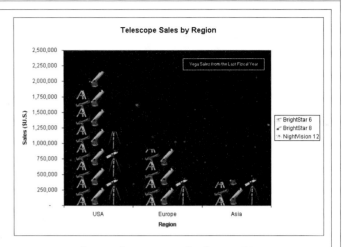

the Stack option stacks the graphic up to the height of the column

Excel provides several ways of adding special effects to your charts, and you must be careful not to overdo it. Some effects, however interesting, can actually make your charts more difficult to read and interpret. Remember also that some of your effects may look good in color, but will not transfer well to a black-and-white printout.

Changing the Axis Scale

Alicia might want you to make one other change to the column chart. She knows that the scale used by the chart is automatically set by Excel. Excel uses the data that you have plotted and determines an appropriate scale for the y-axis, usually designed to cover a range of reasonable values. Alicia wants you to examine the scale that Excel set for this chart to see if a change is warranted. She also thinks that expressing the sales in terms of dollars on the chart is a bit unwieldy for sales of this magnitude. She would rather have the sales expressed in terms of thousands of dollars.

To view the y-axis scale:

1. Click the **Chart Objects** list arrow [   ] on the Chart toolbar, click **Value Axis**, and then click the **Format Axis** button on the Chart toolbar. The Format Axis dialog box opens. You can use this dialog box to format the scale's appearance and to change the range and increments used in the scale.

2. Click the **Scale** tab. See Figure 4-30.

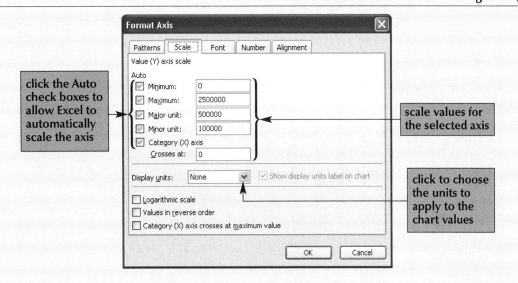

click the Auto check boxes to allow Excel to automatically scale the axis

scale values for the selected axis

click to choose the units to apply to the chart values

There are four values that comprise the scale: the minimum, maximum, major unit, and minor unit. The minimum and maximum values are the smallest and largest tick marks that appear on the axis. The major unit is the increment between the scale's **major tick marks**. The chart also has a second set of tick marks, called **minor tick marks**, that may or may not be displayed. The difference between major and minor tick marks is that axis values appear next to major tick marks, whereas no values appear next to minor tick marks.

In the current chart, the scale that Excel displayed ranges from 0 to 2,500,000 in increments of 500,000. The minor tick mark increment is 100,000, but these tick marks are not displayed on the axes. Alicia wants to reduce the increment value to 250,000 in order to show more detail on the chart. Then she wants to change the display units from none to thousands.

To revise the y-axis scale:

► **1.** Double-click the current entry in the Major unit box, and then type **250000**. Note that when you manually change a scale value its Auto check box is automatically deselected.

► **2.** Click the **Display units** list arrow, and then select **Thousands** in the list.

► **3.** Make sure that the **Show display units label on chart** check box is selected, and then click the **OK** button. Figure 4-31 shows the revised y-axis scale.

Figure 4-31 **Revised scale for the y-axis**

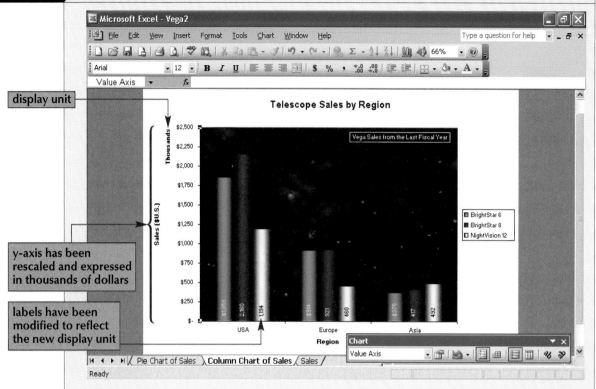

display unit

y-axis has been rescaled and expressed in thousands of dollars

labels have been modified to reflect the new display unit

In this chart, $2,500,000 is displayed as $2,500. Because you have changed the display units in this way, you need to include information about the new value. Excel does this for you by adding the text "Thousands" to the value axis. Also note that the label values for each column now use the thousands display unit, so the Asian sales for the BrightStar 6 are displayed as $375 rather than $375,000.

Pleased with the latest version of the column chart, Alicia now wants you to go back to the pie chart and make some modifications there.

Working with Three-Dimensional Charts

Many of the Excel charts can be displayed either as two-dimensional "flat" charts or as charts that appear in three dimensions. Alicia wants you to change the pie chart to a three-dimensional pie chart. To do this, you have to change the chart type.

To change the pie chart to 3-D:

▶ **1.** Switch to the Pie Chart of Sales chart sheet.

▶ **2.** Click **Chart** on the menu bar, and then click **Chart Type**. The Chart Type dialog box opens.

▶ **3.** Click the second chart sub-type in the top row, as shown in Figure 4-32.

Changing to a 3-D pie chart ◀ **Figure 4-32**

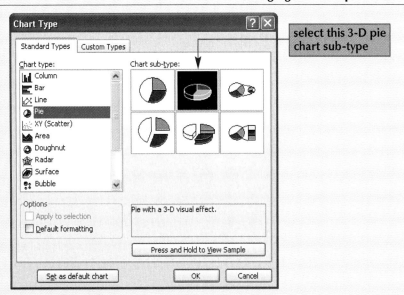

select this 3-D pie chart sub-type

4. Click the **OK** button. Excel displays the pie chart in three dimensions. Note that Excel has retained the rotation you applied to the chart in the last session, and the BrightStar 6 slice is still exploded. See Figure 4-33.

3-D pie chart ◀ **Figure 4-33**

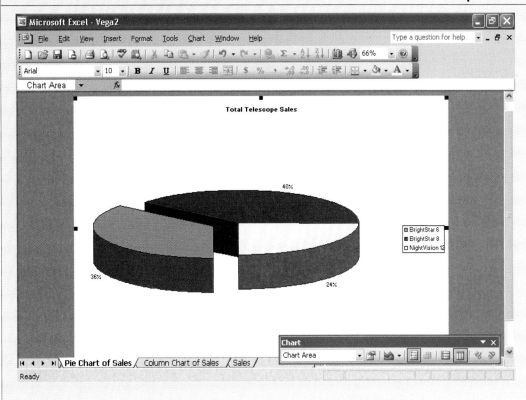

In a 3-D chart, you have several options to modify the 3-D effect. One of these is **elevation**, which is the illusion that you're looking at the 3-D chart from either above or below the chart. Another of these is **perspective**, which is the illusion that some parts of the 3-D chart are farther away from you than others. Finally, you can rotate a 3-D chart to bring different parts of the chart to the forefront. In a pie chart, you can change the elevation and rotation, but not the perspective.

Alicia likes the 3-D view of the pie chart but feels that the angle of the pie is too low. She wants you to change the angle of the pie so that the viewer is looking "down" on the chart more.

To increase the elevation above the pie chart:

1. Click **Chart** on the menu bar, and then click **3-D View**. The 3-D View dialog box opens.

2. Click the **Elevation** up button twice to increase the elevation to **25** degrees. See Figure 4-34. Note that there are also buttons that you can use to rotate the pie chart. Clicking one of the rotation buttons is similar to the rotation setting that you applied to the pie chart at the end of the first session.

| Figure 4-34 | 3-D View dialog box |

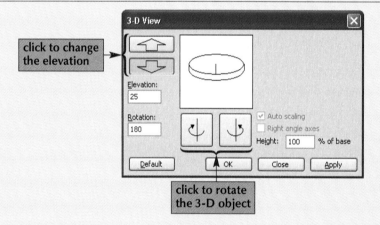

3. Click the **OK** button. Excel redraws the pie chart, giving the illusion that the observer is at an elevation above the chart.

The charts you have created present the sales data effectively, but Alicia also wants to be sure that the top-selling telescope model is clearly illustrated.

Using the Drawing Toolbar

One of the big stories from the past fiscal year was the successful introduction of the NightVision telescopes, and Alicia wants to highlight the fact that the company had in excess of $1,800,000 in sales of the NightVision 12. She has seen charts that contain shapes, like starbursts and block arrows, that give added emphasis to details and facts contained in the chart. Alicia wants to do something similar with the pie chart.

To create a graphical shape, you can use the tools provided on the Drawing toolbar. The Drawing toolbar is a common feature of all Office 2003 products. You can use the Drawing toolbar to add text boxes, lines, block arrows, and other objects to charts and worksheets. In Excel, an **object** is any entity that can be manipulated. A chart is an Excel object, as are its elements. Next, you will learn how to use the Drawing toolbar to create and format one type of object, an AutoShape.

Displaying the Drawing Toolbar

Depending on your Excel configuration, the Drawing toolbar may or may not be displayed in the Excel window when you start Excel. (The default is to not show the toolbar.) As with all toolbars, you can choose to display or hide the Drawing toolbar. Although you can display the Drawing toolbar using the View menu, you will display the toolbar by clicking the Drawing button on the Standard toolbar.

To display the Drawing toolbar:

▶ 1. Click the **Drawing** button ⬚ on the Standard toolbar. The Drawing toolbar appears in the workbook window.

▶ 2. If necessary, drag the Drawing toolbar to the bottom of the worksheet window, and then release the mouse button. The Drawing toolbar should now be anchored to the bottom of the window.

Now you will use the Drawing toolbar to add a drawing object to the pie chart.

Working with AutoShapes

The Drawing toolbar contains a list of predefined shapes called **AutoShapes**. These AutoShapes can be simple squares or circles or more complicated objects such as flow chart objects and block arrows. Once you insert an AutoShape into a chart or worksheet, you can resize and move it, like any other object. You can modify the fill color of an AutoShape, change the border style, and even insert text.

Inserting an AutoShape	Reference Window

- Click the AutoShapes list arrow on the Drawing toolbar.
- Point to the AutoShape category that you want to use, and then click the AutoShape that you want to create.
- Position the crosshair pointer over the location for the AutoShape in the chart or worksheet, and then drag the pointer over the area where you want the shape to appear. To draw an AutoShape in the same proportion as the shape on the palette, press and hold the Shift key as you drag the pointer to draw the shape.
- Release the mouse button.
- To resize an AutoShape, click the shape to select it, and then drag one of the nine selection handles.
- To rotate an AutoShape, click the green rotation handle that is connected to the shape, and drag the handle to rotate the shape.
- To change the shape of the AutoShape, click the yellow diamond tool, and then drag the tool to change the shape.

You will now add a multi-pointed star to the pie chart to highlight the success of the NightVision 12 telescope.

To add a multi-pointed AutoShape star to the pie chart:

▶ **1.** Click the **AutoShapes** list arrow on the Drawing toolbar, point to **Stars and Banners**, and then click the **16-Point Star** AutoShape (second row, second column from the left) on the AutoShapes palette. A ScreenTip appears when you position the pointer over an AutoShape on the palette so you will know which shape you are selecting.

▶ **2.** Move the pointer to the upper-right corner of the chart area, about one inch to the right of the chart title. As you move the pointer over the worksheet, the pointer shape changes to $+$.

To draw an AutoShape in the same proportion as the shape on the palette, you must press and hold the Shift key as you drag the pointer to draw the shape.

▶ **3.** Press and hold the **Shift** key, and then click and drag the pointer down and to the right about one and one-half inches. Note that pressing the Shift key allows you to create a perfect 16-point star; otherwise, the shape might be lopsided.

▶ **4.** Release the mouse button. A 16-point star appears in the upper-right corner of the chart area. See Figure 4-35.

| Figure 4-35 | Adding an AutoShape to the pie chart |

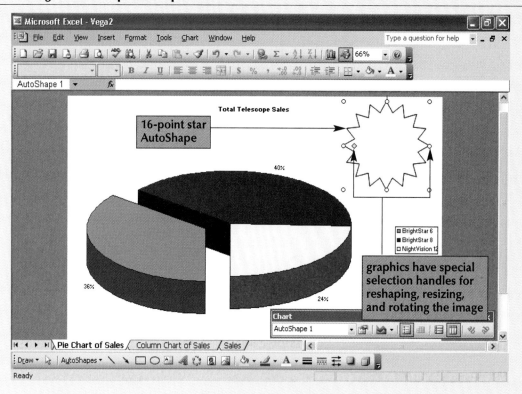

Trouble? If the AutoShape on your screen does not match the size and shape of the AutoShape shown in the figure, you can resize the object again by pressing and holding the Shift key as you drag a selection handle. Or click the Undo button on the Standard toolbar to delete the object, and then repeat Steps 1 through 4 to redraw the AutoShape, being sure to press and hold the Shift key to draw the object proportionally.

You probably noticed that the selection handles of the AutoShape appear as open circles and that there is also a diamond tool. You can use the diamond tool to change the shape of the AutoShape. For example, you can change the size of the jagged points of the star by dragging the diamond tool either toward the center of the star (to increase the size of the points) or away from the center (to decrease the size of the points). You may have also noticed a green selection handle that is attached to the AutoShape through a vertical line. This is a rotation handle. By clicking and dragging this handle, you can rotate the AutoShape.

Formatting an AutoShape

In addition to modifying the shape, size, and rotation of an AutoShape, you can add text to it. To add text to an AutoShape, you first select it and then start typing the desired text. The text will automatically be placed within the boundaries of the shape.

Reference Window

Inserting Text into an AutoShape

- Click the border of the AutoShape to select the object.
- Type the text you want to appear in the AutoShape.
- Select the text within the AutoShape.
- Format the text using the options on the Formatting toolbar.
- Click outside of the shape to deselect it.

To highlight the success of the NightVision 12, you will add the text that Alicia wants to the AutoShape star.

To insert text into the AutoShape:

1. Make sure that the 16-point star is still selected.
2. Type **NightVision 12 Sales Exceed $1.8 Million!**
3. Click **Format** on the menu bar, click **AutoShape** to open the Format AutoShape dialog box, and then click the **Alignment** tab.

   Trouble? If there is no Alignment tab in the dialog box that opens, close the dialog box. Click the AutoShape again, making sure that the object, and not just its frame, is selected. Then repeat Step 3.
4. Click the **Horizontal** list arrow, and then click **Center**.
5. Click the **Vertical** list arrow, click **Center**, and then click the **OK** button.

   Trouble? If the text does not wrap logically within the boundaries of the AutoShape, resize the star to better accommodate the text.

The star with text adds value to the overall appearance of the chart. However, the star could use some background color to make it more visually interesting. In keeping with the other colors you have been using in the charts, you will format the AutoShape by adding a yellow background.

To change the background color of the AutoShape:

1. Make sure the 16-point star is still selected.
2. Click the **Fill Color** list arrow on the Drawing toolbar, and then click the **Ivory** square (sixth row, third column) in the color palette.

   Trouble? If the background color does not change to ivory, you may have selected the text in the star rather than the star itself. Click the Undo button on the Standard toolbar, and then repeat Steps 1 and 2, being sure to select the AutoShape.

The AutoShape definitely looks better with the ivory background. You decide to try one more thing: if adding a shadow effect to the star will be too much or will add depth to the object. To add a shadow effect to an object, you can choose one of the available shadow effects provided on the Drawing toolbar.

To add a drop shadow to the AutoShape:

1. Make sure the 16-point star is still selected.
2. Click the **Shadow Style** button 🔲 on the Drawing toolbar to display the gallery of shadow options.
3. Click **Shadow Style 6** (second row, second column from the left) in the shadow gallery, and then click outside the star to deselect it.

   As a final step, Alicia feels that the pie chart is a little too far to the left. You will move it down and to the right to center it better.
4. Click the **Chart Objects** list arrow [_____] on the Chart toolbar, and then click **Plot Area**.
5. Click on the gray selection border around the plot area, drag the border down and to the right, and then click outside the chart area. Figure 4-36 shows the revised pie chart with the formatted AutoShape and the relocated pie.

Figure 4-36   Drop shadow added to the 16-point star AutoShape

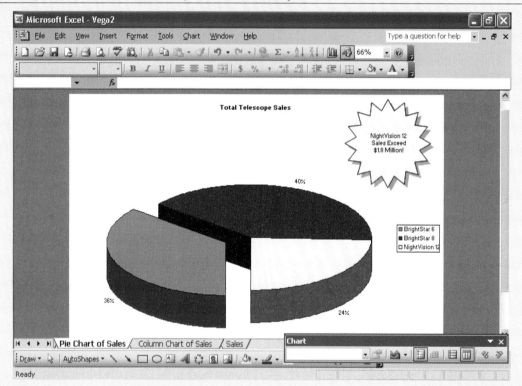

Alicia doesn't want any other changes to be made, so you will hide the Drawing toolbar, which will increase the workspace on your screen.

6. Click the **Drawing** button 🔲 on the Formatting toolbar. The Drawing toolbar closes.

Printing Your Charts

Now that you have completed your work on the two charts for Alicia, you will make hard copies of them. Printing a chart sheet is similar to printing a worksheet. As when printing a worksheet, you should preview the printout before sending the worksheet to the printer. From the Print Preview window, you can add headers and footers and control the page layout, just as you do for printing the contents of your worksheets. You also have the added option of resizing the chart to fit within the confines of a single printed page.

To print both charts at the same time, you will select both chart sheets, open Print Preview, and then set up each chart to print on its own page.

To set up the two charts for printing:

1. Make sure the Pie Chart of Sales worksheet is the current sheet.
2. Press and hold the **Shift** key, and then click the **Column Chart of Sales** tab. Both chart sheets are selected.
3. Click the **Print Preview** button ▨ on the Standard toolbar. The Print Preview window opens, showing the pie chart on the first of two pages.
4. Click the **Setup** button on the Print Preview toolbar to open the Page Setup dialog box. The Page Setup options are similar to the options for printing a worksheet, except that a new dialog box tab, Chart, appears.
5. Click the **Chart** tab. See Figure 4-37.

Chart tab in the Page Setup dialog box ◀ **Figure 4-37**

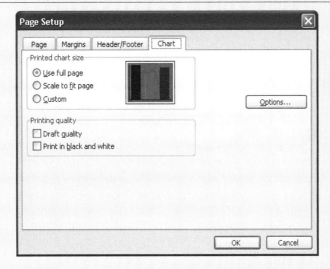

Excel provides three choices for defining the size of a chart printout. These are:

- **Use full page:** The chart is resized to fit the full page, extending to fit the full width and height of the page. The proportions of the chart may change since it is extended in all directions to fit the page. This is the default option.
- **Scale to fit page:** The chart is resized until one of the edges reaches a page margin. The chart expands in both dimensions (width and height) proportionally until one dimension fills the space between the margins.
- **Custom:** The dimensions of the printed chart are specified on the chart sheet using the Zoom tool.

You will use the Scale to fit page option because you do not want to have the charts resized disproportionately.

To set the size of the charts:

▶ **1.** Click the **Scale to fit page** option button, and then click the **OK** button. The Use full page option and the Scale to fit page option will often result in charts that are close in the same size. You may not see much difference in the chart size in the Print Preview window.

▶ **2.** Click the **Next** button to preview the column chart printout.

▶ **3.** Click the **Setup** button, click the **Scale to fit page** option button on the Chart tab, and then click the **OK** button.

▶ **4.** Click the **Print** button to open the Print dialog box, make any necessary changes, and then click the **OK** button to send both chart sheets to the printer.

For now, there are no other changes to be made. Alicia will use the printouts of the charts at the meeting next week.

▶ **5.** Save your changes to the workbook and then close it

Alicia is pleased with the results and will get back to you with any other tasks she might need you to do before the sales meeting next week.

Review

Session 4.2 Quick Check

1. How would you remove a data series from a column chart?
2. How would you change the location (either embedded or as a chart sheet) of a chart?
3. What is the difference between label text, attached text, and unattached text?
4. What is the difference between major tick marks and minor tick marks?
5. How would you change a column chart into a 3-D column chart?
6. What is an AutoShape?
7. Describe the three options for sizing a chart on the printed page.

Review

Tutorial Summary

In this tutorial, you learned how to work with charts in Excel. You saw how to use Excel's Chart Wizard to create a basic chart and learned about the different types of charts that can be created by Excel. You also learned how to embed charts within a worksheet or place them on their own chart sheet in the workbook. You used Excel's editing tools to modify the chart's appearance by inserting additional text, changing font and background colors and images, rotating the chart in three dimensions, and changing the scale of the chart. This tutorial also introduced you to the Drawing toolbar, which you used to create an AutoShape, placing that shape on a chart to provide additional emphasis on key points. Finally, you learned about the different options Excel provides for printing your completed charts.

Key Terms

active chart	chart title	embedded chart
attached text	Chart Wizard	exploded pie chart
AutoShape	data marker	gridline
category values	data series	horizontal axis
chart	data source	label text
chart area	data value	legend
chart sheet	elevation	major gridline

major tick mark	plot area	vertical axis
minor gridline	scale	x-axis
minor tick mark	tick mark	x value
object	unattached text	y-axis
perspective		

Review Assignments

Data File needed for the Review Assignments: VegaUSA1.xls

Alicia has another workbook that shows the monthly United States sales for the three major telescope models. She wants you to create a column chart showing the monthly United States sales figures and a pie chart showing the total sales figures for each telescope model. To complete this task:

1. Open the **VegaUSA1** workbook located in the Tutorial.04\Review folder included with your Data Files, and then save the workbook as **VegaUSA2** to the same folder.
2. Enter your name and the current date in the Documentation sheet, and then switch to the Monthly Sales worksheet.
3. Select the range A6:D18, and then start the Chart Wizard.
4. Use the Chart Wizard to create a column chart, using the first chart sub-type. Specify "United States Telescope Sales" as the chart title, "Month" as the x-axis title, and "Sales ($U.S.)" as the y-axis title. Place the chart on a chart sheet named "Monthly Sales Chart."
5. Format the x-axis labels, changing the alignment to 90 degrees.
6. Change the scale of the y-axis using thousands as the display unit.
7. Change the background color of the plot area to white.
8. Place the chart legend at the bottom of the chart. (*Hint*: Open the Format Legend dialog box and select the Bottom option on the Placement tab.)
9. Use the Drawing toolbar to create an 8-point star located in the upper-left corner of the chart area.
10. Insert the text "NightVision 12 sales remained high in Autumn!" into the 8-point star you just created. Center the text both horizontally and vertically.
11. Change the fill color of the 8-point star to ivory, and apply Shadow Style 1 to the shape.
12. Return to the Monthly Sales worksheet, select the nonadjacent range B6:D6;B19:D19, and use the Chart Wizard to create a pie chart of the data. Assign the chart the title "Pie Chart of Total Sales" and display the sales values next to the pie slices. Place the pie chart in a chart sheet named "Pie Chart of Total Sales."
13. Apply the Late Sunrise fill effect to the pie chart's chart area.
14. Select both charts, and then open the Print Preview window.
15. Use the Setup dialog box to scale both charts to fit their respective pages and to add a footer to the charts displaying your name and the date in the lower-right corner of the page. Print the charts.
16. Save your changes to the workbook and then close it.

Case Problem 1

Data File needed for this Case Problem: CIC1.xls

Cast Iron Concepts Andrea Puest, the regional sales manager of Cast Iron Concepts (CIC), a distributor of cast-iron stoves, is required to present a report of the company's first-quarter sales for the states of New Hampshire, Vermont, and Maine. Her sales data covers four major models: Star Windsor, Box Windsor, West Windsor, and Circle Windsor. The Circle Windsor is CIC's latest entry in the cast-iron stove market.

Andrea will make a presentation of her sales figures next month and has asked for your help in creating a chart showing the sales results. She wants to create a 3-D column chart, with each column representing the sales for a particular model and state. To complete this task:

1. Open the **CIC1** workbook located in the Tutorial.04\Cases folder included with your Data Files, and then save the file as **CIC2** to the same folder.
2. Enter your name and the current date in the Documentation sheet, and then switch to the Sales worksheet.
3. Select the range A5:D9, and then start the Chart Wizard.
4. Use the Chart Wizard to create an embedded 3-D column chart that compares values across categories and across series. The data series in the chart should be organized by columns, not rows. Specify "Windsor Stove Sales" as the chart title. Do not specify titles for the axes. Do not include a legend.
5. Move the embedded chart so that the upper-left corner of the chart is located in cell A11, and then resize the chart so that it covers the range A11:E32.
6. Change the font of the chart title to a 14-point, bold, dark-blue Arial font.
7. Add the subtitle "1/1/2006 - 3/31/2006" as unattached text to the chart. Format the text in an 8-point, bold, dark-blue Arial font and place it under the chart's main title.

Explore
8. Change the color of the chart area to tan.
9. Change the 3-D view of the chart so that its elevation equals 10 degrees, its rotation equals 120 degrees, and its perspective equals 15.
10. Change the font of the y-axis (also called the "series axis") labels (the names of the states) to an 8-point regular Arial font.
11. Change the font of the x-axis labels (the model names) to an 8-point regular Arial font, displayed at a –90 degree angle.

Explore
12. Select the walls of the 3-D plot, and change the wall color to white.
13. Center the contents of the worksheet horizontally on the page, and then add a header that displays your name and the date in the upper-right corner of the worksheet.
14. Preview and then print the worksheet.
15. Save your changes to the workbook, and then close it.

Case Problem 2

Challenge

Broaden your knowledge and challenge your skills by exploring how to use Excel to create a Pareto quality control chart.

Data File needed for this Case Problem: Powder1.xls

Dantalia Baby Powder Kemp Wilson is a quality control engineer for Dantalia Baby Powder. Part of the company's manufacturing process involves a machine called a "filler," which pours a specified amount of powder into bottles. Sometimes the heads on the filler become partially clogged, causing the bottles to be under-filled. If that happens, the bottles must be rejected. On each assembly line, there are a certain number of bottles rejected during each shift.

Kemp's job is to monitor the number of defective bottles and locate the fillers that may have clogged filler heads. One of the tools he uses to do this is a Pareto chart. A Pareto chart is a column chart in which each column represents the total number of defects assigned to different parts of the production process. In this case, the columns would represent the 24 different fillers in the assembly line. The columns are sorted so that the part that caused the most defects is displayed first, the second-most is displayed second, and so forth. Superimposed on the columns is a line that displays the cumulative percentage of defects for all of the parts. Thus, by viewing the cumulative percentages, you can determine, for example, what percentages of the total defects are due to the three worst parts. In this way, Kemp can isolate the problem filler heads and report how much they contribute to the total defects.

Kemp has a worksheet listing the number of defects per filler head from a recent shift. The data is already sorted going from the filler head with the most defects to the one with the fewest. The cumulative percent values have also been calculated already. Kemp wants you to create a Pareto chart based on this data. To complete this task:

1. Open the **Powder1** workbook located in the Tutorial.04\Cases folder included with your Data Files, and then save the file as **Powder2** to the same folder.
2. Enter your name and the current date in the Documentation sheet, and then switch to the Quality Control Data worksheet.
3. Select the range A5:C29, and then start the Chart Wizard.

Explore

4. Use the Chart Wizard to create a custom chart, selecting the Line – Column on 2 Axes option in the Custom Types list box. Specify "Filler Head Under Fills" as the chart title. Specify "Filler Head" as the x-axis title, "Count of Under Fills" as the y-axis title, and "Cumulative Percentage" as the second y-axis title. Do not include a legend. Place the chart on a chart sheet named "Pareto Chart."
5. Change the alignment of the x-axis labels to an angle of 90 degrees.
6. Change the alignment of the second y-axis title to –90 degrees.

Explore
Explore

7. Change the scale of the second y-axis so that the values range from 0 to 1.0.
8. Select the data series that displays the number of defects for each filler head, and add data labels that display the number of defects above each column. Do *not* display labels above the lines that represent the cumulative percentages. (*Hint*: Use the Data Labels tab in the Format Data Series dialog box.)

Explore

9. From the Format Data Series dialog box for the chart's columns, use the Options tab to reduce the gap separating the columns to 0 pixels.
10. Change the fill color of the chart columns and the plot area to white.
11. Examine the Pareto chart, and determine approximately what percentage of the total number of defects can be attributed to the three worst filler heads.
12. Add a header to the Pareto Chart sheet that displays the name of the worksheet in the center and your name and the date on the right of the page, and then print the Pareto chart.
13. Save your changes to the workbook, and then close it.

Challenge

Go beyond what you've learned in the tutorial by exploring how to use Excel to chart stock market data.

Case Problem 3

Data File needed for this Case Problem: Pixal1.xls

Charting Stock Activity You work with Lee Whyte, a stock analyst who plans to publish a Web site on stocks. One component of the Web site will be a five-week record of the activity of various key stocks. Lee has asked for your help in setting up an Excel workbook to keep a running record of the trading volume, open, high, low, and close values of some of the stocks he's tracking.

Lee wants you to create a stock market chart of the activity of Pixal Inc. stock as a sample. The last six weeks of the stock's performance have been saved in a workbook. He wants you to create a chart sheet for the data that has been entered. To complete this task:

1. Open the **Pixal1** workbook located in the Tutorial.04\Cases folder included with your Data Files, and then save the file as **Pixal2** to the same folder.
2. Enter your name and the current date in the Documentation sheet, and then switch to the Pixal Data worksheet.
3. Select the range B6:G36, and then start the Chart Wizard.

4. Use the Chart Wizard to create a stock chart using the Volume-Open-High-Low-Close sub-type. Specify "Pixal Inc." as the chart title. Specify "Date" as the x-axis title, "Volume (mil)" as the y-axis title, and "Price" as the second y-axis title. Remove the gridlines and do not include a legend. Place the chart in a chart sheet named "Pixal Chart."

5. Change the scale of the first y-axis so that the scale ranges from 0 to 5 with a major unit of 0.5.

6. Change the scale of the second y-axis so that the scale ranges from 15 to 21 with a major unit of 1.

7. Change the alignment of the second y-axis title to –90 degrees.

Explore ▶ 8. Change the scale of the x-axis so that the major unit occurs every seven days.

9. Double-click the column data series that displays the volume of shares traded and, using the Options tab, reduce the gap between adjacent columns to 0 pixels.

10. Change the fill color of the plot area to light yellow.

11. Change the font size of the chart title to 16 points.

Explore ▶ 12. In the upper-right corner of the plot area, insert the Rounded Rectangular Callout AutoShape from the Drawing toolbar. Enter the following quote into the AutoShape: "Pixal Inc. is experiencing a tough first quarter" – Stock Reviews
Format the text in a bold, red, 14-point font. Resize the AutoShape if necessary.

13. Add the Shadow Style 6 drop shadow to the AutoShape.

14. Add your name and the date to the right section of the header. Scale the chart to fit the page in landscape orientation.

15. Save the changes, and then print the chart sheet.

Explore ▶ 16. Lee has a new week's worth of data for the Pixal worksheet. Enter the data shown in Figure 4-38 to the table of stock activity, and then modify that chart's data source to include the new data values for each data series.

Figure 4-38 ▶

Date	Volume (mil)	Open	High	Low	Close
2/17/2006	0.35	16.30	16.95	16.75	16.85
2/18/2006	0.45	16.85	17.20	17.05	17.15
2/19/2006	0.52	17.15	17.45	17.25	17.25
2/20/2006	0.40	17.25	17.35	16.95	17.25
2/21/2006	0.38	17.25	17.55	16.75	16.95

17. Save your changes to a new workbook named **Pixal3** in the Cases folder, and then reprint the chart sheet with the new data values. Close the workbook.

Create

Test your knowledge of charts by creating a workbook with an XY (scatter) chart that presents data from a cancer research study.

Case Problem 4

There are no Data Files needed for this Case Problem.

Relating Cancer Rates to Temperature A 1965 study analyzed the relationship between the mean annual temperature in 16 regions in Great Britain and the annual mortality rates in those regions for a certain type of breast cancer. Lynn Watson is working on a symposium on the history of breast cancer research and has asked you to chart the data from this historic study. Figure 4-39 shows a preview of the workbook and chart that you'll create.

Figure 4-39

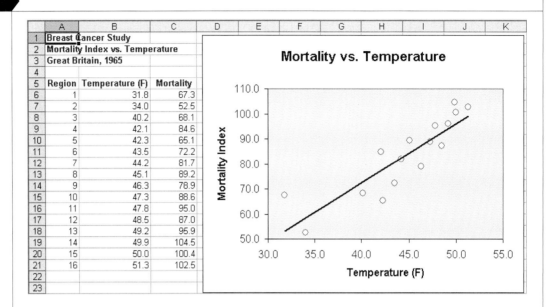

To complete this task:

1. Create a new workbook and save it as **BCancer** in the Tutorial.04\Cases folder included with your Data Files. The workbook should contain a Documentation sheet displaying your name, the date, and the purpose of the workbook. Name one of the other work-sheets "Breast Cancer Data," and then add the titles and data shown in Figure 4-39.

Explore

2. Use the Chart Wizard to create an embedded XY (scatter) chart with no data points connected. Specify "Mortality vs. Temperature" as the chart title. Specify "Temperature (F)" as the title of the x-axis and "Mortality Index" as the title of the y-axis. Remove the gridlines. Do not include a legend. The scatter chart should be embedded on the Breast Cancer Data worksheet.

3. Change the scale of the x-axis to cover the temperature range 30 to 55 degrees Fahrenheit.

4. Change the scale of the y-axis to cover the mortality index range 50 to 110.

Explore

5. Double-click one of the data points in the chart to open the Format Data Series dialog box, and make the following changes to the appearance of the data points:
   - Change the marker style to a circle that is 7 points in size.
   - Change the background color of the circle to white.
   - Change the foreground color of the circle to red.

Explore

6. Open the Add Trendline dialog box from the Chart menu, and select the Linear trend line option on the Type tab. The purpose of the linear trend line is to display whether a linear relationship exists between the 16 regions' mean annual temperature and their annual mortality index. Does it appear that such a relationship exists? What does a high mean annual temperature imply about the annual mortality index?

7. Change the fill color of the plot area to light yellow.

8. Set up the worksheet to print in landscape orientation, centered horizontally and ver-tically on the page. Enter your name and the date in the right section of the page's header. Print the chart.

9. Save your changes to the workbook and close it.

Research

Use the Internet to find and work with data related to the topics presented in this tutorial.

Internet Assignments

The purpose of the Internet Assignments is to challenge you to find information on the Internet that you can use to work effectively with this software. The actual assignments are updated and maintained on the Course Technology Web site. Log on to the Internet and use your Web browser to go to the Student Online Companion for New Perspectives Office 2003 at **www.course.com/np/office2003**. Click the Internet Assignments link, and then navigate to the assignments for this tutorial.

Assess

SAM Assessment and Training

If you have a SAM user profile, you may have access to hands-on instruction, practice, and assessment of the skills covered in this tutorial. Log in to your SAM account and go to your assignments page to see what your instructor has assigned.

Review

Quick Check Answers

Session 4.1

1. A chart type is one of the 14 styles of charts supported by Excel. Each chart type has various alternate formats, called chart sub-types.
2. stock chart
3. A data series is a range of data values that is plotted on a chart.
4. The plot area contains the actual data values that are plotted in the chart, as well as any background colors or images for that plot. The chart area contains the plot area and any other element (such as titles and legend boxes) that may be included in the chart.
5. Gridlines are lines that extend out from the tick marks on either axis into the plot area.
6. embedded charts, which are placed within a worksheet, and chart sheets, which contain only the chart itself
7. pie
8. exploded pie

Session 4.2

1. Click Chart on the menu bar, click Source Data, click the Series tab, select the data series in the Series list box, and then click the Remove button.
2. Click Chart on the menu bar, click Location, and then select a new location.
3. Label text is text that consists of category names, tick mark labels, and legend text. Attached text is text that is attached to other elements of the chart, such as the chart title or axes titles. Unattached text is additional text that is unassociated with any particular element of the chart.
4. Major tick marks are tick marks that appear on the axis alongside the axis values. Minor tick marks do not appear alongside any axis value, but instead are used to provide a finer gradation between major tick marks.
5. Click Chart on the menu bar, click Chart Type, and then select one of the 3-D chart sub-types for the column chart.
6. An AutoShape is a predefined shape available on the Drawing toolbar. You can add an AutoShape to any worksheet or chart. You can change the size or shape of an AutoShape, and you can change its fill color.
7. Use full page, in which the chart is resized to fit the full size of the printed page (the proportions of the chart may change in the resizing); Scale to fit page, in which the chart is resized to fit the page but retains its proportions; and Custom, in which the dimensions of the printed chart are specified in the chart sheet.

Glossary/Index

Task Reference

TASK	PAGE #	RECOMMENDED METHOD
Absolute reference, change press to relative	EX 58-59	Edit the formula, deleting the $ before the column and row references; or F4 to switch between absolute, relative, and mixed references
Action, redo	EX 34	Click
Action, undo	EX 34	Click
Actions, redo several	EX 34	Click , select the action(s) to redo
Actions, undo several	EX 34	Click , select the action(s) to undo
Auto Fill, copy formulas	EX 68	See Reference Window: Copying Formulas Using the Fill Handle
Auto Fill, create series	EX 71	Select the range, drag the fill handle down, release mouse button, click , click the option button to complete series
AutoFormat, apply	EX 125	Select the range, click Format, click AutoFormat, select an AutoFormat design, click OK
AutoShape, add text to	EX 183	See Reference Window: Inserting Text into an AutoShape
AutoShape, insert, reshape, resize and rotate	EX 181	See Reference Window: Inserting an AutoShape
AutoSum, apply	EX 28	Click the cell in which you want the final value to appear, click , select the AutoSum function to apply
Background color, apply	EX 112	Select the range, click the list arrow for , select a color square in the color palette
Background pattern, apply	EX 112	Open the Format Cells dialog box, click the Patterns tab, click the Pattern list arrow, click a pattern in the pattern gallery, click OK
Border, create	EX 109	Click , select a border in the border gallery
Border, draw	EX 109	Click , click , draw the border using the Pencil tool
Cell, clear contents of	EX 32	Click Edit, point to Clear, click Contents; or press Delete
Cell, edit	EX 34	See Reference Window: Editing a Cell
Cell reference, change	EX 59	Press the F4 key to cycle through the difference cell reference modes
Cells, delete	EX 32	Select the cell or range, click Edit, click Delete, select a delete option, click OK; or select the cell or range, click-right the selection, click Delete, select a delete option, click OK
Cells, insert	EX 31	See Reference Window: Inserting Cells into a Worksheet
Cells, merge	EX 115	Select the adjacent cells, open the Format Cells dialog box, click the Alignment tab, select the Merge cells check box, click OK
Cells, merge and center	EX 115	Select the adjacent cells, click
Chart, add data label	EX 167	Select a data marker(s) or data series, click Chart, click Chart Options, click the Data Labels tab, select the data label type, click OK
Chart, add gridline	EX 167	Select the chart, click Chart, click Chart Options, click the Gridlines tab, click the check box for gridline option you want to select, click OK
Chart, add, remove, revise data series	EX 164	See Reference Window: Editing the Data Source of a Chart
Chart, change 3-D elevation	EX 180	Select a 3-D chart, click Chart, click 3-D View, enter the elevation value or click the Elevation Up or Elevation Down button, click OK
Chart, change location	EX 166	Select the chart, click Chart, click Location, specify the new location
Chart, change scale	EX 176–177	Double-click a value on the y-axis, enter the minimum and maximum values for the scale, click OK
Chart, change to 3-D	EX 179	Select the chart, click Chart, click Chart Type, select a 3-D subtype, click OK
Chart, create with Chart Wizard	EX 148	See Reference Window: Creating a Chart Using the Chart Wizard

TASK	PAGE #	RECOMMENDED METHOD
Chart, format data marker	EX 172	Double-click the data marker, select the formatting options using the tabs in the Format Data Series dialog box
Chart, move	EX 158	Select the chart, move the pointer over the chart area, drag the chart to its new location, release the mouse button
Chart, resize	EX 158	Select the chart, move the pointer over a selection handle, drag the handle to resize the chart, release the mouse button
Chart, select	EX 157	Move pointer over a blank area of the chart, and then click
Chart, update	EX 159	Enter new values for the chart's data source and the chart is automatically updated
Chart, use background image in	EX 175	Double-click the plot area, click the Patterns tab, click Fill Effects, click the Picture tab, click Select Picture, locate and select the background image file, click Insert, click OK twice
Chart axis title, add or edit	EX 155	Select the chart, click Chart, click Chart Options, click the Titles tab, click on the Category (X) axis text box and type the text for the title, click in the Values (Y) axis text box and type the text for the title, click OK
Chart data markers, change fill color	EX 172	Double-click the data marker, click the Patterns tab, click Fill Effects, click the Gradient tab, select the color and related color options, click OK
Chart text, format	EX 168	Select the chart label, click a button on the Formatting toolbar; or double-click the chart label, select the formatting options using the tabs in the Format Data Label dialog box
Chart text, insert new unattached	EX 171	See Reference Window: Inserting Unattached Text into a Chart
Chart title, add or edit	EX 155	Select the chart, click Chart, click Chart Options, click the Titles tab, click in the Chart title text box type the text for title, click OK
Chart Wizard, start	EX 148	Click 📊
Column, change width	EX 19	See Reference Window: Changing the Column Width or Row Height
Column, delete	EX 32	Select the column, click Edit, click Delete; or select the column, click-right the selection, click Delete
Column, hide	EX 116	Select the headings for the columns you want to hide, right-click the selection, click Hide
Column, insert	EX 31	See Reference Window: Inserting a Row and Column into a Worksheet
Column, select	EX 25	Click the column heading of the column you want to select. To select a range of columns, click the first column heading in the range, hold down the Shift key and click the last column in the range.
Column, unhide	EX 116	Select the column headings left and right of the hidden columns, right-click the selection, click Unhide
Columns, repeat in printout	EX 133	Open the Page Setup dialog box, click the Sheet tab, click the Column to repeat at left box, click the column that contains the information you want repeated, click OK
Date, insert current	EX 72	Insert the TODAY() or NOW() function
Dates, fill in using Auto Fill	EX 71	Select the cell containing the initial date, drag and drop the fill handle to fill in the rest of the dates. Click 🔽, select option to fill in days, weekdays, months, or years
Drawing toolbar, display	EX 181	Click View, point to Toolbars, click Drawing; or click 🖉
Excel, start	EX 5	Click Start, point to All Programs, point to Microsoft Office, click Microsoft Office Excel 2003
Font, change color	EX 104	Select the text, click 🅰️▾, select a color from the color palette
Font, change size	EX 103	Click 10 ▾, click a size
Font, change style	EX 103	Click **B**, click *I*, or click U
Font, change typeface	EX 103	Click Arial ▾, click a font
Format Cells dialog box, open	EX 101	Click Format, click Cells

TASK	PAGE #	RECOMMENDED METHOD
Format, apply Currency Style, Percent Style, or Comma Style	EX 97-99	Click $, click % or click , , or open the Format Cells dialog box, click the Number tab, select a style, specify style-related options, click OK
Format, clear	EX 119	Click Edit, point to Clear, click Formats
Format, copy using Format Painter	EX 99	See Reference Window: Copying Formatting Using the Format Painter
Format, decrease decimal places	EX 97	Click ·00
Format, find and replace	EX 120	See Reference Window: Finding and Replacing a Format
Format, increase decimal places	EX 99	Click ·0
Formula, copy	EX 56	See Reference Window: Copying and Pasting a Cell or Range
Formula, copy using the fill handle	EX 68	See Reference Window: Copying Formulas Using the Fill Handle
Formula, enter using keyboard	EX 15	See Reference Window: Entering a Formula
Formula, enter using mouse	EX 15	See Reference Window: Entering a Formula
Formula, insert	EX 15	See Reference Window: Entering a Formula
Formulas, show/hide	EX 42	Press the Ctrl + ` (grave accent) keys to display or hide the formulas in the worksheet cells
Function, insert using Insert Function dialog box	EX 65	Click *fx* on the Formula bar, select the function from the Insert Function dialog box, complete the Function Arguments dialog box
Header/footer, create	EX 128	Open the Page Setup dialog box, click the Header/Footer tab, click the Header list arrow or the Footer list arrow, select an available header or footer, click OK
Header/footer, create custom	EX 129	Open Page Setup dialog box, click the Header/Footer tab, click the Custom Header or Customer Footer button, complete the header/footer related boxes, click OK
Logical function, insert	EX 83	Use the IF function
Magnification, changing	EX 62	See Reference Window: Changing the Zoom Magnification of the Workbook Window
Mortgage, calculate monthly payment	EX 78	Use the PMT function
Mortgage, calculate the interest rate of	EX 80	Use the RATE function
Mortgage, calculate the number of payments	EX 80	Use the NPER function
Mortgage, calculate total value of	EX 80	Use the PV function
Page, change orientation	EX 40	Open the Page Setup dialog box, click the Page tab, click the Landscape or Portrait option button
Page, set margins	EX 127	Open the Page Setup dialog box, click the Margins tab, specify the width of the margins, click OK
Page break preview, switch to	EX 131	Click View on the menu bar, click Page Break Preview
Page Setup dialog box, open	EX 40	Click File, click Page Setup; or click the Setup button on the Print Preview toolbar
Pie chart, create	EX 159	Select the row or column of data values to be charted, click , select Pie in the list of chart types, select a sub-type, complete the remaining Chart Wizard dialog boxes
Pie chart, explode piece(s)	EX 162	See Reference Window: Creating an Exploded Pie Chart
Pie chart, rotate	EX 161	Double-click the pie in the pie chart, click the Options tab, enter a new value in the Angle of First Slice box, click OK
Print area, define	EX 131	Select the range, click File, point to Print Area, click Set Print Area
Range, copy	EX 27	Select the cell or range, hold down the Ctrl key and drag the selection to the new location, release the Ctrl key and mouse button
Range, move	EX 26	Select the cell or range, drag the selection to the new location, release the mouse button
Range, select adjacent	EX 24	See Reference Window: Selecting Adjacent or Nonadjacent Ranges of Cells
Range, select nonadjacent	EX 24	See Reference Window: Selecting Adjacent or Nonadjacent Ranges of Cells

TASK	PAGE #	RECOMMENDED METHOD
Relative reference, change to absolute	EX 58–59	Type $ before the column and row references; or press the F4 key
Row, change height	EX 19	See Reference Window: Changing the Column Width or Row Height
Row, delete	EX 33	Select the row, click Edit, click Delete; or select the row, right-click the selection, click Delete
Row, hide	EX 116	Select the headings for the rows you want to hide, right-click the selection, click Hide
Row, insert	EX 31	See Reference Window: Inserting a Row or Column into a Worksheet
Rows, repeat in printout	EX 133	Open the Page Setup dialog box, click the Sheet tab, click the Row to repeat at top box, click the row that contains the information
Row, select	EX 25	Click the heading of the row you want to select. To select a range of rows, click the first row heading in the range, hold down the Shift key and click the last row in the range
Row, unhide	EX 116	Select the rows headings above and below the hidden rows, right-click the selection, click Unhide
Sheet tabs, format	EX 119	Right-click the sheet tab, click Tab Color, select a color from the color palette
Spelling, check	EX 38	Click ![ABC check icon]
Style, apply	EX 123	Select the range, click Format, click Style, select a style, click OK
Style, create	EX 122	Select the cell that contains the formatting you want to use as the basis of the new style, click Format, click Style, type a name for the style, click Modify, specify format options using the Format Cells dialog box, click OK, click OK
Style, modify	EX 124	Select the range, click Format, click Style, click Modify, change style attributes, click OK
Text, align within a cell	EX 105	Click ![align left], click ![align center], or click ![align right]; or open Format Cells dialog box, click the Alignment tab, select a text alignment, click OK
Text, increase or decrease indent of	EX 106	Click ![increase indent] or ![decrease indent]
Text, enter into cell	EX 11	Click the cell, type text entry, press Enter
Text, enter multiple lines in a cell	EX 12	See Reference Window: Entering Multiple Lines of Text Within a Cell
Text, enter using AutoComplete	EX 17	Type the first letter of text entry you've entered in the worksheet, press Enter or Tab to complete the text entry displayed by AutoComplete
Text, wrap in cell	EX 107	Open the Format Cells dialog box, click the Alignment tab, select the Wrap text check box, click OK
Workbook, preview	EX 39	Click ![preview icon]; or click the Preview button in the Print dialog box
Workbook, print	EX 39	Click ![print icon]; or click File, click Print, select printer and print-related options, click OK
Workbook, save	EX 22	Click File, click Save, locate the folder and drive where you want to save the file, type a filename, click Save
Workbook, save in a different format	EX 22	Open the Save or Save As dialog box, display the location where you want to save the file, enter a filename, click the Save as type list arrow, select the file format you want to apply, click Save
Worksheet, add background image	EX 117	See Reference Window: Adding a Background Image to the Worksheet
Worksheet, copy	EX 37	See Reference Window: Moving or Copying a Worksheet
Worksheet, delete	EX 35	Click the sheet tab, click Edit, click Delete Sheet; or right-click the sheet tab, click Delete
Worksheet, insert	EX 35	Click Insert, click Worksheet; or right-click a sheet tab, click Insert, click Worksheet icon, click OK
Worksheets, move	EX 37	See Reference Window: Moving or Copying a Worksheet
Worksheet, rename	EX 36	Double-click the sheet tab that you want to rename, type a new name, press Enter
Worksheets, move between	EX 9	Click the sheet tab for the worksheet you want to view; or click one of the tab scrolling buttons and then click the sheet tab